SPRING TWO THOUSAND FIVE
LECTURES
MARTELL LECTURE

Steven

HOLL

Steven Holl founded Steven Holl Architects in New York in 1976 as a design-oriented office, with a current staff of 25.

wednesday
april 1
5.30pm
Crosby 301

The firm has been internationally recognized for quality and excellence in design. Recent projects include the Expansion of the Nelson Atkins Museum of Art in Kansas City, Undergraduate Dormitories at the Massachusetts Institute of Technology, the expansion and renovation of the Natural History Museum of Los Angeles County; a new marina development in Beirut, Lebanon, and a new building for the Department of Art and Art History at the University of Iowa.

Time Magazine named Steven Holl as America's Best Architect, for 'buildings that satisfy the spirit as well as the eye.' Most recently Steven Holl was honored by the Smithsonian Institution with the Cooper Hewitt National Design Award in Architecture.

UB

THE STATE UNIVERSITY OF NEW YORK UNIVERSITY AT BUFFALO
SCHOOL OF ARCHITECTURE AND PLANNING

"URBANISMS"

STEVEN HOLL
steven holl architects | new york
www.stevenholl.com

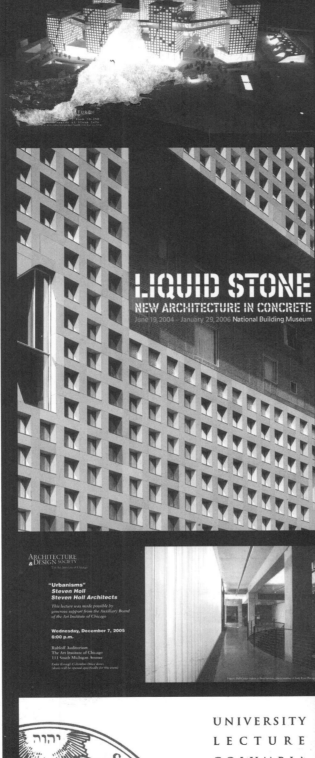

LIQUID STONE
NEW ARCHITECTURE IN CONCRETE
June 19, 2004 – January 29, 2006 National Building Museum

ARCHITECTURE & DESIGN SOCIETY
The Art Institute of Chicago

"Urbanisms"
Steven Holl
Steven Holl Architects

This lecture was made possible by generous support from the Auxiliary Board of the Art Institute of Chicago

Wednesday, December 7, 2005
6:00 p.m.

Rubloff Auditorium
The Art Institute of Chicago
111 South Michigan Avenue

Enter through Columbus Drive doors.
(doors will be opened specifically for this event)

UNIVERSITY
LECTURE
COLUMBIA
UNIVERSITY

SIGILLVM · C
VIDEBIMVS LVMEN

Professor of Architecture at the Graduate School of Architecture, Planning and Preservation, Columbia University

"Urbanisms"

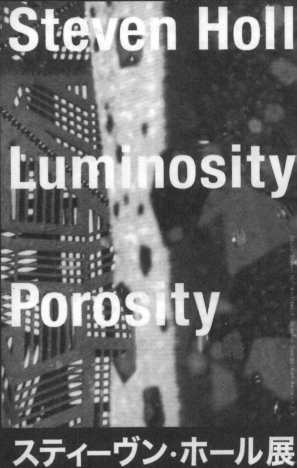

Steven Holl
Luminosity
Porosity

スティーヴン・ホール展

2006年6月2日[FRI]—7月29日[SAT] GALLERY・MA

開館時間＝11:00—18:00(金曜日のみ19:00まで)／日曜・月曜・祝日休館／入場無料
企画＝ギャラリー・間運営委員会(安藤忠雄／川上元美／黒川雅之／杉本貴志)
主催＝ギャラリー・間　後援＝(社)東京建築士会／(社)東京都建築士事務所協会
(社)日本建築家協会関東甲信越支部／(社)日本建築学会関東支部
東京アメリカンセンター　協賛＝TOTO

GALLERY・MA
間

INVITATION
本券をお持ちの方、先着200名様にポスターをさしあげます。

You are cordially invited to attend the dedication of the
NEW HIGGINS HALL
CENTER SECTION
PRATT INSTITUTE SCHOOL OF ARCHITECTURE

THURSDAY
SEPTEMBER 22

Steven Holl *Architecture Spoken*

Steven Holl *Architecture Spoken*

With a foreword by Lebbeus Woods

RIZZOLI NEW YORK

Foreword *Lebbeus Woods*

Steven Holl tells his own story pretty well. In his lectures and writings, he confides to us his aspirations for architecture and the sources of his ideas. In the interviews, appearing at the end of this book, he candidly talks about the struggles he has had over the past quarter-century getting his designs built—and struggles he has certainly had, right up to the present. Becoming well known—well, famous—has not made the task any easier. Part of his fame is a reputation for being demanding and uncompromising with his clients, in pursuit of the realization of his concepts, *his* architecture. Clients may be attracted to him for exactly these qualities, but—as any architect whose fame rests on innovative design will testify—working with an enamored client is seldom easy. Once the romance cools down, as it always does when hardcore issues such as program and budget are engaged, the toughest part of the struggle begins. This is when the architect's character is most solely tested. Steve (I will call him that, given our long friendship) has a remarkably good record for keeping clients *and* building the architecture he wants.

There is no single factor in his achieving this record. However, having the wisdom and strength to turn away commissions that will probably end in rupture or compromise is certainly a major part of the story. That can be especially difficult to do when financial times are hard, when commissions are scarce, and when the ability to hold together even a small staff necessary to practice architecture as the art of building is threatened. Steve has faced more than one of such moments and knows he may face them again. Certain kinds of clients—usually those with blatantly commercial projects, where a lobby or entrance or facade by a famous architect, a signature piece, will elevate an otherwise mundane project—show up continually and they are willing to pay well. Steve's oeuvre contains none of this kind of work, which says a great deal of sureness of himself.

Self-assurance, I believe, comes from self-knowledge. I do not think Steve has ever had any doubts about who he is and what he wants to accomplish. Also, he developed his core ideas very early and therefore has not had to grope around for precepts that will guide his designs. This is not to say that he merely plugs in a set of preconceived concepts whenever he confronts a new project. Rather, he has on the one hand a set of operating principles that narrow the possibilities for any given project. He will never, for example, make overt reference to any building other than his own. On the other hand, he has a repertoire of forms and spatial conditions developed over many years of exploratory drawing—he makes a new watercolor every morning—that have been tested over two decades of building practice. Every building designed by him bears the stamp of his style of thinking and shaping, regardless of the wide differences that often exist between his individual projects.

I met Steve in the late seventies, when he had first come to New York from his home state of Washington by way of San Francisco and the Architectural Association in London. He had worked with Bill Stout and encouraged him to found his architecture bookstore, and in

London had met Zaha Hadid, then a student of Rem Koolhaas, and studied at the AA, brushing up against the postmodernist eclecticism that had taken shape there. I think the experience only confirmed his modernist predilections and gave him a lasting distaste for historical allusions in architecture, which was then so much in vogue. At the same time, it was too late to really be a modernist, so he, like Koolhaas and Hadid, were engaged in finding ways to incorporate modernism's forms, and what they saw as its critical spirit, into new, more complex, modes of architecture.

The London experience was formative for another reason: it had broadened his world. The young man from the wilds of the American far west had tasted European sophistication in thinking and talking about architecture, giving him a more nuanced idea about the role of ideas in the conception and design of buildings than he had found in America. It is not surprising that the first serious notice of his work was to be, a few years later, in Holland, Germany, and Italy, where his idiosyncratic mix of modernist formalism and existential philosophy could be fully appreciated. More about that later.

I never discussed with Steve why he came to New York, but always assumed it was for the same reasons I did. New York at that time, more than today, was a singular locus of commercial, pop-cultural, intellectual, and artistic activities. It had a mythical quality that came to an abrupt end on 9/11, when its feeling of sanctuary was destroyed along with the Twin Towers. But in the late seventies, it seemed a unique haven for creativity, and great things seemed possible, even if it meant an uphill struggle against New York's money-driven culture. It was the place where a young, talented, and ambitious architect could make a mark, through drawing, writing, and if lucky enough, through building. True, the city had few examples of innovative architecture. Postmodern towers were sprouting everywhere, standard commercial office buildings adorned by domes, spires, classical, or art-deco touches meant to make them fashionable, but hardly daring. Offering some hope of the triumph of art over greed was Breuer's Whitney Museum, Roche's Ford Foundation Building, and of course Paul Rudoph's fabled apartment, which was glassy, glossy, but thoroughly modernist in spirit. Among older buildings, the Seagram Building, the UN complex, Lever House, the Daily News building, even the RCA Building were examples of the power of new ideas over expediency. Anyway, it was enough to sustain the myth of New York as a capital of innovation. It had an irresistible allure for young and ambitious talent looking for major challenges and opportunities.

When Steve and I met, we were both living and working in, shall we say, humble circumstances, really only illegal cracks in the city's matrix of rentable spaces. I lived in a small shoebox of a "loft" way downtown, in which I had installed a twenty-five-foot-long drawing board that pretty much filled it. The occasional rat, coming in through holes in the floor, was testament to its domestic fragility. Steve had a small, cubelike space, near 23rd Street, in a vast, nearly abandoned department store building from the nineteenth century. Because the building had no lock on the front door, anyone visiting him in the winter had to step over homeless people huddled in the run-down lobby to escape the cold wind. Inside his small space it was warm, clean, and orderly. He remodeled it into levels for sleeping and working, which was necessary, because from the start he had an office, with at least one person working for him at any given time. The lone window looked out on the oldest Jewish cemetery in the city, a fact that Steve seemed very proud of.

Steve set up shop in New York as though he intended to stay. Besides his office, he founded Pamphlet Architecture, an architectural monograph series that included issues by a number of young architects with heady ideas and high hopes, including himself. Of the first five issues he made two. Others that followed included Lars Lerup, myself, Mark Mack, and Zaha Hadid. The architects designed their own pamphlets, according to a few rigorous guidelines set by Steve. One of the rules was that you could not put your name on the cover, just the pamphlet number. This spoke eloquently of his idealism: we were not to be self-promoters, but workers in the fields of architecture. Architecture was the "star." I have never forgotten his adamancy on this point and am still moved by it. Bill Stout's book-shop always bought a hundred copies, thereby subsidizing the printing costs. They were sold to bookshops and packed and shipped by Steve and his assistant.

Steve and I were introduced by Andrew MacNair, who at that time worked at the Institute for Architecture and Urban Studies, as editor of its newspaper *Skyline*. Andrew was one of the first to publish the work of young, unknown architects, and was a good friend and advo-cate. The IAUS was at that time a pretty high-powered machine, founded and directed by Peter Eisenman, financed by Philip Johnson, attracting the likes of Kenneth Frampton, Anthony Vidler, Diana Agrest, Joan Copjec, and a score of rising international luminaries, such as Rem Koolhaas and Aldo Rossi. Steve and I were definitely on the outside looking in, but it was a fascinating scene, one that gave New York a reason to consider itself a center of advanced architectural thinking.

Steve's most ardent admiration, however, was not for the intellectual glamour of the Institute, but for the school of architecture at the Cooper Union, where under the direction of John Hejduk, strange new ideas were being experimented with by the students, led by a fac-ulty that included Hejduk, Raimund Abraham, Bernard Tschumi, and Ricardo Scofidio. Postmodern pastiche was not allowed, and the place had a monastery-like quality that appealed to Steve. He genuinely revered Hejduk's poetical, idiosyncratic architecture, which had evolved from Mies and Corbusier and the more ethical line of modernist thinking.

Eventually, after a few years of writing, drawing, exhibiting unbuilt projects, and teaching—he began at Columbia in 1982—Steve got some things built. A pool house in Connecticut, an apartment on Fifth Avenue, and—most important—a showroom for furniture, uptown at the corner of 72nd and Madison, practically the center of the world. It got a huge amount of critical attention in New York, Europe, and Asia. Everyone recognized that it was something new, extending the vocabulary of modernism, but without the usual postmodernist irony. The showroom was straightforward, readable, crystalline in its precision and details, and—something really astonishing—it exhibited an entirely new sensitivity to industrial materials such as copper, steel, and glass. Like the Barcelona Pavilion of an earlier, more radical generation, it was a temporary architecture that showed a hopeful way forward, out of the dead-end of a prevailing, shallow eclecticism. I think it had a tremendous impact at the time, especially on young European architects.

It was clear from the beginning that Steve's architecture was original in the way it took the familiar and transformed it into something new. With few exceptions, he has never relied on radical shape-making to give his work a radical edge. Rather, he relies on fresh ways of looking at ordinary things and events. So he spends as much time as he can reading, drawing, and thinking.

Ideas are, and always have been, very important to Steve. It is not theories of architecture that have shaped his point of view, but concepts emerging from philosophy and science. Ideas addressing the world at large have served as both inspirations for his projects and as standards of thought against which to measure his own. He sees architecture not as an isolated specialty—however exalted—answerable only to its own formal rules, but as an art serving wide and diverse human interests. Most architects shy away from such aspirations, for fear that their work will suffer from comparison with broader, more comprehensive ideas, but in this regard Steve is fearless. He engages the headiest concepts straightforwardly and without apology, as though doing so were simply a responsibility of practice.

Of particular interest to him is phenomenology. The philosophy and science of perception, of the body and its interactions with the physical world, are natural companions of architectural thinking, but rarely used. Steve correlates them with the materiality and the shaping that architecture—especially his architecture—brings to the world. In several books he spells out very explicitly how buildings create a framework for understanding our experiences. Indeed, architecture is an essential, affective instrument of knowledge. In *Parallax*, he writes, "The urgent need of a thought-to-feeling bridge today is a main polemic of this book….A scientist's world of statistics, cause and effect, and space-time—created with precise thought—is separate from the world of emotion and will. Thought and feeling should merge to provide *a new catalyst for the imagination* [my italics]….For architecture's inspirations every possible world at every scale must be explored. Eternities exist in the smallest detail."

Here Steve goes beyond Mies's "God is in the details." His ambition is to build the perceptual bridge between different worlds that will at the same time be the conceptual one. He wants everyone, not just scholars and aesthetes, to be able to cross it, so it must engage not just the intellect, not just the senses, but *the imagination*. In short, he wants architecture to inspire us. To do that it must, he believes, be inspired by new insights and revelations. This is what separates him from most architects practicing today.

It does not come as a surprise that light is the phenomenon that is Steve's major preoccupation. We inhabit a world that we know primarily through vision, and light is its medium. In many passages in his books he writes eloquently of his experiences of light in places as diverse as the chapel at Ronchamp and a Tarkovsky film. Architecture shapes light, giving it structure and form, giving it meaning in a cognitive sense by making it comprehensible. But light remains elusive, ever-shifting, grounding us even while it draws us irresistibly into mysteries where only imagination can guide us. Steve's Chapel of St. Ignatius in Seattle and his Light Laboratory at Cranbrook are overt essays in the evocative power of light, but all of his projects, especially the museums, are in one way or another celebrations of light and its counterpart, shadow. This is especially true of their interior spaces, which, in their innovative vision of natural and artificial light, are unique in contemporary architecture.

As an architect inspired by ideas, Steve could not help but become engaged with questions about the city and the state of urban design. His concern has gone far beyond the usual issues of placing individual buildings sensitively in their sites and has taken on larger-scale issues of urban patterns and growth. His earliest published work on urbanism was *The Alphabetical City*, summarizing his detailed, scholarly research from the seventies of existing building types devised for urban grids. It contained nothing of his own design, but made a plea for architects, city officials, and developers to reassess historical urban building patterns and regard them with more respect in their future plans—a quite modest, even conservative, position. By the mid-eighties, he had become more bold, more sure of his own phenomenology and architecture. Arguing for an experiential, hence fragmentary, approach, his proposal for the Milan Porta Vittoria is a convincing, even masterly, vision of perceptually interlocking urban spaces shaped by Hollian buildings of varying types, all characterized by their striking fusion of the familiar and the extraordinary. For his Edge of the City proposals of the mid-nineties, his polemic was more blunt—he writes, "There is a fatigue in urban planning ideas today. We see old academic planners making reports, maps, and long-range plans that are ignored by high-paced capitalist development....The issues of urban planning remain as crucial as ever, thus requiring new strategies and enthusiasm." At the same time, his ideas had become more epically American: "The edge of a city is a philosophical region where city and natural landscape overlap and exist without choice or expectation. This zone calls for visions and projections that delineate the boundary between the urban and the rural....Traditional planning methods are no longer adequate to address this edge." With this he launched daringly large-scale proposals for the highly differing edges of Cleveland, Dallas, Phoenix, and New York—a bravura design performance based on his usual, painstakingly thorough research. Where his earlier urban proposals were mostly ignored, this amazing project—self-commissioned because he thought it necessary—was savagely dismissed by one prominent critic and damned with faint praise by others, who felt Steven Holl should stay within the bounds of building design that had made him famous. Accustomed to struggles for the realization of his concepts and projects, he absorbed the comments and moved on.

I will close with a little-known aspect of Steve's way of thinking and working. From the beginning he has actively sought criticism of his designs from his peers. At certain points in the design process he will invite a respected colleague—including those with whom he sometimes competes for commissions—to his office, and present his ideas and work on a project at some preliminary or developmental stage. The colleague is invited to comment freely and, after overcoming his or her own incredulity, usually does. Steve listens, nods, discusses without a shred of defensiveness. Reflecting his years of teaching, this openness testifies to Steve's wisdom in seeking out honest and often tough critiques, his eagerness to learn, and his deep respect for the ideas of others. Clearly, these are the same qualities of character that enable him to see the familiar in new ways and to innovate so consistently in his designs.

Occasionally, in the late seventies, Steve and I would meet for lunch. Our favorite spot was the Square Diner below Canal Street, which we agreed had the best all-you-can-eat-for-a-dollar bean soup in town. Our conversations were usually focused on architecture, about which we often disagreed. The differences between us were apparent from the beginning. While we were both making drawings of imaginary projects—we had no clients—it was clear that Steve wanted to realize his ideas in building, while I enjoyed the freedom of drawing architecture as the realization of my ideas and saw the clients required to build as interference. He was listening to Bartók. I was listening to Wagner. He was reading Merleau-Ponty. I was reading Joseph Campbell and Robert Graves. He was inspired by urban building typologies. I was inspired by the crumbling feel of the city in the midst of its growth. He said tomayto, I said tomahto. But we didn't call the whole thing off. In fact, we both got something out of our differences, as we do to this day.

This book gives us new insights into the evolving thinking, methods, and productions of a unique and gifted architect. Let us read as well as look, slowly and deliberately. There is a story here that, as he might have it, bridges many possible, and wonderful, worlds.

28 July 2006
New York City

11

CLASSICAL		MODERN
ABSOLUTE	絕對的	RELATIVE
ESSENCE	元素	MATTER
ANALOGICAL	仿真的	MECHANICAL
RITUAL	儀式性的	FUNCTIONAL
SYMBOLIC	象徵性的	DOGMATIC
EVOCATIVE	觸動性的	ABSENT
HIERARCHICAL	等級制的	POSITIONAL
CONTINUOUS	連續的	DISCONTINUOUS
UNIFORM	統一的	VARIABLE
PREDICTABLE	預料的	MEASURABLE
NORM		TYPE
PROTOLOGICAL	原型	TYPOLOGICAL
FORMAL	形式	ABSTRACT

Architecture Spoken *Steven Holl*

To name an object is to suppress three-fourths of the enjoyment...to suggest is the dream.
–Stéphane Malarmé

Each time I speak in a public lecture, I organize my current projects to illustrate a general argument. The lectures provide a chance to grapple with issues and ideas. Questions can yield a feedback and dialogue. In a public lecture it is possible to present issues without becoming too serious—especially with questions afterward.

This collection of recent projects under the title *Architecture Spoken* is likewise gathered in four chapters chronologically parallel to the polemic of four talks.

> *Pro-Kyoto*: an argument for resistance and environmental resolve in the face of a belligerent USA government's refusal to join an important global shift
>
> *Compression*: an argument for architectural intensity
>
> *Porosity*: an experimental plea as well as a scalar shift
>
> *Urbanisms*: a rethinking toward 21st-century orderings with architecture as a catalyst

These four chapters are followed by the antecedent of this book, which was begun in 2004 with interviews by the critic and curator Mildred Friedman. We have included the raw texts as basic unedited "anecdotes" to the projects presented. The spoken word, like a text recorded around the table at a dinner party, has rhythms of ordinary speech with casual language.

These personal stories about a difficult process frame the struggles for architecture. Architecture is the most fragile of arts during inception but the joy of its realization and experiential emotion endures.

New York City

PRO KYOTO

April 18, 2001
Cornell University, Steinberg Hall
Ithaca, N.Y., U.S.A.

October 1, 2001
Washington University, School of Architecture
St. Louis, U.S.A.

October 20, 2001
Abaco Cultural Association
Vicenza, Italy

December 17, 2001
Beijing University
Beijing, China

February 25, 2002
Vassar College, Agnes Rindge Claflin Lecture
Poughkeepsie, N.Y., U.S.A.

April 22, 2002
New Jersey Institute of Technology, School of Architecture
Newark, N.J., U.S.A.

I would like to begin this lecture with a few paragraphs from the translator's introduction to *The Art of War* by Sun Tzu, who wrote about invincibility, victory without battle:

> The central figure of this novel is a magical monkey who founds a monkey civilization and becomes its leader by establishing a territory for the monkeys. Subsequently the monkey overcomes a "devil confusing the world," and steals the devil's sword. Returning to his own land with the devil's sword, the monkey king takes up the practice of swordsmanship. He even teaches his monkey subjects to make toy weapons and regalia to play at war. Unfortunately, though the ruler of a nation, the martial monkey king is not yet ruler of himself. The monkey king in the story exercised power without wisdom, disrupting the natural order and generally raising hell until he ran into the limits of matter, where he was finally trapped.[1]

> Now the monkey pleads with the saint for his release. The saint grants this on the condition that the monkey devote himself to the quest for higher enlightenment, not only for himself but for society at large. Finally, before letting the monkey go to set out on the long road ahead, as a precaution the saint places a ring around the monkey's head, a ring that will tighten and cause the monkey severe pain whenever a certain spell invoking compassion is said in response to any new misbehavior on the part of the monkey.[2]

In Kyoto I visited the Ryoanji Temple many times while building in Japan. The rock garden of the temple is considered to be its masterpiece. The garden is in the *Karesansui* or "dry landscape" style. Fifteen rocks of various sizes are arranged on white gravel in such a manner that from any angle you can see only 14 of them at once. Once you reach spiritual enlightenment, you can see the invisible stone.

My first encounter with these gardens was on a cold January morning. Upon entering the temple grounds, we placed shoes, as required, in a wooden shoe rack and stepped onto the well-worn floorboards of the temple. I realized how cold it was as I moved through the paper-screened walkway and felt the cold boards through my thin cotton socks with two icy holes. At the edge of the main garden, with its 15 upright stones in a field of immaculately raked white gravel, only the vapor of our breath broke the stillness. The wide-boarded platform was perfectly proportioned for sitting cross-legged in the upright posture of the monks. From our central position at the garden's edge, we could visually measure the distance between the upright stones, each separated by the length of an outstretched arm and hand according to perspective and foreshortening. The abstraction of this place, with its extreme minimalism and horizontal orthogonality, seemed to transcend culture, history, and the limits of time.

The rock garden was framed by a low rectangular wall of "boiled clay," which had a wonderful uneven pattern like clouds in a watercolor. The wooden decking was so old that time had raised its grain, and these wrinkled ridges could be felt, like an ancient, shriveled monk whose bones showed through his skin. Although the paper screens in the temple were pulled shut, the dim glow of light filtering through them illuminated black and white Sumi ink paintings, which covered some of the interior walls. Inside, I remember wonderful smells from the freshly woven tatami mats.

a projective lens, the hypnotically abstract spaces of Ryoanji magnified seasonal changes. The spatial/material/seasonal connection seemed so subtle and intense as if it were revealing some hidden, vital force: a life principle illuminated through the phenomenology of architecture. Merging and shifting perspectival views, details of joinery, the textures, the smells, and sounds all combined and expressed in this architecture of gravel, paper, and wood.

In Japan we built Void Space/Hinged Space Housing and Makuhari Housing as experiments with new urban standards. Fukuoka engages the surrounding city from hinged space to the silence of void space. Four active north-facing voids interlock with four quiet south-facing voids to bring a sense of the sacred into direct contact with everyday domestic life. The building, with its street-aligned shops and intentionally simple facades, is seen as part of a city in its effort to form space. Space is its medium, from urban to private, hinged space.

Makurari Housing was built on mud. The new town is sited on dredged fill at the rim of Tokyo Bay. People get around by a high-speed train. A variety of programming provided to minimize the need of cars for which a naturally ventilated garage was built. Our concept proposes the inter-relation of two distinct types: silent heavyweight buildings and active lightweight structures. The silent buildings shape the forms of urban space and passage with apartments entered via the inner garden courts. Inside these apartments, advanced recycling sorting is required for all waste. Inspired by Basho's book, *The Narrow Road to the Deep North*, the semipublic inner gardens and the perspectival arrangement of activist houses form an "inner journey."

We have designed an oceanic retreat in Kaua'i, Hawaii, incorporating the tectonics of its precarious site: located on the leading edge plate which has moved across a volcanic hot spot at a constant rate of 3.5 inches per year. The sectional stepping of the large room in the main house is in increments of 3.5 inches (one year/one step). Roofs of the stained concrete structures are covered in photovoltaic solar panels, heating and cooling the entire project. The corner terrace holds a lap pool built of volcanic stone from near the site.

Recently, in the *New York Times*, there was the article "How Coal Got Its Glow Back," detailing the American energy industry's dramatic fossil fuel increases. *(New York Times, Sunday, July 22, 2001).*

The lecture title Pro-Kyoto refers to the failure of the U.S. and specifically of the Bush administration to endorse the Kyoto Protocol.

Currently Denmark is the leading wind power nation in the world, an unrivalled hub of knowledge, expertise, and advanced technology. More than 20 percent of the Danish electricity consumption will soon be covered by clean energy from wind turbines.

We designed Toolenburg-Zuid Housing in Amsterdam with maximal ecological goals. Each part of the project relates to the environment of the whole, with each part designed to optimize its particular sustainable design. For example, floating villas take advantage of rainwater recycling and the checkerboard garden houses optimize sunlight hours through the use of photovoltaics.

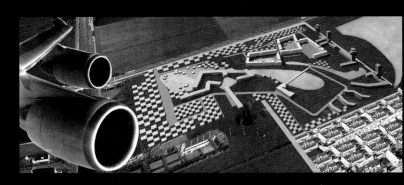

Throughout the project, maximum use is made of passive solar energy, natural ventilation, and green spaces. Recycling and composting facilities provide nutrients to the landscape—produce waste from the organic café fertilizes individual vegetable gardens; and sewage is minimized through gray water recycling. Ecological ideals are offered along with the ultramodern style of spaces, materials, and detail.

The Whitney Water Purification Facility and Park in Connecticut fuses the architecture of the water purification plant with the landscape to form a public park. Purifying 15 million gallons of water per day, the new treatment facility operates at the molecular level. For example, in the ozonation portion, oxygen O_2 becomes O_3 and is bubbled through the water to purify bacteria. The scale change from molecular in the purification process to the landscape above is celebrated in an interpretation of microscopic morphologies as landscape sectors. The overall park is thus comprised of six sectors, analogous to the six stages of the water treatment in the plant below.

Following the natural laws of gravity, water flows across the site and within the purification plant. Gardens filter and store storm water to prevent runoff to neighboring sites. A geothermal groundwater heat pump system of 88 wells provides a renewable energy source for heating and cooling the building, and avoids the environmental impact associated with fossil fuel energy use. The building systems use no HCFCs, CFCs, or halons.

Above the treatment facility is a 30,000-square-foot green roof, the largest in Connecticut. The roof increases the insulation, prevents a heat island effect, and controls storm water runoff. The green roof is a low-maintenance system and no "lawn cutting" or irrigation is required. Most of the plants will grow to about 6 inches in height, and will spread to form full coverage within two growing seasons.

Whether at the scale of dense city fragments, or the rural landscape with the solitary house, a deeper, more comprehensive vision of humans and the earth they inhabit is an urgent issue for architecture. Architecture enacts an authentic connection of nature, society and humanity. The 21st century presents us with one-third of the earth already developed, much of it in sprawling waste. A fundamental change of attitude, a revisioning of values must take place.

The following chart prepared as a tribute to the great critic Colin Rowe, charts a 21st-century architecture.

I would like to conclude with two quotes from *The Art of War*: Confucius said, "If I bring up one corner, and those to whom I am speaking cannot come back with the other three: I don't talk to them anymore. I just go away."[3]

Confucius continues:

> To sense and comprehend after action is not worthy of being called comprehension. To know after seeing is not worthy of being called knowing. These three are far from the way of sensing and response. Indeed to be able to do something before it exists, see something before it sprouts, are abilities that develop interdependently. Then nothing is sensed but is comprehended, nothing is undertaken without response, nowhere does one go without benefit.[4]

1 Tzu, Sun. *The Art of War*. Boston: Shambhala Publications, 1988, 15
2 *ibid*, 16
3 *ibid*, 37
4 *ibid*, 15

Table # 1 Architecture and New Architecture

	Classic	Modern (20th century)	21st Century
1.	Absolute	Relative	Interactive
2.	Fixed	Stable	Dynamic
3.	Physical-Metaphysical	Physical-Real	Virtual-Real
4.	Space and Time	Space-Time	Space-Time-Information
5.	Essence	Matter	Information
6.	Single	Divided	Diverse
7.	Analogical	Mechanical	Digital
8.	Ritual	Functional	Operative
9.	Symbolic	Dogmatic	Contingent
10.	Harmonious	Autonomous	Accorded
11.	Evocative	Absent	Reactive
12.	Hierarchical	Positional	Tactical
13.	Continuous	Discontinuous	Intermittent
14.	Compact	Fragmented	Fractal
15.	Uniform	Variable	Evolutional
16.	Exact	Precise	Combinatory
17.	Predictable	Measurable	Differential
18.	Norm	Type	Gene
19.	Proto-logical	Typo-logical	Topo-logical
20.	Formal	Abstract	Mixed
21.	Figurative	Structural	Infrastructural
22.	Solemn	Severe	Easygoing
23.	Ceremonial	Strict	Uninhibited
24.	Pure	Purist	Crossbred
25.	Code	Relationship	Combination
26.	Control	Order	Synergy
27.	Flat (2d)	Volume	Landscape
28.	Composition	Position	Disposition

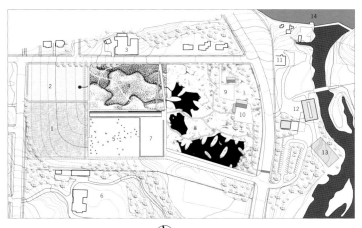

SITE PLAN ⌐————⌐ 150' ⊕

1 Wave Meadow
2 Chlorophyl Park
3 Pumping Station
4 Turbulent Lawn
5 Bubbling Marsh (Plant below)
6 Public Park
7 Filter Court

8 Wetland Ponds
9 Historic Boarding House
10 Historic Barn
11 Water Center
12 Museum
13 Auditorium/Community Center
14 Lake

WHITNEY WATER PURIFICATION FACILITY AND PARK

South Central Connecticut
1998–2005

This water purification plant and park uses water and its purification process as the guiding metaphors for its design. Its program consists of water treatment facilities located beneath a public park and a 360-foot-long stainless-steel sliver that encloses the client's public and operational programs. Like an inverted drop of water, the sliver expresses the workings of the plant below. Its shape creates a curvilinear interior space open to a large window view of the surrounding landscape while its exterior reflects the horizon in the landscape.

The public park is comprised of six sectors that are analogous to the six stages of the water treatment in the plant. The change in scale from molecular scale of the purification process below ground to the landscape above is celebrated in an interpretation of microscopic morphologies as landscape sectors. The park's "micro to macro" reinterpretation results in unexpected and challenging material-spatial aspects. For example, in a field formed by the green roof, which corresponds to ozonation bubbling, there are "bubble" skylight lenses that bring natural light to the treatment plant below. In the landscape area corresponding to filtration, vine wall elements on trellises define a public entrance court. Following the natural laws of gravity, water flows across the site and within the purification plant. As the water courses through its turns and transformations toward its final clean state, it creates microprogram potentials within the vast space of the new park. Aligned along the base of the sliver are water pumps that distribute clean water to the region.

Given the urgent need to manage and conserve water resources, this project is an example of today's best sustainable design measures and water shed management practices. Indeed, it even includes the enlargement of an existing wetland into a vibrant microenvironment that increases biodiversity.

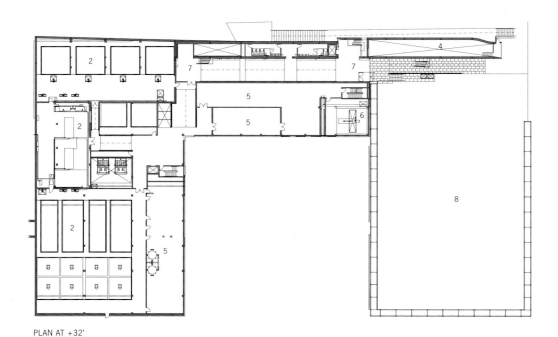

PLAN AT +32'

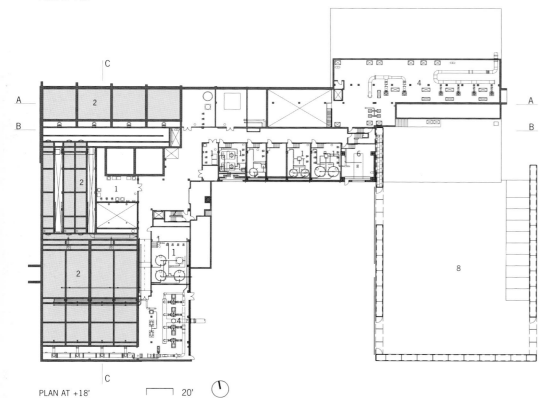

PLAN AT +18'   ⊢—⊣ 20'   ①

1 Chemical Storage
2 Process Area
3 Pump Room
4 Mechanical/Electrical
5 Residuals
6 Water Storage
7 Lobby/Exhibition Space
8 Filter Court

22

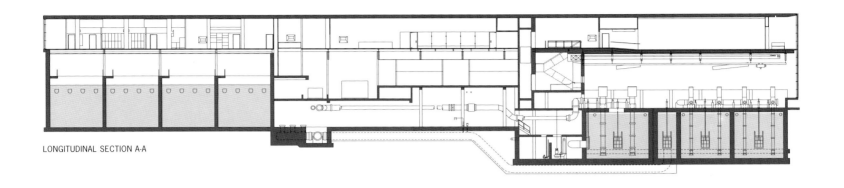

LONGITUDINAL SECTION A-A

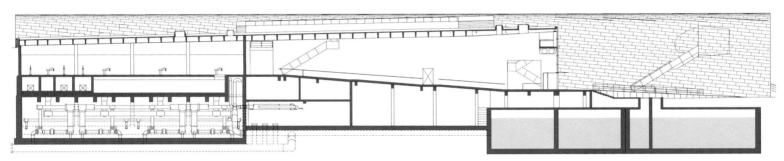

LONGITUDINAL SECTION B-B

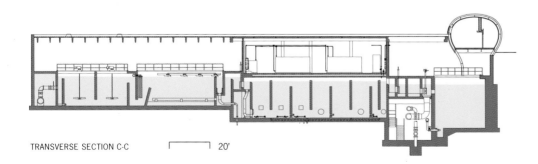

TRANSVERSE SECTION C-C   20'

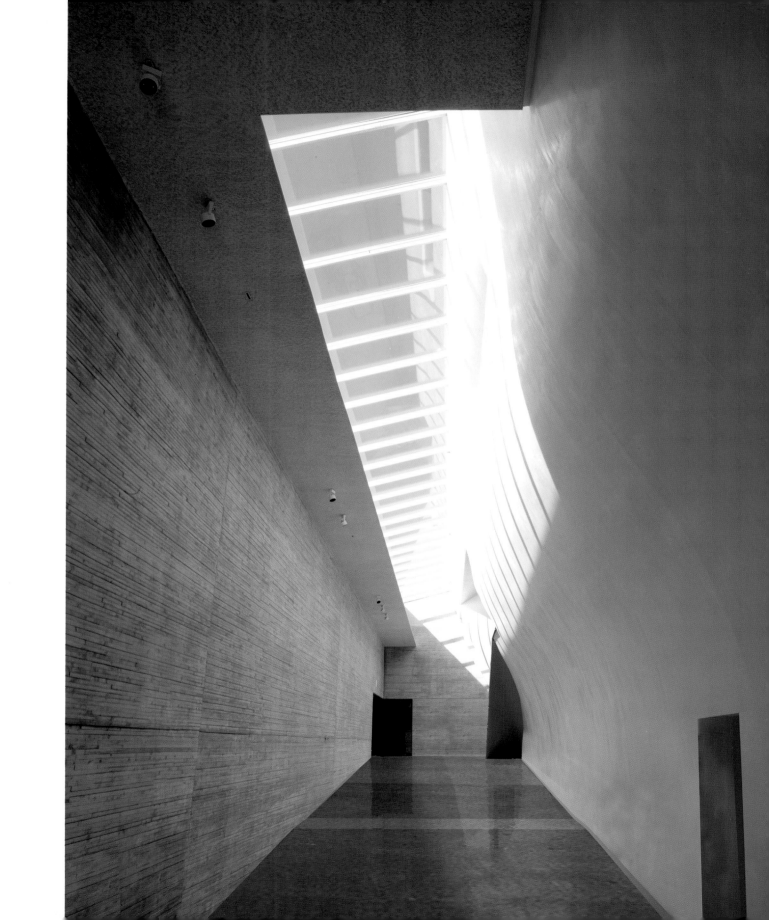

OCEANIC RETREAT

Kaua'i, Hawaii

2001

The form for this private residence refers to its setting on the northwest prow of Kaua'i, an area prone to extremely strong hurricane winds and on the leading edge of a tectonic Pacific Ocean plate that has moved across a volcanic hot spot at a constant rate of 3.5 inches per year. Like two continents separated by a tectonic shift, an imaginary erosion creates two L-shaped forms: a main house and a guest house. The large room in the main house is based on the concept of a sectional stepping with increments of 3.5 inches (one year/one step). The roofs of the two stained-concrete structures are covered in photovoltaic solar panels, which reverse meter into the Kaua'i power grid. Volcanic stone found near the site was used to build the lap pool courtyard.

By imagining a datum parallel to the horizon that has struck the concrete house as a way of carving views and organization, space flows through the house like water; the plan and section contain, drop, embank, and then release the space down the curvilinear path through the natural gardens and finally to the ocean.

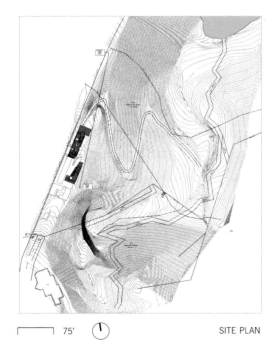

75'   SITE PLAN

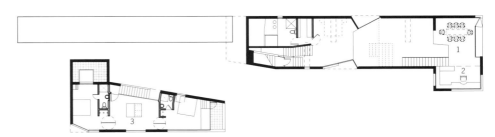

SECOND FLOOR PLAN

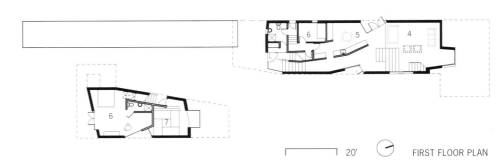

20'   FIRST FLOOR PLAN

1 Dining
2 Studio
3 Guest
4 Living
5 Kitchen
6 Guest
7 Yoga

THE SWISS RESIDENCE

Washington, D.C.

2001–2006

Sited on a hill with a direct view through the trees to the Washington Monument in the distance, the conceptual starting point of this house was a diagonal line of overlapping spaces drawn through a cruciform courtyard plan. The residence and caretaker's house are positioned on a plateau at the highest point of the site and as a result official arrival spaces and ceremony spaces are connected along this diagonal line.

Each of the house's functions connects directly to an outdoor space. A large paved square serves as driveway and grand arrival point overlooking a park and existing chancery building. From the entrance hall, one can see diagonally through the building to the terrace with a view of the Washington Monument. Private living quarters are on the level above. Juggling its many uses, the building is a multifunctional microcosm of private life, work space, and of official reception and service areas.

In addition to being a home, the residence of the Swiss ambassador to Washington, D.C., is a cultural institution and an example of national architecture. It is constructed according to the Swiss Minergie standard with the south facades using passive solar energy. Materials used include charcoal integral color concrete trimmed in local slate and sand-blasted structural glass planks. The sedum green roof features PVC panels. The existing natural landscape will be clarified with new walkways and trees, while the plateau of the residence defines an arrival square, a reception courtyard, and an herb garden.

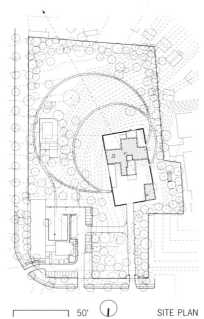

50'   SITE PLAN

SECOND FLOOR PLAN

⊏———⊐ 20' ⊕ FIRST FLOOR PLAN

1 Main Entrance Hall
2 Dining and Reception Area
3 Service
4 Herb Garden
5 Reception Terrace
6 Reflection Pool
7 Caretaker's House
8 Embassador's Private Quarters
9 Guest Suites
10 Staff

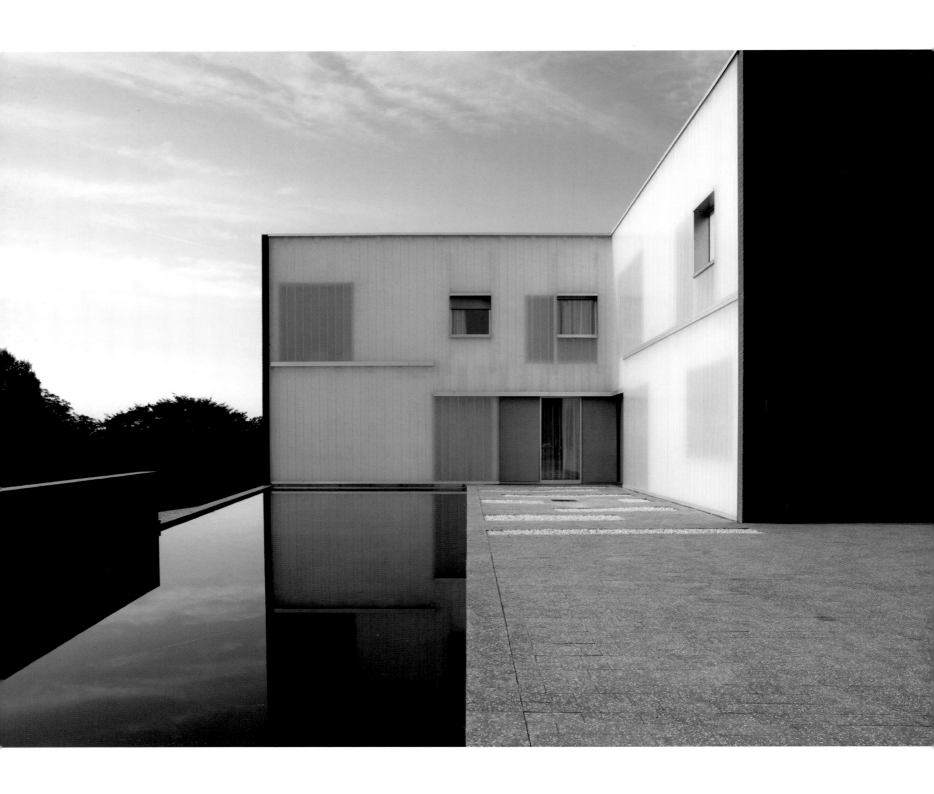

Opposite: A diagonal cut connects the main entry, the entry hall, and the exterior courtyard with the Washington Monument in the distance.

Above left: Public functions level.

Above right: Stairs to the ambassador's living level on the second floor.

Above right: View from the art room down toward the entry hall.

Opposite: A sedum green roof.

September 11, 2003
SCI-Arc
Los Angeles, California, U.S.A.

October 31, 2003
Inaugural David J. Azrieli Lecture in Architecture
McGill University
Montreal, Canada

March 12, 2004
The Central House of Architects
Moscow, Russia

March 17, 2004
American University of Beirut
Beirut, Lebanon

March 21, 2004
Triennale Hall
Milan, Italy

February 16, 2004
Princeton University, School of Architecture
Princeton, New Jersey, U.S.A.

Tonight I would like to experiment with what is at t
the compression of a manifold of things into a fev
lecture, this will be an experiment in doubt.

What I am trying to explore by the idea of comp
tion of a multiplicity of things into something cor
irreducible. It cannot be reduced to anything less

Compression, or densification, is one of my aspir
the condensation of a manifold of requirements:
details, via a single concept that yields exh
phenomena. The reducible properties in architec
have to deal with on a daily basis: How much do
is the building? How dramatically inventive is it? I tl
subjects but tonight I am actually questioning
excess of value that is intense enough. For me,
tion via concept into a meaning, inseparable fror
And that is why I prefer to use the word compres

Over the past 25 years I have constantly tried to
tions in architecture. I always work parallel: I try to
I am trying to create. Let me read some things fr

The first book that I wrote was *Anchoring* (1989)
exhibition at the Museum of Modern Art. The follo
manifesto:

> An idea is the force that drives the desig
> device that can be left unsaid. An idea gatl
> fold aspects of the building into a whole.
> place, it gathers the meaning of a situation

So it is about compression.

An ideal exists in the specific, an absolute i

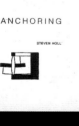

ANCHORING

STEVEN HOLL

In this way limited concept can be more than idea driving design. It can establish a miniature utopian focus. An organizing idea is a hidden thread connecting disparate parts with exact intention. An architecture based on "limited concept" begins with dissimilarity and variation. It illuminates the singularity of a specific situation.

The argument is for an architecture that is unique to site and situation. Every project has a beginning point in its locus, a universal condition in the specific. This is an interesting philosophy, but does it mean that there is nothing in general that we can say about architecture?

I started to doubt, because what I want to say with the word "compression" is not literal. Tension, a kind of elasticity, is the essence of the thought. Literally compression refers to something that is smashing into something else. But that is not what I mean by the word compression. I want to boil everything down into the one word. Why?

In 1993, a few years after *Anchoring*, I wrote *Questions of Perception: A Phenomenology of Architecture* together with Alberto Perez-Gomez and Juhani Pallasmaa. The breakthrough in this book was not to speak of the specifics of the site. I divided the book into phenomenal zones such as "Enmeshed Experience: The Merging of Object and Field." I wanted to explain the moment when you walk through a space when the texture, when the light, when it all merges into a single experience. This notion of phenomenology seemed to be a measure, not a philosophy. It became something that I could move forward with.

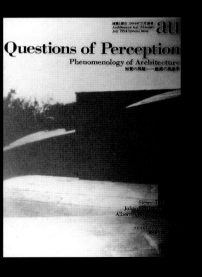

In 2000 I felt the turn of a century should provoke excitement and I wrote the book *Parallax*. It was about using science as an armature to explore architecture. I feel that ideas for architecture could come from outside. This book was a real experiment. The table of contents moves on the Fulcrum of Doubt…working with doubt.

The book attempted to affirm a spirit in architecture and discoveries in science and perception and tried to explore the relation of one to the other. Science remains essentially mysterious, yet our daily scientific and phenomenal experiences shape our lives; experience sets a new frame from which we interpret what we perceive. Perhaps one of the best examples for that is the Aurora Borealis, the Northern Lights. In *Parallax*, the Aurora Borealis is an example of the solar wind crackling against Earth's magnetic field lines. Curtains of light: electrons from the solar wind rain down along Earth's magnetic field lines. Color depends on the type of atom or molecule stuck by the charged particles. The Northern Lights are historically poetic and mythical—today full of new feelings.

Parallax is an argument for a way to break out of habitual ways of working. After that I am beginning to doubt myself again.

n the poetry of Paul Celan, especially in his collection of 1967 titled *Threadsuns*, the consolidation of words in each poem achieves meanngs of mysterious intensity. This is one of the poems:

> Before it,
> in the slated watershield, the
> three standing whales
> head the ball
>
> A right eye
> Flashes.

My wife, the artist Solange Fabião, and I think that this translation by Pierre Joris doesn't reflect the original poem in German. This is our translation:

> There,
> in the slated watershield, the
> three standing whales
> twistheads
>
> A right eye
> flashes.

Celan believed in being, in working at all costs, in a realm where clarity was law. He collapses the mind/spirit/language matters onto the anatomical/organic by expanding the vocabulary of the poems into the ields of psycho-physiology. I think that it had a way of compression, a multiplicity of thoughts into a kind of way beyond haiku.

n some ways this analogy that I am groping for is really not yet clear in architecture. In sculpture it is. Just think of the work of Cy Twombly and Giacometti. A work as Giacometti's *The Palace at 4 AM* is of amazing ntensity, compression, and a promise of lightness. In an analogous

compression, the sculpture of Cy Twombly achieves rare and subtle density. It is not a literal hardness or heaviness, nor is it an elaborated conceptual thought, but a congealment over time of incomparable power, from lightweight materials, trash almost. Perhaps the fact that over a working period of more than 40 years Twombly has produced so few sculptural works accounts for part of this intensity. These works of Twombly and Giacometti contain strange elements of compression: the illusive quality that I am after.

To get back to architecture as a form of compression, the analogue concept sketch begins the process of a design experiment. It is a fact that we need to use all the resources that computerized architectural production may offer. However, I believe the idea of a small watercolor sketch fuses intuition with a concept and embodies hopes and desires. This direct mind/eye/hand interaction constitutes a link between all the synapses of the mind to circumambient reality.

A much wider range of circuits of decision is opened by this process than by any current digital setup. Harnessed to the supercharged power of computerized production, the initial idea in the analogue drawing has the potential to embody the spirit that animated its conception. With the advent of new technologies, the initial watercolor can be transformed into a digital hybrid. While the speed in which we can now move from concept sketch to spatial geometry and physical model is provocative, the initial sketch still begins the process and is an important form of compression.

Holl, Steven. *Anchoring*. New York: Princeton Architectural Press, 1989, 9

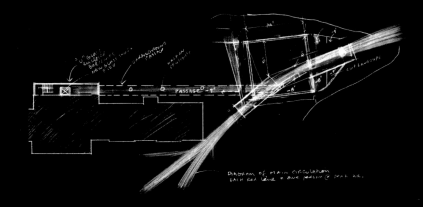

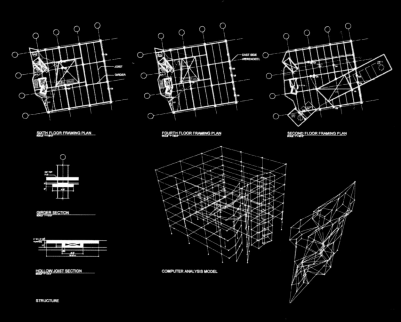

KNUT HAMSUN CENTER

Hamarøy, Norway
1994–

Knut Hamsun, Norway's most inventive twentieth-century writer, fabricated new forms of expression in his first novel, *Hunger*. He went on to found a truly modern school of fiction with his works *Pan*, *Mysteries*, and *Growth of the Soil*. This center dedicated to Hamsun is located above the Arctic Circle near the village of Hamarøy on the farm where the writer grew up. The 600-square-meter center includes exhibition areas, a library and reading room, a café, and an auditorium equipped with the latest film projection equipment. (Hamsun's writings have been particularly inspiring to filmmakers, which is evident in the more than 17 films based on his work.)

The building is conceived as an archetypal and intensified compression of spirit in space and light, concretizing a Hamsun character in architectonic terms. The concept for the museum, "Building as a Body: Battleground of Invisible Forces," is realized from inside and out. Here the wood exterior is punctuated by hidden impulses piercing through the surface: An "empty violin case" balcony has phenomenal sound properties, while a viewing balcony is like the "girl with sleeves rolled up polishing yellow panes."

Many other aspects of the building use the vernacular style as inspiration for reinterpretation. The tarred black wood exterior skin is characteristic of the great wooden stave Norse churches. On the roof garden, long grass refers to traditional Norwegian sod roofs in a modern way. The rough white-painted concrete interiors are characterized by diagonal rays of light calculated to ricochet through the section on certain days of the year. These strange, surprising, and phenomenal experiences in space, perspective, and light provide an inspiring frame for exhibitions.

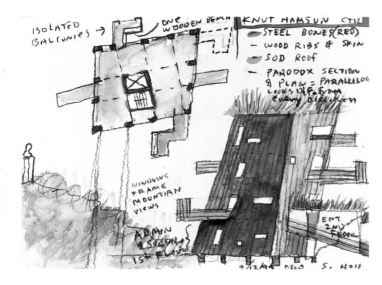

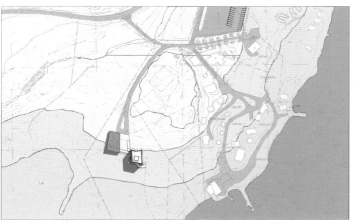

250'   SITE PLAN

Left: View of the first site (1997).

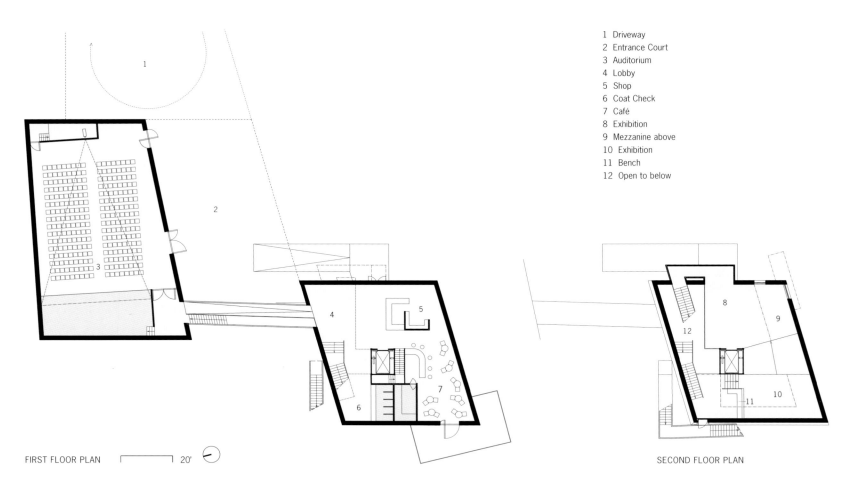

1 Driveway
2 Entrance Court
3 Auditorium
4 Lobby
5 Shop
6 Coat Check
7 Café
8 Exhibition
9 Mezzanine above
10 Exhibition
11 Bench
12 Open to below

FIRST FLOOR PLAN ⊢———⊣ 20'

SECOND FLOOR PLAN

Concept! BUILDING = A BODY — battleground
of invisible forces.

KNUT
HAMSUN
CTR

1. SPINE ELEVATOR, BONE STAIR
2. BIG BROWN DOG COLLAR of MEXICAN SILVER
3. WOMEN w/ TWO BLUE FEATHERS IN HATS, PLAID HANKERCHIEF
4. GIRL w/ SLEEVES ROLLED UP PUBLISHING ...

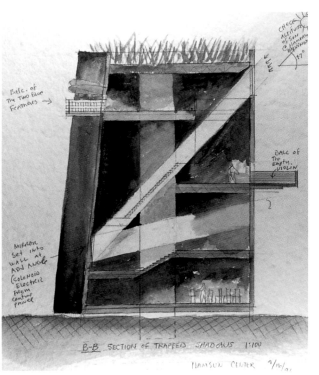

B-B SECTION OF TRAPPED SHADOWS 1:100

HAMSUN CENTER 7/16/?

54

Above: Entrance and information desk.

1 Lobby
2 Reception
3 Café
4 Coat Check
5 Mechanical
6 Exhibition
7 Mezzanine
8 Apartment beyond
9 Loft
10 Library and Reading Room
11 Office beyond
12 Roof Terrace Pavilion

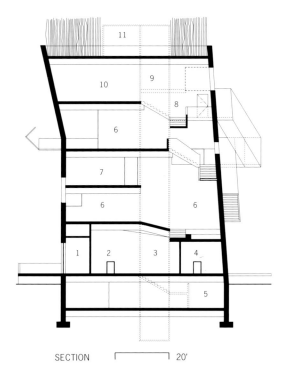

SECTION   20'

CHAPEL OF ST. IGNATIUS

Seattle, Washington

1994–1997

[St. Ignatius] returns to his metaphor of light: the light to perceive what can best be decided upon must come down from the first and supreme wisdom...

- David Lonsdale S.J., *Eyes to See, Ears to Hear*

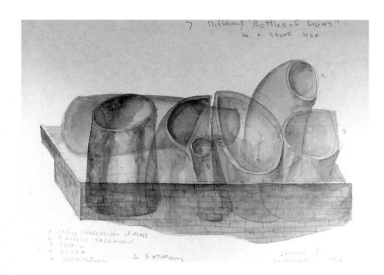

In the Jesuits' "spiritual exercises," no single method is prescribed—instead "different methods helped different people." Thus, a unity of differences gathered into one.

Seven bottles of light in a stone box; the metaphor of light is shaped in different volumes emerging from the roof whose irregularities aim at different qualities of light. North-, east-, south, and west-facing light all gather together for one united ceremony.

Each of the light volumes corresponds to a part of the program of Jesuit Catholic worship. The south-facing light corresponds to the procession, a fundamental part of the mass. The north-facing city light corresponds to the Chapel of the Blessed Sacrament and to the mission of outreach to the community. The main worship space has a volume of east and west light. At night, which is the particular time of gatherings for mass in this university chapel, the light volumes are like beacons shining in all directions out across the campus. Much like when staring at a blue rectangle and then a white surface, one can experience the visual phenomena of complementary colors (i.e. one will see a yellow rectangle), this arrangement contributes to the twofold merging of concept and phenomena in the chapel.

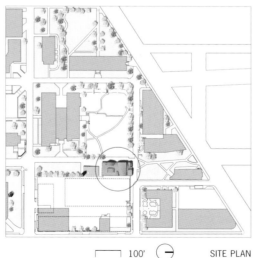

100'　SITE PLAN

The chapel is sited to form a new campus quadrangle green space to the north, the west, and in the future, to the east. The elongated rectangular plan is especially suited to defining campus space as well as the processional and gathering space within. Directly to the south of the chapel is a reflecting pond or "thinking field."

Opposite: Carved cedar entry doors with seven lights.

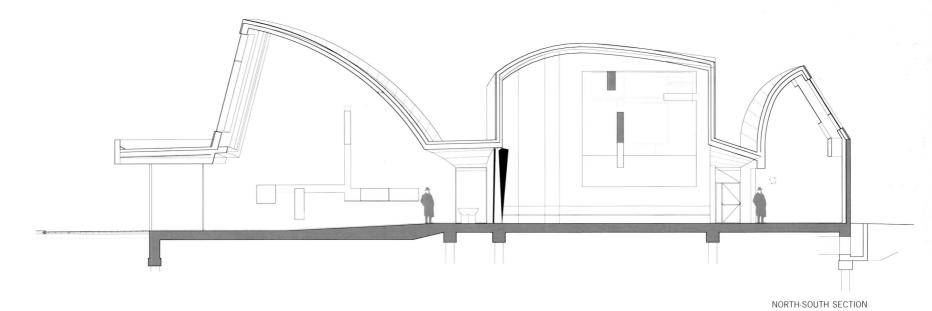

NORTH-SOUTH SECTION

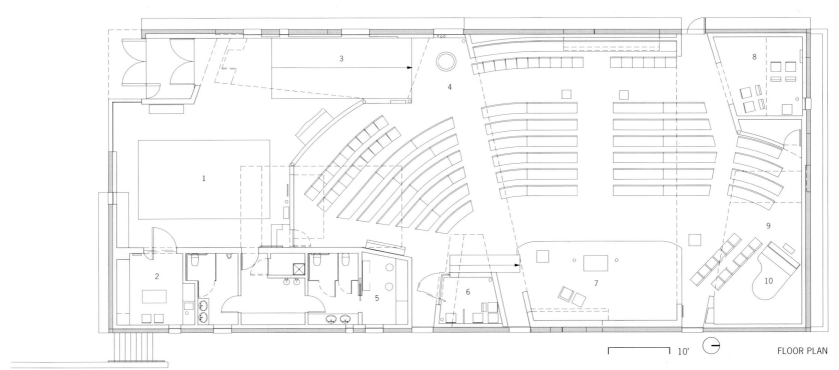

10'   FLOOR PLAN

1 Narthex   6 Reconciliation Chapel
2 Vesting Sacristy   7 Altar
3 Procession   8 Blessed Sacrament Chapel
4 Baptistry   9 Choir
5 Bride's room   10 Piano

Opposite: Narthex with four cast-glass windows, analogous to the four weeks of "spiritual exercises."

Right, top: The "Arth" week cast-glass window.

Right, bottom: Bronze entry door handle.

COLLEGE OF ARCHITECTURE, ART AND PLANNING
CORNELL UNIVERSITY

Ithaca, New York
2001

The concept of this building is organized around the idea of the tesseract or hypercube (an open bracket). Scientifically, a tesseract is the four-dimensional analogue to a cube (a square is to a cube as a cube is to a tesseract). Internally this cube develops non-Euclidean properties, which are experientially evident in the overlapping interior perspectives of the building. Thus, the review rooms—the heart of an architecture studio education—are in the central overlapping cubes.

The loftlike studio spaces form an open bracket made operative by the infrastructural tesseract zone, which is pulled inside-out, forming the west facade. The tesseract zone is embedded in the open bracket as a shifting intermittent section with alignments to the landscape of the site: the bottom of Fall Creek gorge, the distant view of Cayuga Lake, and the angle of the sun (47.5° at the equinox).

The site for the new College of Architecture building, Milstein Hall, is located at the northeast corner of the arts quad and north of the Fall Creek gorge bridge, a main thoroughfare for pedestrian traffic onto campus. The building offers a campus passage at its ground plane, which is open to all and makes a new connection to the existing architecture school building, Sibley Hall. Placed in this way, with the shop and lecture hall opening directly onto it, the passage functions as the "social condenser" for the arts quad.

Construction in precast concrete planks and beams is complemented by the simplicity of structural channel glass planks on three facades (with translucent insulation) and juxtaposed with aluminum in different states for the tesseract wall (foamed aluminum, bead-blasted, and direct digital-cut sheets). The translucent insulation in the glass planks brings softly molded light into the studios, while the rooms of the tesseract wall can be fully darkened to accommodate digital media.

150' SITE PLAN

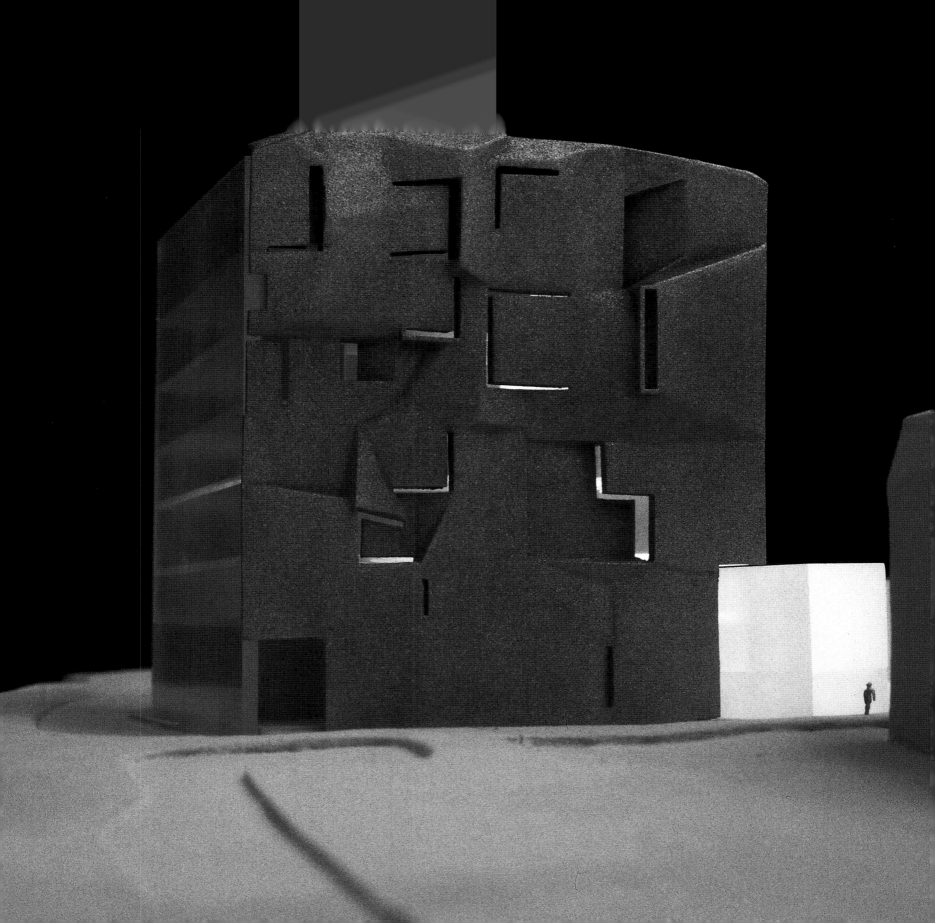

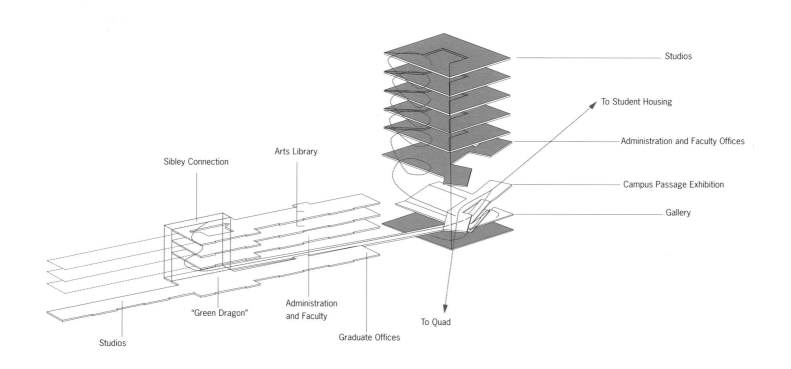

Studios

To Student Housing

Administration and Faculty Offices

Campus Passage Exhibition

Gallery

Sibley Connection

Arts Library

"Green Dragon"

Administration
and Faculty

Graduate Offices

To Quad

Studios

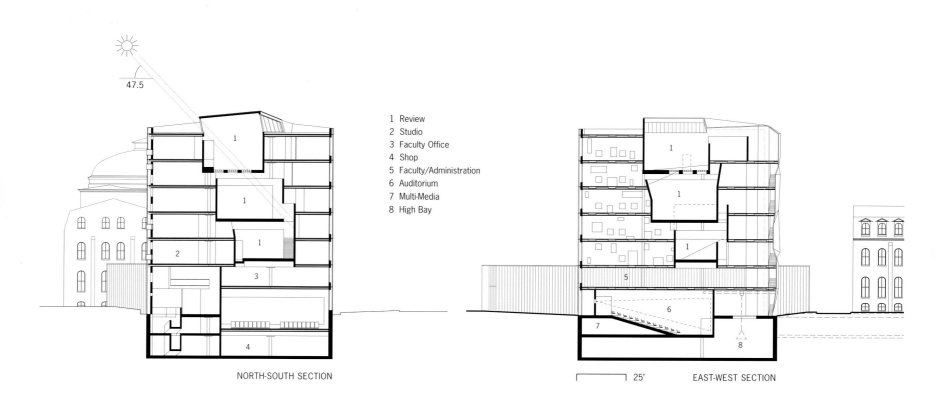

47.5

1 Review
2 Studio
3 Faculty Office
4 Shop
5 Faculty/Administration
6 Auditorium
7 Multi-Media
8 High Bay

NORTH-SOUTH SECTION

25'   EAST-WEST SECTION

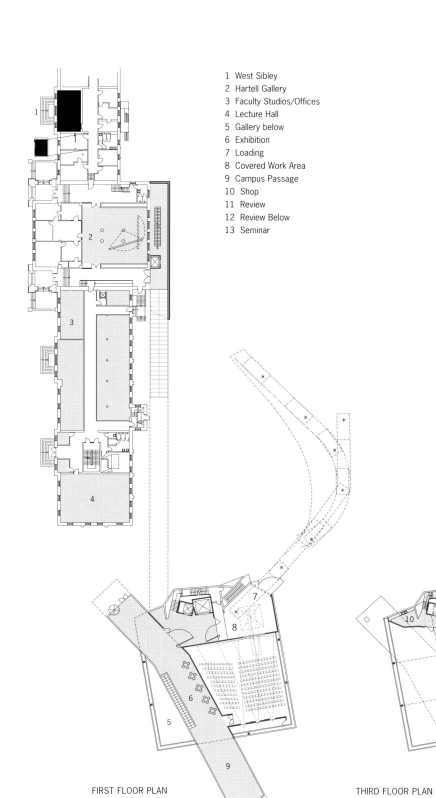

1 West Sibley
2 Hartell Gallery
3 Faculty Studios/Offices
4 Lecture Hall
5 Gallery below
6 Exhibition
7 Loading
8 Covered Work Area
9 Campus Passage
10 Shop
11 Review
12 Review Below
13 Seminar

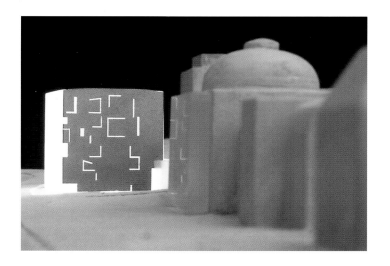

Top: Foamed-aluminum "tesseract" wall at west.
Above: Solar stack-glass-plank wall at south.

FIRST FLOOR PLAN

THIRD FLOOR PLAN

SIXTH FLOOR PLAN   40'

WRITING WITH LIGHT HOUSE

Long Island, New York
2001–2004

The concept of this linear wooden beach house was inspired by its close proximity to the studio of the painter Jackson Pollock. Several free-form designs were made based on his 1949 painting *Seven in Eight*. Also, the wooden balloon-frame construction references the strip-wood fencing along the neighboring sand dunes and ocean.

To open up the house's interior to the bay and the north view of the Atlantic Ocean required closing its south side for privacy. Thus, the final scheme brackets the internal energy in an open frame, through which the sun projects lines. Strips of white light inscribe and bend through the interior according to the dynamics of the season and time of day. Guest rooms swirl around the double-level living room from which one ascends to a pool suspended over the garage. From this upper pool court, the Atlantic Ocean is visible.

concept = "writing with
LIGHT"
LINEAR STRIPS of sunlight
inscribe and bend
internal spaces
dynamically in time

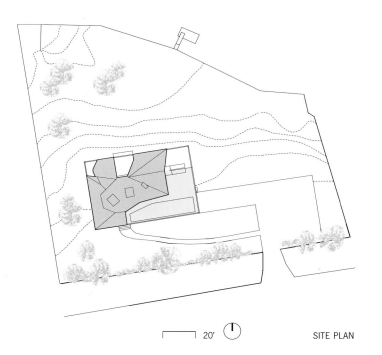

20'   SITE PLAN

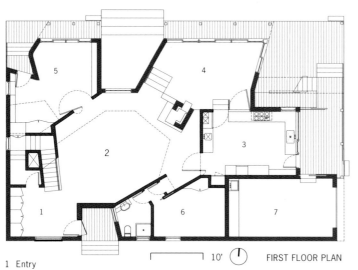

1 Entry
2 Living
3 Kitchen
4 Dining
5 Library
6 Guest 1
7 Garage

10' FIRST FLOOR PLAN

8   Master Bedroom
9   Guest 2
10 Guest 3
11 Lap Pool

SECOND FLOOR PLAN

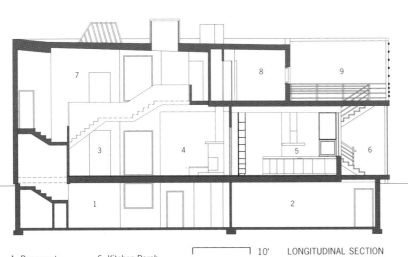

1 Basement	6 Kitchen Porch
2 Utility Room	7 Guest 3 beyond
3 Library beyond	8 Master Bath
4 Living	9 Pool Porch
5 Kitchen	

⊢——————⊣ 10' LONGITUDINAL SECTION

TRANSVERSE SECTION

1 Basement
2 Library
3 Living
4 Guest 3
5 Guest 2

NAIL COLLECTOR'S HOUSE

Essex, New York

2001–2004

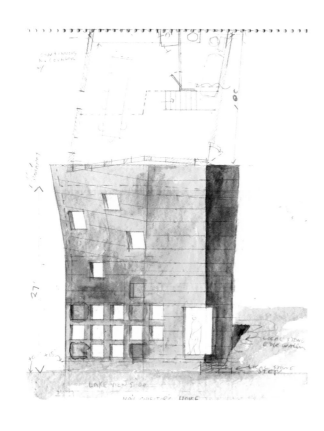

Overlooking the expanse of Lake Champlain and located in the 19th-century town of Essex, this 1,200-square-foot house for a writer is sited on a former nail factory foundation. (The owner has gathered over the years a collection of square-head 19th-century nails from the site.)

Inspired by Homer's *The Odyssey*, the house's windows correspond to the 24 chapters of that epic poem and are organized to project "Fingers of Light" into the interior volume. The main northeast wall has 14 windows and the southeast and southwest walls contain five windows, while the northwest wall has none.

The largely open interior ascends counterclockwise through a series of spaces pierced by the light of the windows. A "prow" thrust toward Lake Champlain completes this upward spiral of space. White plaster walls, hickory floors, and cartridge brass siding nailed in pattern over a wood frame create a tactile weathering for this structure—a poetic reinterpretation of the industrial history of the site and of the pre–Civil War architecture of Essex.

SITE PLAN

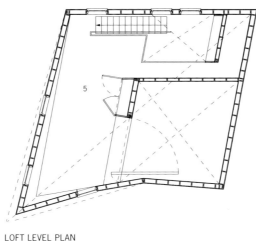

LOFT LEVEL PLAN

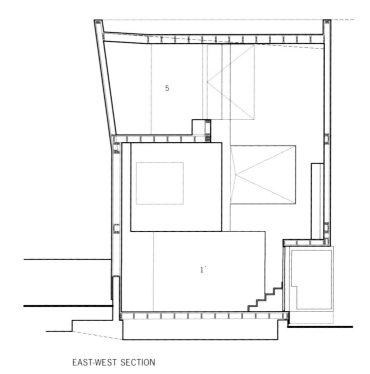

EAST-WEST SECTION

1 Entry
2 Living
3 Kitchen
4 Studio
5 Loft

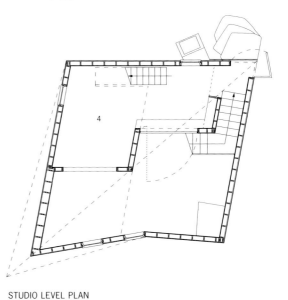

FIRST LEVEL PLAN ⊢――――⊣ 8' ①

STUDIO LEVEL PLAN

TURBULENCE HOUSE

Abiquiu, New Mexico
2001–2004

Adjacent to two adobe courtyard houses built by the artist Richard Tuttle, this small construction is sited atop a windy desert mesa. Its form, imagined like the tip of an iceberg indicating a much larger form below, allows turbulent wind to blow through the center. The artist's friend, Kiki Smith, calls it a "brooch pinned to the mesa."

The stressed-skin and aluminum-rib construction was digitally prefabricated in Kansas City then bolted together on-site. A total of 31 metal panels, each with a unique shape, were fabricated to form the shell of the house. The metal fabricator utilized digital definition combined with crafts-manship to produce intricate shapes. By means of parametric logic, materials were converted into engineered assemblies with an accuracy once considered impossible.

A second Turbulence House, made for an exhibition in Vicenza, Italy, is now located in a private sculpture park in Schio, Italy.

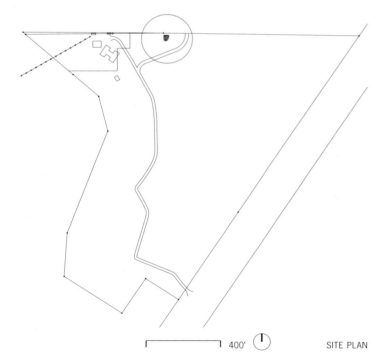

400'   SITE PLAN

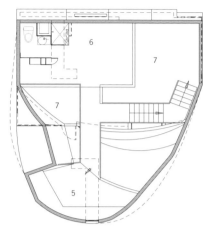

SECOND FLOOR PLAN

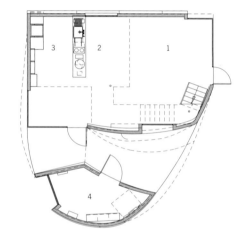

|___|___| 10' ⊙ FIRST FLOOR PLAN

1 Living
2 Dining
3 Kitchen
4 Storage
5 Study
6 Sleeping Loft/Bath
7 Open to below

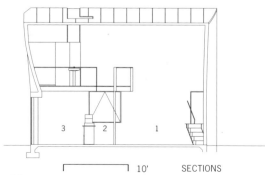

|___|___| 10' SECTIONS

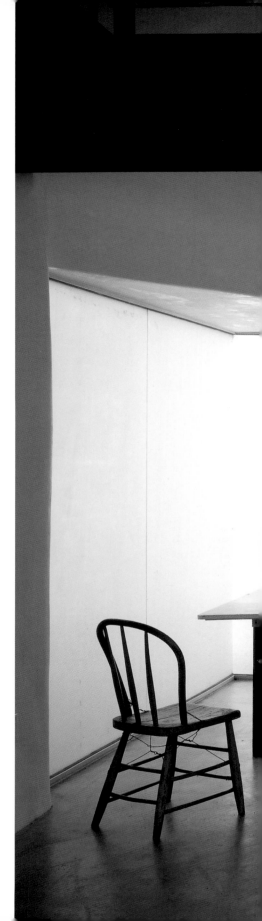

PLANAR HOUSE

Arizona

2002–2005

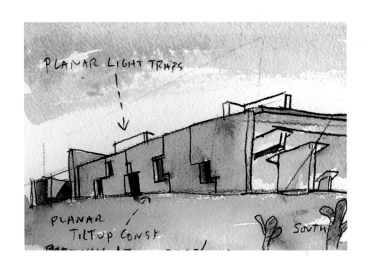

This house is a part of, and vessel for, a large contemporary art collection. Great 20th-century works by Bruce Nauman, Robert Ryman, Jeff Koons, and Jannis Kounellis are part of the collection, which includes important video artworks.

Constructed of tilt-up concrete, the flat and rotated nature of the walls merges with the simple orthogonal requirements for displaying art. Light and air chimneys connected to cooling pools articulate the planar geometry. From a courtyard experienced at the entry of sequence, a ramp leads to a rooftop sculpture garden—a place of silence and reflection.

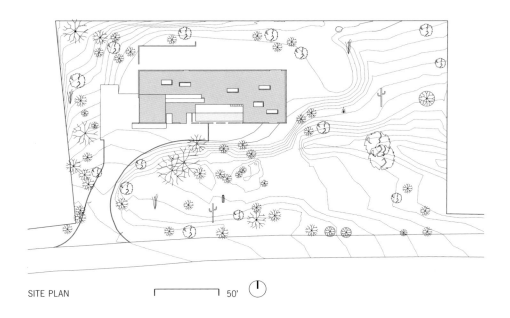

SITE PLAN   50'

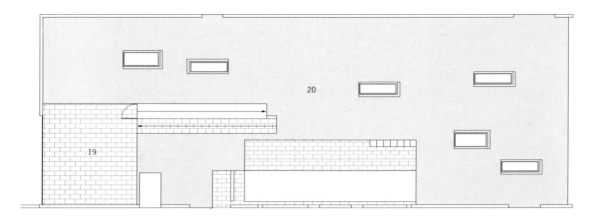

ROOF PLAN

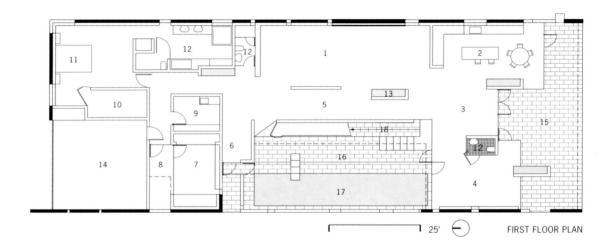

25' FIRST FLOOR PLAN

1 Living
2 Kitchen
3 Dining
4 Study
5 Gallery
6 Entry
7 Library
8 Outdoor Court
9 Laundry
10 Closet
11 Bedroom
12 Bathroom
13 Cool Pool
14 Garage
15 Camelback Porch
16 Pool Court
17 Lap Pool
18 Ramp to Sculpture Terrace
19 Sculpture Terrace
20 Terrace

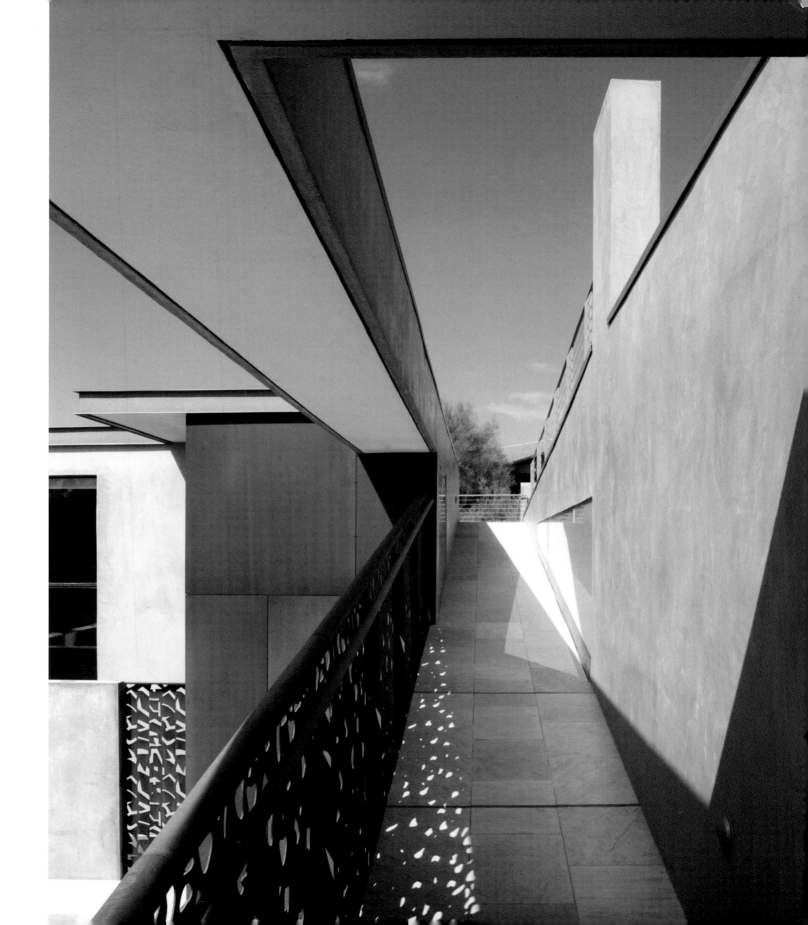

October 27, 2004
Iowa State University, School of Architecture
Ames, Iowa, U.S.A.

January 25, 2005
University of Toronto,
School of Architecture, Landscape, and Design
Toronto, Canada

March 7, 2005
Carleton University and
the National Gallery of Canada
Ottawa, Canada

March 9, 2005
National Building Museum for Liquid Stone Exhibition
Washington D.C., U.S.A.

April 1, 2005
University of Buffalo
Buffalo, New York, U.S.A.

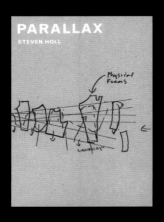

This talk is an experimental one, something that I have been working on that comes out of my interest in phenomenology. I always read the science section of the *New York Times* from cover to cover. This type of knowledge needs to be part of an architect's inspiration. In the 2000 book *Parallax* the table of contents included a word that I liked: porosity. I find it works well as a lens for phenomenological questions. Recently my work has focused on a series of experiments in porosity.

In my work I am moving this concept from the typological to the topological. I started my career at the end of the Italian Rationalist movement and, in my early research, we catalogued building types, which were documented in books like *The Alphabetical City* and *Urban and Rural House Types in North America*. I thought that it was possible to go from typology to a new architecture, but I found this was a dead end. Coincidentally, I was traveling across Canada in 1984, and on the journey I ended up talking all night with a philosopher about Merleau-Ponty. The train went through a spiral tunnel, and I like to think that this was where I changed my philosophy. It was a bit like having a sex change. If you ever have the opportunity to go from Toronto to Banff on the trans-Canadian railway, this spiral tunnel is a spectacular and strange experience.

In 1938, when Alvar Aalto was experimenting with the designs for the Villa Mairea, Le Corbusier's Villa Savoye had been completed for seven years. While both of these villas became iconic examples of modern architecture, their approach is almost opposing, regarding the connection between the architecture and the site. Poised in the center of a great field, the Villa Savoye is the extreme autonomous object sitting on pilotis in a geometric and pure contrast to the landscape. Merged with the birch forest, the Villa Mairea, with its lashed poles and partial sod roofs, fuses with the landscape. These two villas, though nearly the same size and program, are antithetical as a white cube and a sponge; as distinct as the typological is from the topological.

Earlier, the "organic architecture" of Frank Lloyd Wright's Usonian Houses aspired to deep integration of house and landscape, but somehow Aalto had made this aspiration into a new icon with the Villa Mairea. Was it the witty and irreverent collage technique that seemed so free compared to Wright's geometric consistency? Was it the purposely primitive detailing in lashed-together pole clusters, latticework, and leather-wrapped door handles? Was it the quote of new "white architecture" blurred with partially plastered and lumpy brick finish? Expressing Frank Lloyd Wright's earlier principle, somehow Villa Mairea came to symbolize fusion with the landscape in a new way.

The elevated cube of Villa Savoye was radically clear—with the free facade, free plan, roof gardens, pilotis, and horizontal strip windows. In fact, Le Corbusier's 1926 manifesto, *The Five Points of the New Architecture* were virtually and literally characterized in this house. But the Villa Savoye had vanishing points; normal perspectives. Aalto had built a villa without vanishing points. The Villa Mairea dilates space, merging and interlocking with the landscape outside. You cannot turn around in the Villa Mairea without sensing these overlapping fields of vision. While a walk through the Villa Savoye's strict geometry evokes the fixed certainty of a manifesto on Purism, a walk through the Villa Mairea is to experience phenomenological acceptance of uncertainty— as if Aalto was working with uncertainty itself.

And here is where the doubts begin, when trying to elevate the work as a model. Western perspective is time-fixed, while Eastern perspective exists outside of time. This episodic and partial perspective seems to be everywhere in Aalto's merging of birch forest and villa, creating a sort of "time porosity." In writing about the "transvaluation of architectural principles," Pierluigi Nicolin wrote, "The challenge involves crossing, albeit symbolically, a strong and ancient boundary—that between nature and artifice, between what is there because it comes from within and what is there because it has been constructed." Aalto's Villa Mairea opens a porous lens on that "ancient boundary."[1]

It was this initial examination of Aalto's Villa Mairea that inspired our further research into the multiple identities and forms porosity can accommodate—Porosity: Literal, Phenomenal, Urban.

We have spent a number of years conducting research into the multiple identities and forms of porosity. The former arguments for the porosity of architecture, urbanism, and landscape can be reinforced with a testament for the porosity of spirit and matter as well as light's effect through form, shade, and shadow. Rather than a preoccupation with solid, independent objectlike forms, it is experiential phenomena of spatial sequences within, around, and between which triggers emotions and joy in the experience of architecture. The phenomenal properties of light reflected or refracted over a delicately faceting form transcend the formal aspects of the making of faceted forms. The forms pick up the glowing yellow-orange light of the setting sun, which changes every day in their faceted surfaces. Likewise, a digitally perforated porous skin penetrated by low horizontal sun multiplies its presence in pins of light with a corresponding web of shadows. When sunlight is projected through trees in a dapple of white light and black shadow on a wall, this dancing variegation exhilarates. Natural light and shadow have the psychological power to inspire and encourage. When the seasonal change of the sun angle is multiplied by variations from sunrise to sunset, porosity, when fused with light, attains choreographic virtuosity.

As a thought experiment, we organized a few of our recent projects in relation to this model. Our first realized project along the theme of Porosity was designed in 1996: the Sarphatistraat offices of the social housing company Het Oosten. These provided the experimental potential to build an analogy to a Menger sponge. The overall porosity is the same in section, plan and elevation. These phenomenal properties of literal porosity took on an aim of urban porosity in the design from 1999 for the student dormitory Simmons Hall at MIT. Exploring the phenomenal aspect, we see the School of Art and Art History in Iowa, and discover how light and land can contribute to an elemental porosity. Urban porosity at the scale of a "city within a city" is attempted in our eight-tower project of the Linked Hybrid in Beijing designed in 2003.

New, digitally driven techniques have provided a previously unattainable degree of porosity in membranes, surfaces, and solids, opening up possibilities for a 21st-century architecture of new phenomenal properties. However, power of technique, no matter how omnipotent, requires a human motive, and a connection of spirit and matter. Otherwise all our works are relegated to empty show or the dilettante facile act of manipulating fashion. If the digitally activating hardware and software are on the objective side and the mind-originating thoughts are on the subjective side, it is a fusion of objective-subjective that connects matter and spirit.

How can this simple principle be given teeth? Especially problematic is the fact that language misrepresents the phenomenal effects of our conceptual acts. Some sort of intuition or "subjective ideal" is necessary as a force to drive the objective. Power of technique in the final physical forms is devoid of character in itself. It is in the sensory experience of the mind that reflective thought completes its existence.

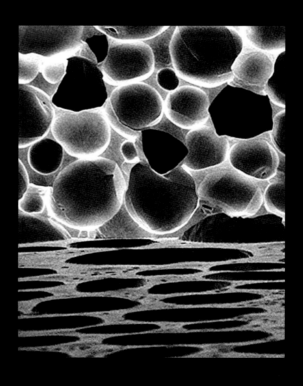

1 Nicolin, Pierluigi. "Steven Holl and Nihilism." *Domus*, February, 2004

SARPHATISTRAAT OFFICES

Amsterdam, the Netherlands
1996–2000

In Amsterdam, on the Singel Canal, this renovated building is the former federal warehouse of medical supplies. The main structure is a four-story brick U merging internally with a new "sponge" pavilion on the canal. While the exterior expression is one of complementary contrast (existing brick adjacent to new perforated copper), the interior strategy is one of fusion.

The porous architecture of the rectangular pavilion is inscribed with a concept from the music of Morton Feldman's *Patterns in a Chromatic Field*. The ambition to achieve a space of gossamer optic phenomena with chance-located reflected color is especially effective at night when the color patches paint and reflect in the canal. The layers of perforated materials, from copper on the exterior to plywood on the interior, contain all services such as lighting, supply, and return air grilles. The perforated screens developed in three dimensions are analogous to the Menger sponge principle of openings continuously cut in planes approaching zero volume. "Chromatic Space" is formed by light bounced between the building's layers. At night, light trapped between screens sometimes appears as thick floating blocks of color. At other times the passing sun creates a throbbing color wash or moving moiré patterns.

The complex is entered through the original 20th-century brick courtyard. Passing through the interior reveals gradually more porous spaces until reaching the Menger sponge pavilion overlooking the canal. While the major portion of the 50,000-square-foot project is workspace for the social housing company's employees, the large sponge space is open to receive all uses from public gatherings to performance events. Given back to the community, the immediate canal edge has a new boardwalk.

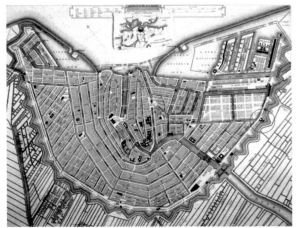

SITE PLAN

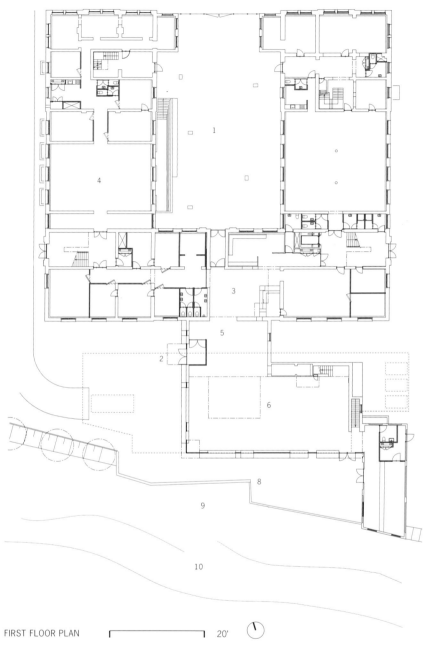

FIRST FLOOR PLAN |‾‾‾‾‾‾‾‾‾‾‾| 20' ⊕

1 Main Entrance
2 Entrance
3 Main Lobby
4 Offices
5 Lobby/Exhibition
6 Conference/Restaurant
7 Kitchen
8 Outdoor Seating Area
9 Boat Landing
10 River

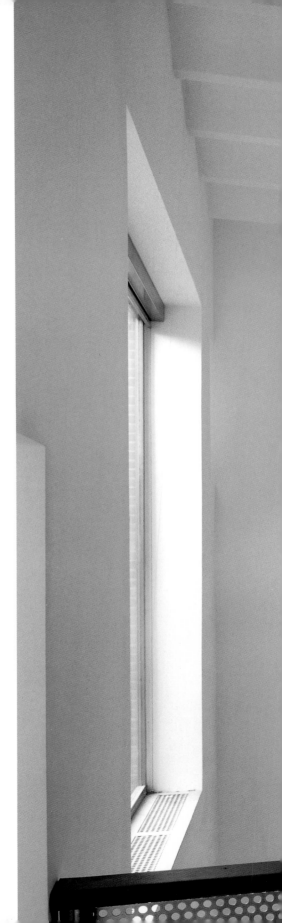

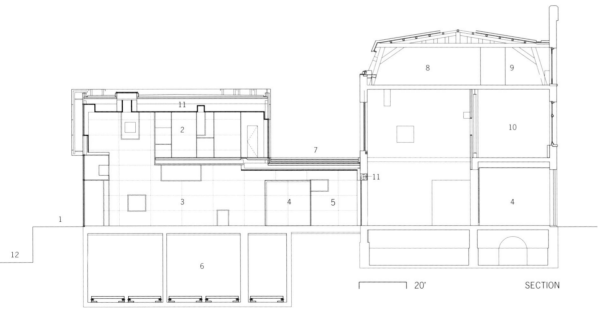

20' SECTION

1 Public Boardwalk
2 Mezzanine/Meeting Room
3 Conference/Restaurant
4 Vestibule
5 Lobby/Exhibition
6 Mechanical/Parking

7 Water Pond
8 Project Leaders
9 Staff Project Development
10 Library/Reading
11 Air Supply
12 Canal

SIMMONS HALL
MASSACHUSETTS INSTITUTE OF TECHNOLOGY

Cambridge, Massachusetts

1992–2002

This 350-bed residence is envisioned as part of the city form and campus form with a concept of "porosity" along Vassar Street. It is a vertical slice of a city—ten stories tall and 330 feet long. The urban concept provides amenities to students within the dormitory such as a 125-seat theater, as well as a night café. House dining is on street level, like a street-front restaurant with a special awning and outdoor tables. The corridors connecting the rooms are like streets (11 feet wide). As in Alvar Aalto's Baker House, here, the hallway has a function akin to a public place or a lounge within a greater urban experience.

The sponge concept for the Simmons Hall transforms a porous building morphology via a series of programmatic and biotechnical functions. The overall building mass has five large-scale openings. These roughly correspond to main entrances, view corridors, and the main outdoor activity terraces of the dormitory connected to programs such as the gymnasium.

The next scale of opening creates vertical porosity in the block, with a ruled surface system freely connected to sponge prints, plan to section. These large, dynamic openings (roughly corresponding to the "houses" in the dorm) are the "lungs" of the building, bringing natural light down and moving air up through the section.

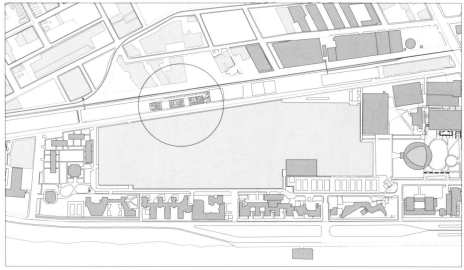

SITE PLAN   250'

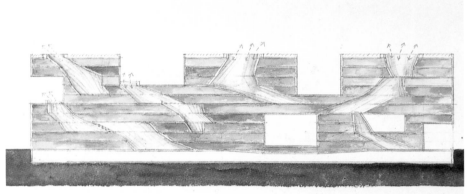

M.I.T. 2001 (POUROSITY) SPONGE
LIGHT & AIR VENTILATION (AIR DRAWN
UP THROUGH MAIN "LUNGS" VIA SLOW RPM FANS
OPERATED BY ROOF TOP PHOTOVOLTAIC CELLS)

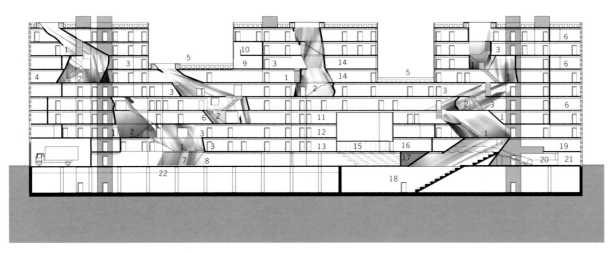

EAST-WEST SECTION ⌐———⌐ 25'

1 Group Study
2 Group Lounge
3 GRA
4 Terrace
5 Roof Terrace
6 Visiting Scholar
7 House Dining
8 Kitchen beyond

9 Exercise
10 Weights
11 House Master
12 Housemaster Reception
13 Passage to Lobby
14 Associate Housemaster
15 Glass Passage
16 Group Studies

17 Meditation Room
18 Multipurpose Room
19 Small Group Studies
20 Lobby
21 House Lounge
22 Mechanical Distribution Zone

1 House Dining
2 Multipurpose Room
3 Lobby
4 Group Study
5 GRA
6 Glass Passage
7 Group Lounge
8 Visiting Scholar

FIRST FLOOR PLAN

THIRD FLOOR PLAN

SIXTH FLOOR PLAN

EIGHTH FLOOR PLAN

25'

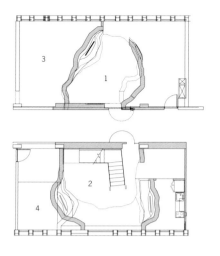

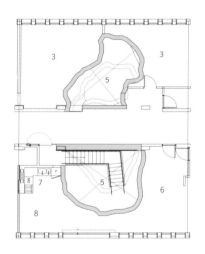

1 Group Study
2 Group Lounge
3 Student Double
4 Student Single
5 Open to below
6 Associate House Master
7 Kitchen
8 Study

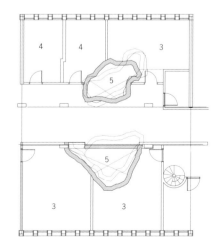

10'

Left, top: Certain dorm rooms enjoy the deformation of the space.

Left, bottom: Yoda taps him on the shoulder.

Opposite: The student lounge space intersects with the facade grid.

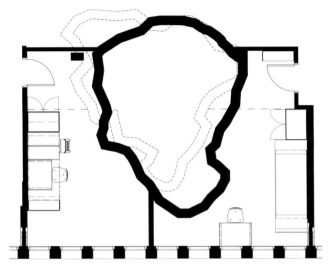

SINGLE ROOM WITH ATRIUM

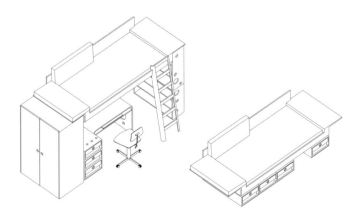

SINGLE ROOM FURNITURE

SCHOOL OF ART AND ART HISTORY, UNIVERSITY OF IOWA

Iowa City, Iowa

1999–2006

Located adjacent to a lagoon and a limestone cliff, the site for the School of Art and Art History at the University of Iowa is a special condition. The existing building is a brick structure with a central body and flanking wings built in 1937 along the Iowa River. The Iowa City grid extends across the river to the limestone bluffs, where it breaks up. The new School of Art and Art History straddles these two morphologies. A 1960s addition to the school extends along the river and joins the building, covering the river-facing entrance.

The new building partially bridges the lagoon and partially connects the organic geometry of the limestone bluff. Implied, rather than actual, the volumes are outlined in the disposition of spaces. Rather than an object, the building is like a "formless" instrument. Flat or curved planes are slotted together or assembled with hinged sections. Flexible spaces open out from studios in warm weather. The school's architecture represents a hybrid vision of the future: half bridge/half loft, half theory/half practice, and half human/half scientific.

The architecture of the building explores formless geometries in its disposition of spaces and combinations of routes. As a working and flexible teaching instrument, the building connects interior functions in spatial overlap at its center. This space is envisioned as a social condenser where ongoing work can be observed. Around the perimeter, the spaces overlook, overlap, and engage the natural landscape of the surroundings. The dispersion and "fuzziness" of the edges is seen as a positive way to embrace phenomena such as sunlight reflected from water on the lagoon and the up-reflected white light of freshly fallen snow in wintertime.

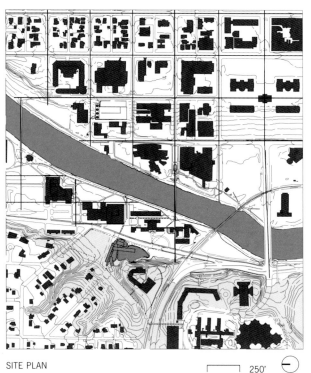

SITE PLAN   250'

Opposite: The library bridge is reflected in the entry-level glass.

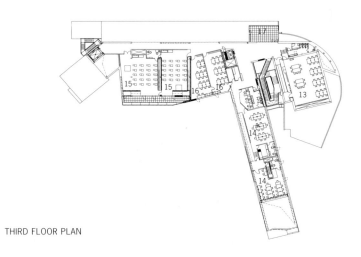

THIRD FLOOR PLAN

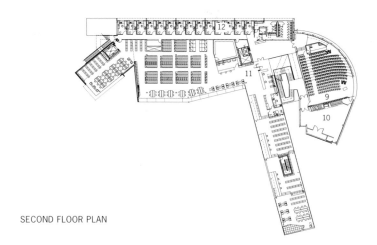

SECOND FLOOR PLAN

1 Entrance
2 Forum
3 Gallery
4 Administration
5 Cafe
6 Student Advisors
7 Art History Lecture Rooms
8 Office of Visual Material
9 Auditorium
10 Media Theater
11 Art Library
12 Faculty Office
13 Graduate Design Studio
14 Digital Studio
15 Painting Studio
16 Design Studio
17 Terrace

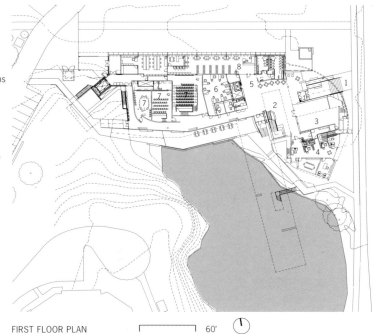

FIRST FLOOR PLAN   60'

Left: The main staircase is hung off the structure with steel rods.

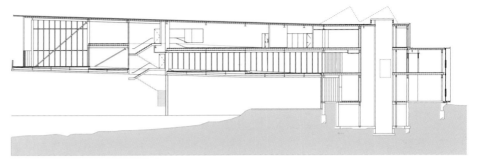

LONGINTUDINAL WEST SECTION

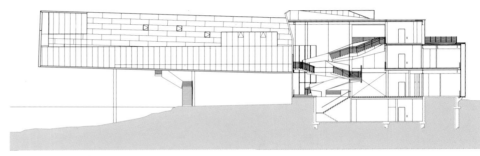

SECTION THROUGH INTERDISCIPLINARY COMMUNITY FORUM

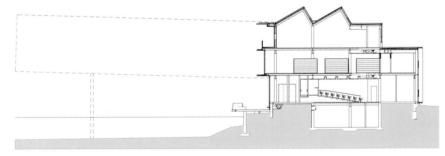

WEST CROSS-SECTION

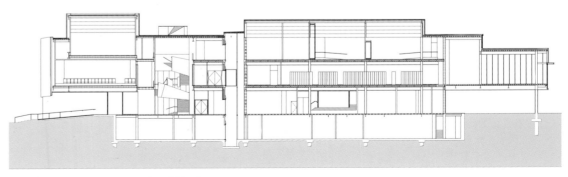

SOUTH CROSS-SECTION 30'

141

143

Left, top: A cubic reading room at the end of the library bridge.

Left, bottom: A special balcony outside the cubic reading room.

LINKED HYBRID

Beijing, China

2003–

Current development in Beijing is almost entirely focused on "object buildings" and freestanding towers. But the aspiration of the developer of Linked Hybrid was for an ultramodern expression of 21st-century ecological urban living in this 200,000-square-meter (roughly 2.15 million-square-foot) complex. For this project, urban space is envisioned as city within a city with all the activities and programs that can support the daily life of more than 2,500 inhabitants: cafés, delis, laundry, dry cleaners, and florists. The eight towers are linked at the 20th floor by a ring of cafés and services.

With more than 700 apartments sited adjacent to the old city wall of Beijing, Linked Hybrid is concerned with filmic urban space around, over, and through multifaceted spatial layers. Focused on the experience of the body passing through spaces, the towers are organized according to movement, timing, and sequence, generating random citylike relationships.

The polychrome architecture of ancient China inspires a new phenomenal dimension that especially inscribes the spatiality of the night. The undersides of the cantilevered portions are colored membranes that glow in the light of the night. Misting fountains from the water retention basin activate this light in colorful clouds, while the floating cineplex centerpiece has partial images of its ongoing films projected on its undersides and reflected in the water.

Feng Shui principles employed throughout the project provide special aspects such as "beamless" ceilings. Each apartment has two exposures with no interior hallways.

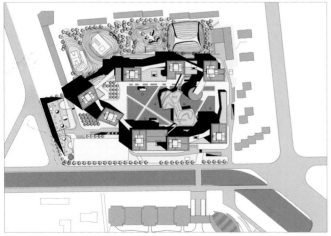

200'   SITE PLAN

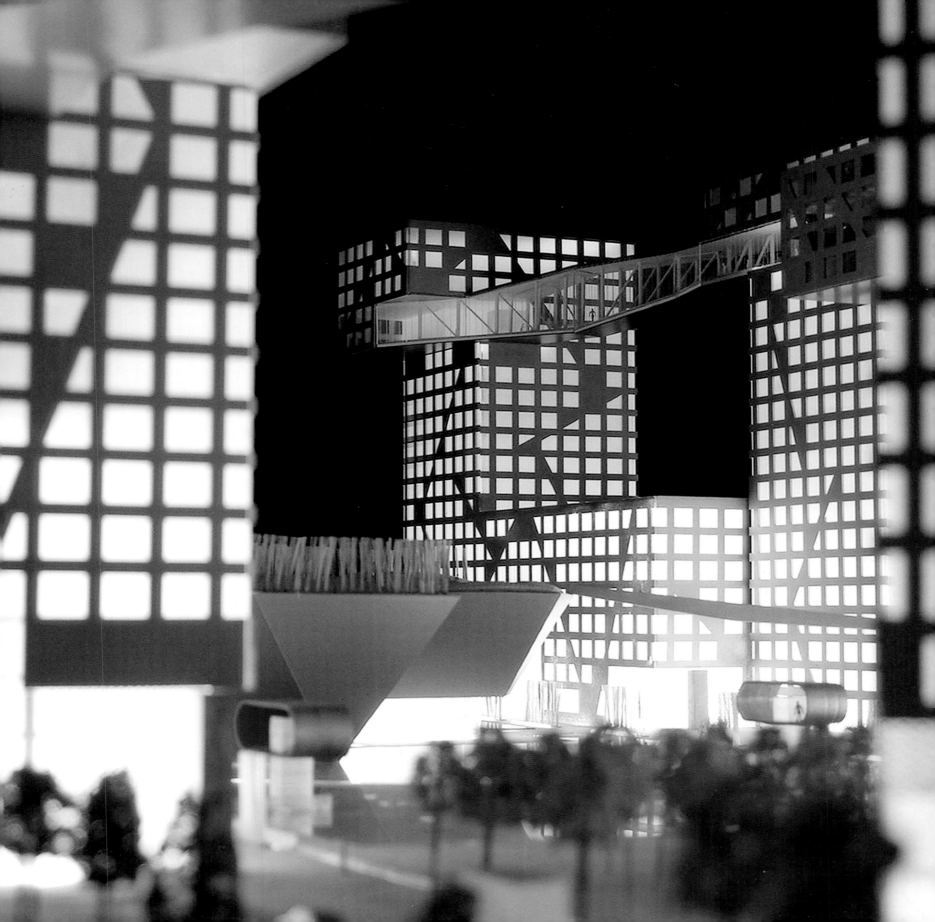

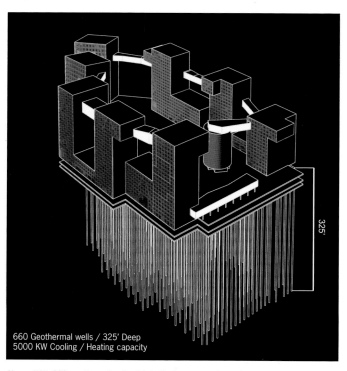

660 Geothermal wells / 325' Deep
5000 KW Cooling / Heating capacity

Above: With 660 geothermal wells, this is the largest geothermal-heated and -cooled complex in the history of residental construction in China.

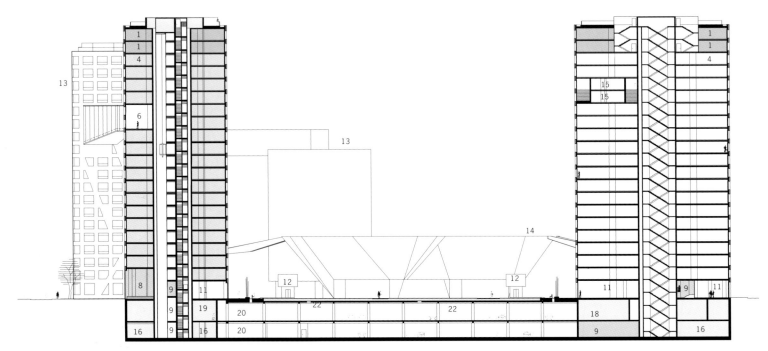

NORTH-SOUTH SECTION

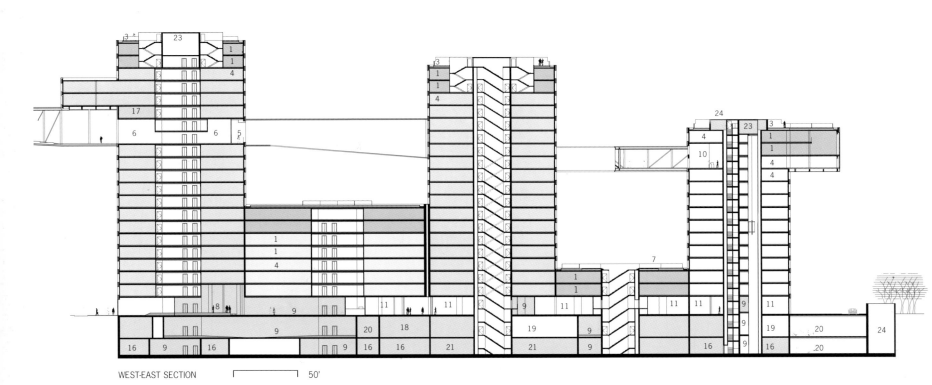

WEST-EAST SECTION   50'

Right: A central recycled-water pond of the water-filtering system is fed by the gray water pipes of the separate apartments.

1 Duplex
2 Duplex Roof Garden
3 Private Roof Garden
4 Typical Apartment
5 Terrace
6 Art Gallery
7 Public Roof Garden
8 Main Lobby
9 Lobby
10 Bar
11 Commercial
12 Tea House Beyond
13 Tower beyond
14 Cinematheque beyond
15 Locker Room
16 Service
17 Mechanical room
18 Trash/Recycling
19 Bycicle Parking
20 Parking
21 Storage
22 Pool Lense
23 Water Tank
24 Exhaust Fans/Air

Left: A swimming pool and spa are suspended within the bridge links.

Opposite, top: The "Five Mounds" landscape.

Opposite, bottom: The central pond with natural vegetation.

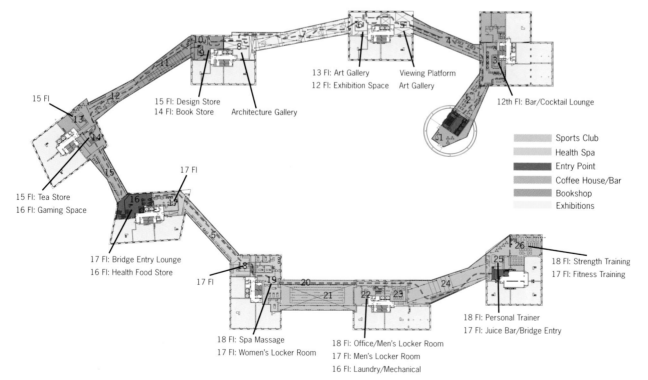

13 Fl: Art Gallery
12 Fl: Exhibition Space

Viewing Platform
Art Gallery

12th Fl: Bar/Cocktail Lounge

15 Fl

15 Fl: Design Store
14 Fl: Book Store

Architecture Gallery

15 Fl: Tea Store
16 Fl: Gaming Space

17 Fl

17 Fl: Bridge Entry Lounge
16 Fl: Health Food Store

17 Fl

18 Fl: Spa Massage
17 Fl: Women's Locker Room

18 Fl: Office/Men's Locker Room
17 Fl: Men's Locker Room
16 Fl: Laundry/Mechanical

18 Fl: Strength Training
17 Fl: Fitness Training

18 Fl: Personal Trainer
17 Fl: Juice Bar/Bridge Entry

Sports Club
Health Spa
Entry Point
Coffee House/Bar
Bookshop
Exhibitions

1 Listening Lounge
2 Ultra Lounge
3 Bar/Cocktail Lounge
4 Dining Deck
5 Viewing Platform
6 Exhibition Space, Art Gallery
7 Sculpture/Architecture Gallery
8 Architecture Gallery
9 Design Store
10 Reading Room
11 Book Event Space
12 Cafe Seating
13 Coffee Shop
14 Tea Store
15 Tea Seating
16 Bridge Entry Lounge
17 Hair/Nail Salon
18 Meeting Place
19 Spa/Massage
20 Suspended Catwalk
21 3-lane Pool
22 Office/Men's Locker Room
23 Spinning Room
24 Group Exercise Space
25 Personal Trainer
26 Strength Training

TYPICAL APARTMENT WITH DIAGONAL VIEWS ACROSS "HINGED-SPACE"

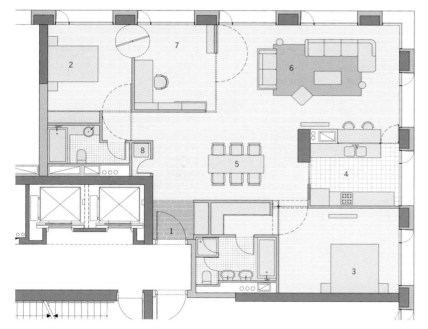

TYPICAL APARTMENT WITH "HINGED-SPACE DOORS"

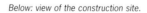

10'

1 Entry
2 Bedroom
3 Master Bedroom
4 Kitchen
5 Dining
6 Living
7 Multi-use Space (Study Room/Guest Room)
8 Bathroom

Opposite: The model apartment is equipped with custom light fixtures; dining chairs by Alvaro Siza.

Below: view of the construction site.

154

September 22, 2005
New Higgins Hall Center Section Dedication
Pratt Institute, School of Architecture
Brooklyn, N.Y., U.S.A.

November 1, 2005
University Lecture
The Rotunda, Columbia University
New York City, U.S.A.

December 7, 2005
The Art Institute of Chicago
Chicago, U.S.A.

April 4, 2006
School of Architecture
Massachusetts Institute of Technology
Cambridge, Mass., U.S.A.

May 26, 2006
Modern Group, Green Architecture Seminar
Beijing, China

June 2, 2006
Opening event for Luminosity/Porosity
Gallery MA
Tokyo, Japan

I would like to dedicate this lecture to my professor from the University of Washington, who died in 2000, Professor Herman Pundt. This man was an inspiration to me; he was a very passionate teacher. When I first came to the University of Washington in 1967 as a student, he gave a lecture called "The Spirit and the Purpose of Teaching." He began the lecture with a slide of Frank Lloyd Wright surrounded by interns at a drafting table. Wright had no university degree and never formally taught, but he shared his knowledge, his idea, and his enthusiasm. Herman Pundt only wrote one book, *Schinkel's Berlin*. It is basically, conceptually, the glue that I use to hold my lecture together in a sense that architecture is an urban act. In *Schinkel's Berlin* he looks at Schinkel's work and its relationship to every aspect of the city.

The title of this talk, *Urbanisms*, takes a look at architecture as a catalyst for urban developments. It is as visual as it is verbal. I try to close the gap between what you *say* and what you *see*; I'm interested in the distinction between "saying and showing." Like Ludwig Wittgenstein's Picture Theory of Meaning, I would argue for a Phenomenal Theory of Urbanism.

The phenomenal qualities of the light and space of particular cities is part of the important characteristics determining their qualities of life. It is strange that few urban planners speak of these things when preparing reports and books that, after political action, have huge effects on the experience, forms, and spaces of cities (some disastrous). If modern medicine has finally realized the power of the irrational psyche in psychosomatic illness, in the near future urban planners might realize that the experiential and phenomenal power of cities cannot be completely rationalized and must be studied subjectively.

Urbanisms is an argument for new densely packed urban visions from the standpoint of the natural landscape via new architectural projects. I crafted this talk to try to wrench together a variety of my projects. They are efforts to speak about architecture as a catalyst: a driving, impor-

NEW CITY
1. FRAGMENTS

tant element that always has urban consequences. In other words, with the smallness of the earth and what we know about it, every act of building is in some way an urban act.

I arranged this talk in five sections: *City Fragments, Porosity, Insertions, Precincts,* and *Fusion.*

I am interested in the *fragments,* the pieces, of cities. It can be about the edge of the city or the possibility of creating new cities from scratch. And why not, why are we not making new cities from scratch? For the World Trade Center site in New York we developed a hybrid urban vision of a new multiuse skyscraper technology. It was sectionally developed as much as it was planimetrically developed.

Another important thing for me is the notion of *urban porosity.* I see it being followed by *social porosity* and *literal porosity.*

By inserting architectural elements into complex urban situations (*insertions*), we found that we can generate new emotions. Architectural insertions can change weightiness into lightness, and lifeless into liveliness or vice-versa depending on the specific situation. The expansion to the College of Architecture and Landscape Architecture at the University of Minnesota, with both its interior and exterior spaces, promotes campus activity and pedestrian circulation while providing a unified facility for the architecture and landscape architecture schools on campus. The Center Section at Pratt Institute is an urban insertion between two historically protected buildings at the Pratt School of Architecture. The concept of the project: to pull the floor levels through from the north and south buildings creating a new "dissonant zone" where students gather.

For the competition of a new cinema complex in Busan, Korea, we wanted to make the six cinemas represent collapsed time. We stacked the cinema vertically in an exposed planar architecture. The different halls draw the surrounding plan elements inward to their planar interiors and the site is ordered as a public plaza. In Knokke-Heist, Belgium, we

2. POROSITY
LITERAL, PHENOMENAL AND URBAN

URBAN
3. INSERTIONS

are working on the Sail Hybrid, an urban insertion activating the center of the city.

Even at a small scale, architecture can preserve many natural landscapes and create a mini-urbanity. I call these projects *Precincts.* For instance, in Langenlois, Austria, we designed a visitors center and hotel for a winery. The project is organized in three parts—under the ground, in the ground, and above the ground—and is a precinct complex linked to the historical town.

In the last category, *Fusion,* I will address four museums that represent a fusion between architecture, urbanism, and landscape. Kiasma lies in the heart of Helsinki, Finland, at the foot of the parliament building to the west, with Eliel Saarinen's Helsinki Station to the east, and Alvar Aalto's Finlandia Hall to the north. The concept of Kiasma involves the building's mass intertwining with the geometry of the city and landscape, which are reflected in the shape of the building. An implicit cultural line curves to link the building to Finlandia Hall while it also engages a "natural line" connecting to the back landscape and Töölö Bay. For the addition and renovation of the Nelson-Atkins Museum of Art, Kansas City, we imagined glass lenses emerging from new sculpture gardens bringing light to the galleries, fusing landscape with architecture. In Biarritz, France, we are creating the Cité du Surf et de L'Océan. On axis with the ocean, toward the west, the project's site is slightly cupped on the edges, connecting the forms with the landscape while simultaneously concealing flanking parked cars. The building shape is intended to create a central gathering plaza, open to sky and sea, with the horizon in the distance. The project integrates seamlessly into the surrounding landscape. The Herning Center of the Arts, sited on a completely flat Jutland field, began as a vision of fusing landscape and architecture. It is important to clarify that this aspiration is distinct from suburban sprawl with its indiscriminate spread of houses and lawns and its auto dependency. The aim of fusion concerns public space and institutional works, which would ideally work together with dense pack housing and pedestrian accessed commercial zones, like the town of Herning.

My argument for the architectural project as an urban catalyst is an argument for idealistic incremental actions instead of master plans. Master plans, endlessly debated and politically positioned, move too slowly in the 21st century to be effective. Usually they are altered beyond recognition or shelved.

Of course we need well-planned overall visions, especially in transportation and infrastructure, but our urban experience is shaped through the realization of specific architectural projects.

Especially with the rapid growth in Asia, the effective realization depends on incorporating visions and ideals in the individual projects.

In 1950 the poet Charles Olsen said, "The central fact of America is Space." At the close of the 20th century Harold Bloom said, "Our central fact is Time." We are now at a turning point: *Macrocosm* is Earth, the planet, and the site-frame of a *Microcosm*. It is a catalyst for change: Architecture.

In conclusion these categories make up an argument for diverse urbanisms which, from the point of view of the natural landscape, are conservative. However, from the point of view of architectural project. they radically refocus the potential for experimental works. As a catalyst they give a unique response to circumstance and site.

COLLEGE OF ARCHITECTURE AND LANDSCAPE ARCHITECTURE
UNIVERSITY OF MINNESOTA

Minneapolis, Minnesota
1990–2002

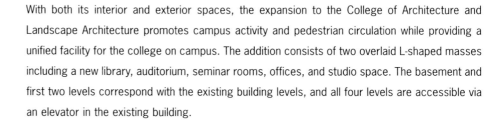

With both its interior and exterior spaces, the expansion to the College of Architecture and Landscape Architecture promotes campus activity and pedestrian circulation while providing a unified facility for the college on campus. The addition consists of two overlaid L-shaped masses including a new library, auditorium, seminar rooms, offices, and studio space. The basement and first two levels correspond with the existing building levels, and all four levels are accessible via an elevator in the existing building.

The addition is a complement and counterpoint to the existing building with its centralized 100-foot-square atrium built in 1958 by Thorshov and Cerny. While the existing building is centralized and homogeneous, the new addition offers peripheral views and morphological multiplicity. The existing building is centripetal, with four right angles framing four views onto the same court; the addition is centrifugal, with four obtuse angles opening to views on four different exterior landscapes. In complement to the horizontal facade of the existing building, the new addition has vertical elevations at the ends of each arm that stand as virtual towers, "shafts of space" activating the campus site.

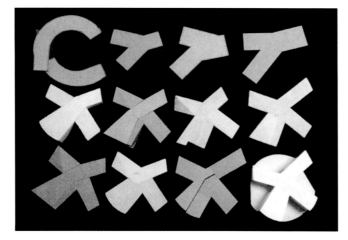

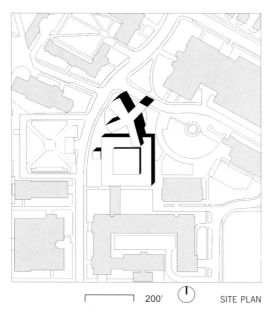

200' SITE PLAN

Opposite: Light-diffusing glass-plank wall in the library.

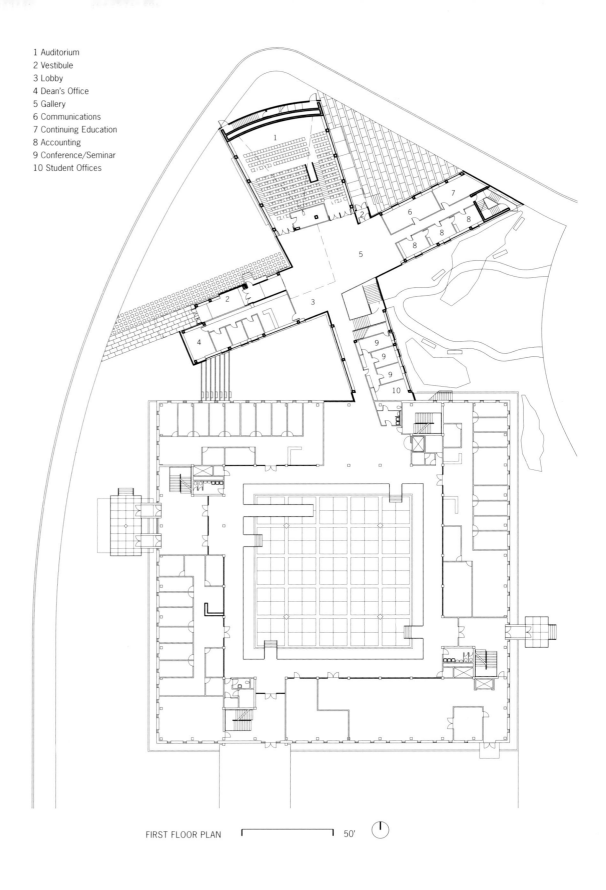

1 Auditorium
2 Vestibule
3 Lobby
4 Dean's Office
5 Gallery
6 Communications
7 Continuing Education
8 Accounting
9 Conference/Seminar
10 Student Offices

FIRST FLOOR PLAN   50'

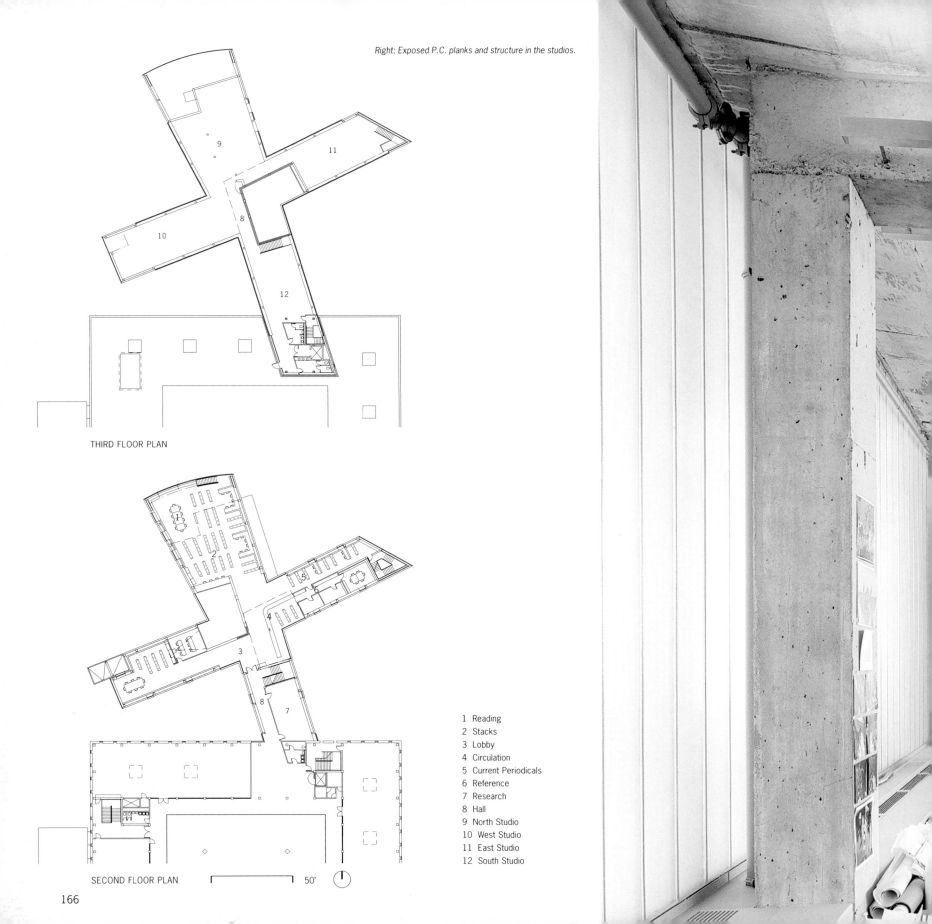

THIRD FLOOR PLAN

SECOND FLOOR PLAN |⊢——————| 50' ⊕

1 Reading
2 Stacks
3 Lobby
4 Circulation
5 Current Periodicals
6 Reference
7 Research
8 Hall
9 North Studio
10 West Studio
11 East Studio
12 South Studio

EXIT>

Right: A required exit composed of concrete and light.

KIASMA MUSEUM OF CONTEMPORARY ART

Helsinki, Finland
1992–1998

The concept of Kiasma involves the building's mass intertwining with the geometry of the city and landscape, which are reflected in the shape of the building.

Particular to Helsinki is the horizontal natural light of the northern latitudes. The slight variation in room shape and size due to the gently curving section of the building allows natural light to enter in several different ways. This asymmetrically drives movement through a series of spatial sequences. In this regard the overall design becomes a slightly warped "gallery of rooms," where the spatial flow emerges from the combination of the horizontal light-catching section and the continuity of the internal space. This curved unfolding sequence provides elements of both mystery and surprise, which do not exist in a typical single- or double-loaded orthogonal arrangement of space. Instead, the visitor is confronted with a continuous unfolding of an infinite series of changing perspectives that connect the internal experience to the overall concept of intertwining or Kiasma.

With Kiasma, there is a hope to confirm that architecture, art, and culture are not separate disciplines but are all integral parts of the city and landscape. Through care in development of details and the materials, the new museum provides a dynamic yet subtle spatial form, extending toward the city in the south and the landscape to the north. The geometry has an interior mystery and an exterior horizon, which, like two hands clasping each other, form the architectonic equivalent of a public invitation. Referring to the landscape the interiors are reversible, and form the site that in this special place and circumstance is a synthesis of building and landscape... a Kiasma.

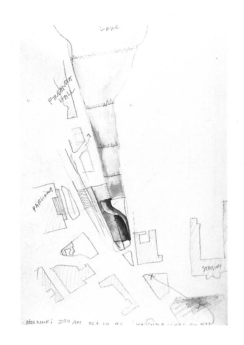

1500'   SITE PLAN

Opposite: The sanded aluminum facade is punctured to reveal the intertwining stairs.

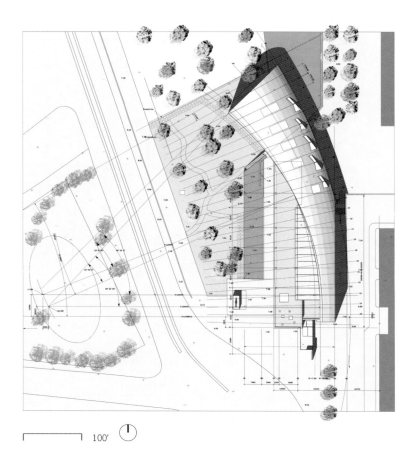

100'

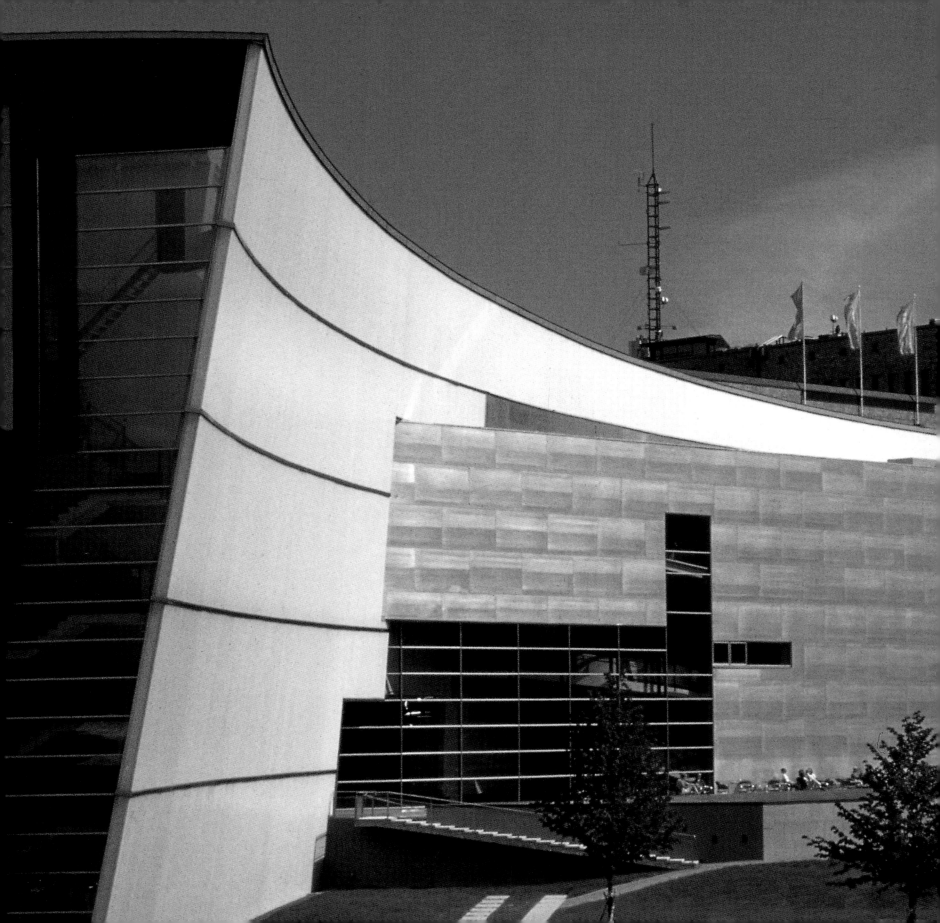

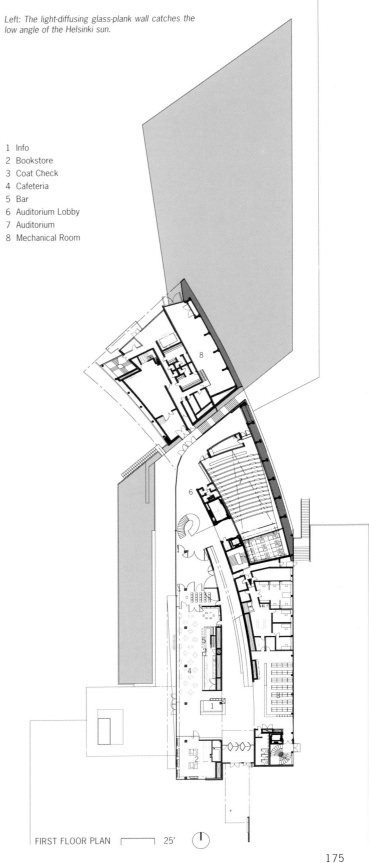

Left: The light-diffusing glass-plank wall catches the low angle of the Helsinki sun.

1 Info
2 Bookstore
3 Coat Check
4 Cafeteria
5 Bar
6 Auditorium Lobby
7 Auditorium
8 Mechanical Room

FIRST FLOOR PLAN   25'

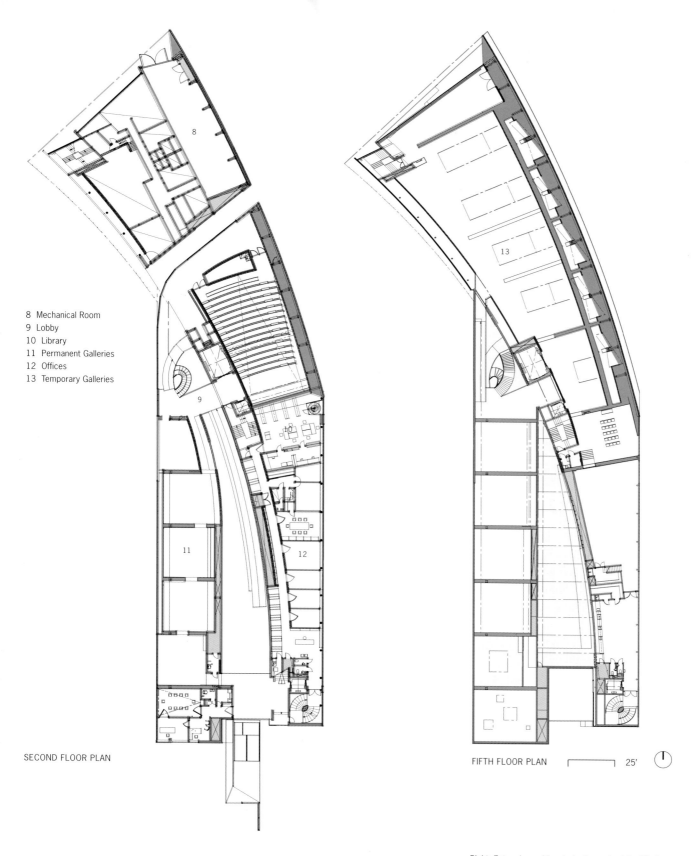

8 Mechanical Room
9 Lobby
10 Library
11 Permanent Galleries
12 Offices
13 Temporary Galleries

SECOND FLOOR PLAN

FIFTH FLOOR PLAN └─────┘ 25' ①

Right: Entry plaza with exterior lamps by Juhani Pallasmaa.

Opposite: Main entry ramp to the second-floor gallery.

Above, left: Opening Day, May 31, 1998.

Above, right: The intertwining central stairs.

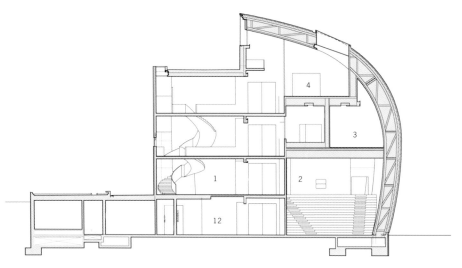

SECTION A-A

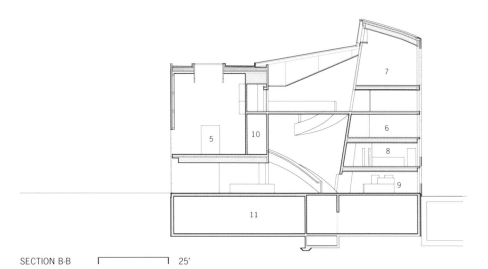

SECTION B-B |———————| 25'

1 Lobby
2 Auditorium
3 Gallery
4 Temporary Exhibition
5 Double-height Permanent Exhibition
6 Permanent Exhibition

7 Workshop for Children
8 Secretary
9 Cloakroom
10 Storage
11 Artwork Storage
12 Packing and Assembling

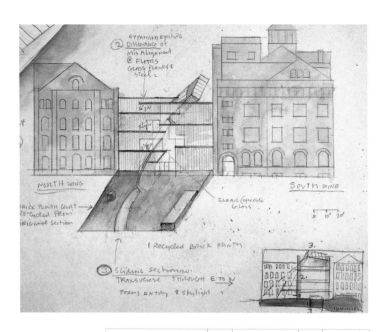

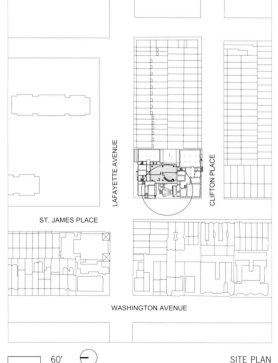

ST. JAMES PLACE

WASHINGTON AVENUE

LAFAYETTE AVENUE

CLIFTON PLACE

60'   SITE PLAN

HIGGINS HALL CENTER SECTION
PRATT INSTITUTE

Brooklyn, New York
1997–2005

The new Higgins Hall Center Section is an urban insertion that connects the sections of the two adjacent historic landmarked buildings. Floor plates of the north and south wings do not align, and thus by drawing this misalignment into the new glass section to meet at the center, a "dissonant zone" is created, which marks the new entry to the school.

The two masonry buildings, together with the new glass insertion, form an H in plan. New courts facing east and west are paved in the reused red brick, which was salvaged following a fire that took place on the site in 1996. Rising from the burnt brick is a concrete frame supported on six columns spanned with concrete and sheathed with structural glass planks. An economical industrial material with translucent insulation, the planks span between floors, creating a translucent glow at night.

The east-facing court overlooks the green yards of the inner block, while the west court is shaped as the main front on St. James Place. A two-throated skylight marks the top of this center wing, joining two types of light: south light and north light, analogous to harmonious sounds in a dissonant chord.

1 Entry
2 Lobby
3 Lower Lobby
4 Reception
5 Student Services
6 Administrative Office
7 Gallery
8 Sculpture Terrace
9 Slope
10 Ramp
11 Studio
12 Classroom/Seminar
13 Faculty Offices

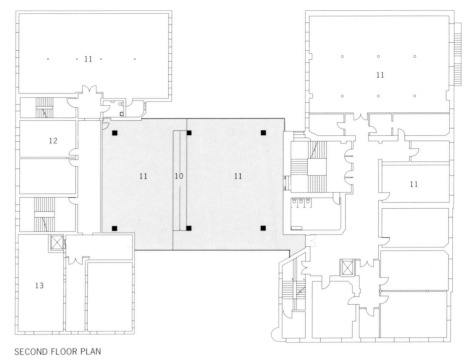

SECOND FLOOR PLAN

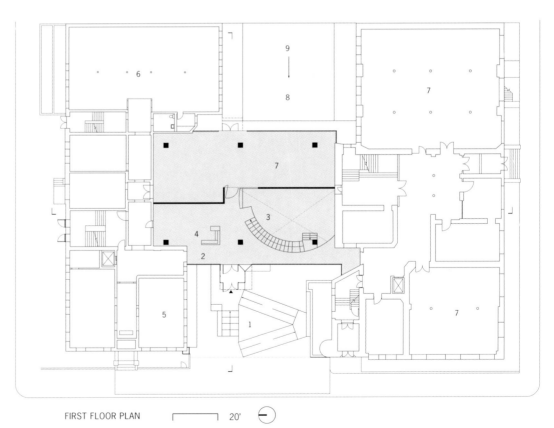

FIRST FLOOR PLAN   20'

Left: The ramp slices through the studio spaces, turning the body's movement perpendicular to the view of the exterior.

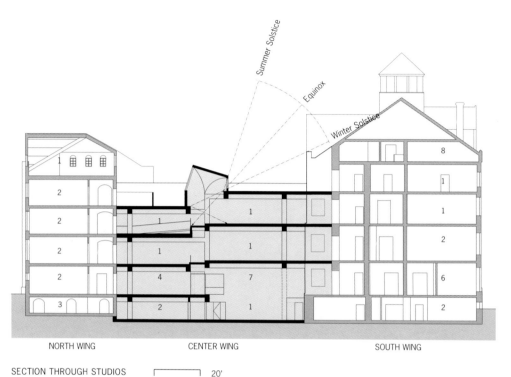

Summer Solstice

Equinox

Winter Solstice

			8
1			1
2		1	1
2		1	1
2	4	7	6
3	2	1	2

NORTH WING   CENTER WING   SOUTH WING

SECTION THROUGH STUDIOS   ⌐————⌐   20'

1 Studios
2 Classrooms
3 Office
4 Lobby
5 Lower Lobby
6 Gallery
7 Gallery behind
8 Attic

Right: Where the ramp slices through the volume, space and vision is pushed upward and downward.

190

LOISIUM VISITOR CENTER AND HOTEL

Langenlois, Austria
2001–2005

On the edge of the town of Langenlois, 60 minutes by car west of Vienna, on a gently south-sloping vineyard, a new wine center and visitor facilities were built to celebrate the rich local heritage of a magnificent wine vault system. This historic subterranean network, which includes 900-year-old stone vaults, underlies the urban plan of the town.

The project is composed of three parts: the existing vaults (which were made accessible to visitors), the visitor center, and the hotel and spa. The three elements of the project stand in relation to a geometric field of vineyards, the landscape of wine production: under the ground (the existing vaults), in the ground (visitor center and ramp connection), and over the ground (hotel and spa).

Wine Visitor Center

The simple volume is cut and sliced via the vault morphology to create a rich interior light. Some of the deep cuts are glazed in recycled bottle glass with rich green hues that cast their lustrous light on the interior. Partially set into the earth of the vineyard, the slight forward tilt of the structure indicates its subterranean connection. Upon entering, the visitor perceives a volume of space and steps out to the vineyard. A footpath leads down to the entrance of the vault system. The return journey is made through a ramped passage dappled with light refracted through a reflecting pool.

Hotel and Spa

The square plan of the hotel is aligned with the strict geometry of the surrounding vineyard rows, and offers a variety of activities and room types. The earthlike materials and palette combined with the views of the surrounding landscape create a strong connection of the hotel to its context. While the ground floor is transparent and open, the two upper floors are more private. A courtyard and terrace provide outdoor seating.

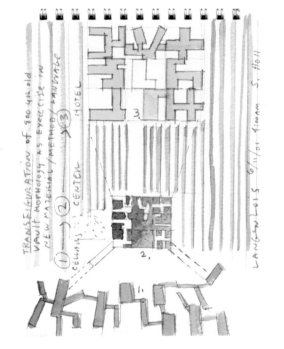

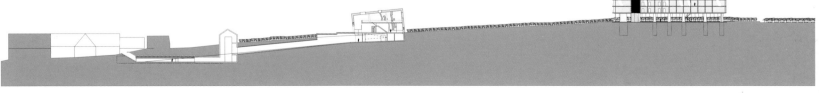

SITE SECTION   Under   In   Over

⊢———⊣ 100'

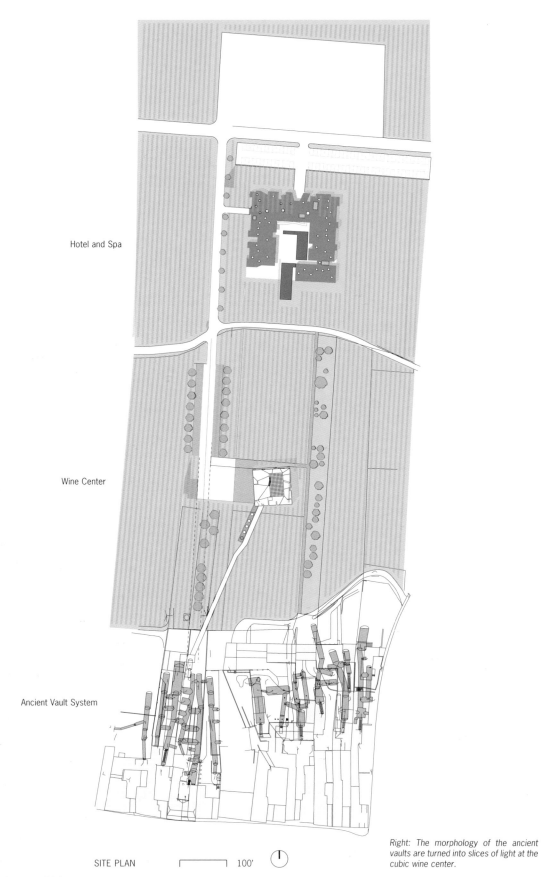

Hotel and Spa

Wine Center

Ancient Vault System

SITE PLAN ⊢——————⊣ 100' ①

194

Right: The morphology of the ancient vaults are turned into slices of light at the cubic wine center.

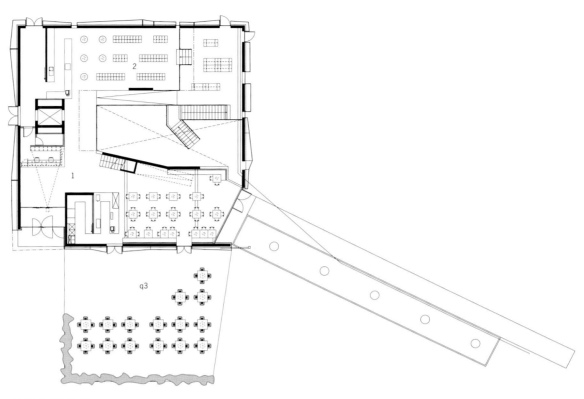

FIRST FLOOR PLAN

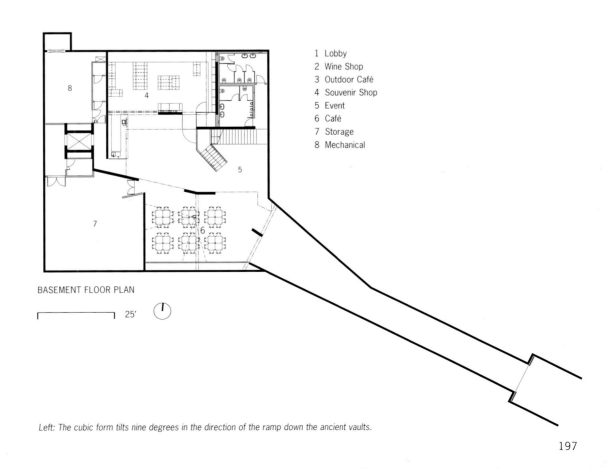

BASEMENT FLOOR PLAN

|—————| 25' (↻)

1 Lobby
2 Wine Shop
3 Outdoor Café
4 Souvenir Shop
5 Event
6 Café
7 Storage
8 Mechanical

Left: The cubic form tilts nine degrees in the direction of the ramp down the ancient vaults.

Opposite: Sunlight filtered through the recycled green bottle-glass.

HOTEL SECOND FLOOR PLAN

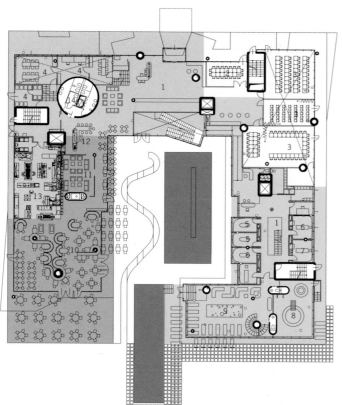

1 Lobby
2 Meeting Room
3 Auditorium/Meeting Room
4 Office
5 Hairdresser
6 Spa Wet Treatment
7 Vichy Shower
8 Fitness
9 Spa Resting Area
10 Restaurant
11 Smoking Lounge
12 Bar
13 Kitchen
14 Restroom
15 Hotel Rooms

HOTEL FIRST FLOOR PLAN   ⊢———⊣ 25'   ①

Right: View from the hotel's courtyard toward the wine center and the town of Langenlois.

Above: The vault morphology becomes sand-cast aluminum door handles.

1 Guestroom
2 Hallway
3 Bathroom
4 Restaurant
5 Manicure/Pedicure
6 Spa Treatment
7 Office
8 Lobby
9 Spa

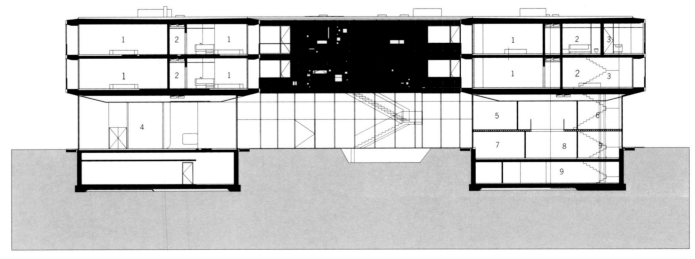

HOTEL SECTION ⊏───⊐ 25'

NELSON-ATKINS MUSEUM OF ART ADDITION

Kansas City, Missouri
1999–2007

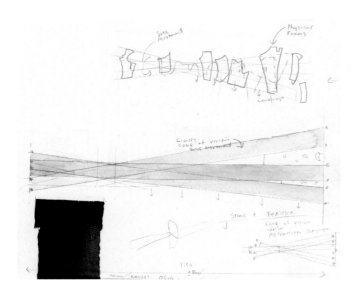

The expansion of the Nelson-Atkins Museum of Art fuses architecture with landscape to create an experiential architecture that unfolds for visitors as it is perceived through each individual's movement through space and time. The new addition engages the existing sculpture garden, transforming the entire museum site into the precinct of the visitor's experience.

Extending along the eastern edge of the campus, the addition is distinguished by five glass lenses, traversing from the existing building through the sculpture park to form new spaces and angles of vision. This innovative merging of landscape, architecture, and art was executed through close collaboration with museum curators and artists to achieve a dynamic and supportive relationship between art and architecture.

The sculpture garden continues up and over the gallery roofs, creating sculpture courts between the five lenses, while also providing green roofs to achieve high insulation and to control storm water. The meandering path in the sculpture garden above has its sinuous complement in the open flow of the new galleries. Glass lenses bring different qualities of light to the galleries while the sculpture garden's pathways wind through them.

At the heart of the addition's lenses is a structural concept merged with a light and air distributor concept: "Breathing T's" transport light down into the galleries along their curved undersides while carrying the glass in suspension. Circulation and exhibition merge as visitors can look from one level to another, from inside to outside. The double-glass cavities of the lenses gather sun-heated air in winter and exhaust it in summer. Optimum light levels for all types of art or media installations and seasonal flexibility requirements are ensured through the use of computer-controlled screens and of special translucent insulating material embedded in the glass cavities.

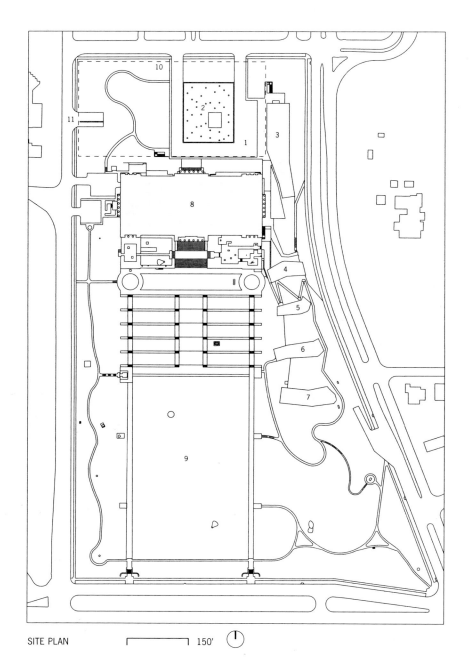

SITE PLAN ⌐────────┐ 150' ◯

1 Entry Plaza
2 Reflecting Poll
3 Lens 1 Upper Lobby
4 Lens 2
5 Lens 3
6 Lens 4
7 Lens 5
8 Existing Museum
9 Existing Sculpture Lawn
10 Garage Below
11 Garage Entrance

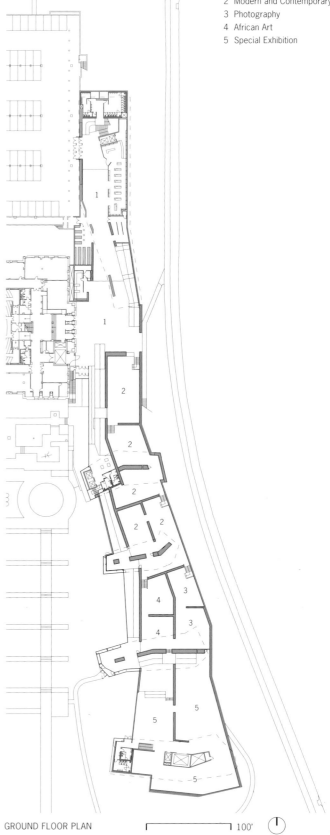

1 Lower Lobby
2 Modern and Contemporary Art
3 Photography
4 African Art
5 Special Exhibition

GROUND FLOOR PLAN   ⊢————————⊣ 100'

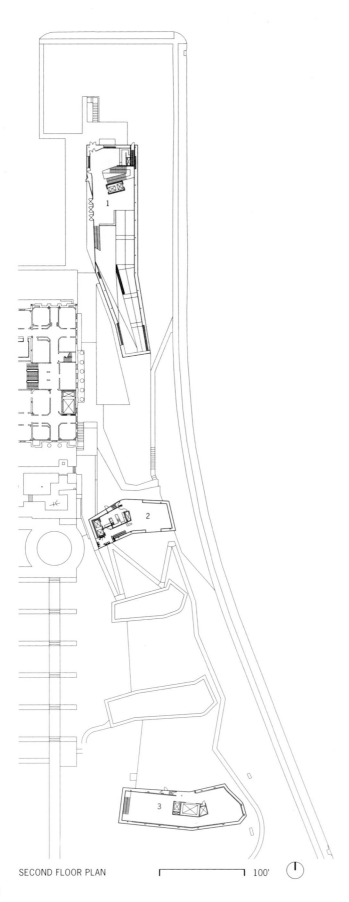

SECOND FLOOR PLAN  100'

LIBRARY LEVEL PLAN

1 Upper Lobby
2 Trustees Garden Dining Room
3 Special Exhibitions
4 Library

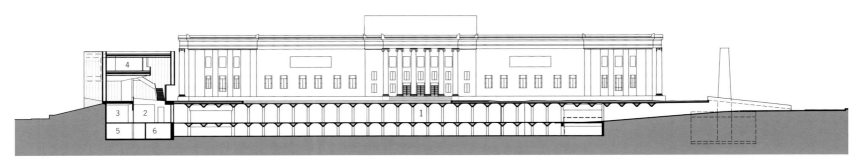

CROSS SECTION THROUGH MAIN LOBBY & GARAGE

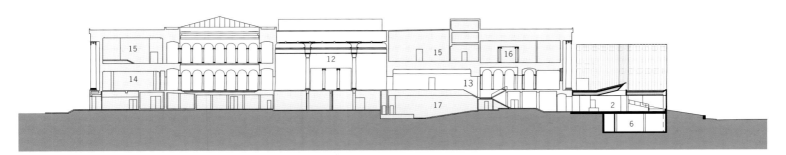

CROSS SECTION THROUGH LOWER LOBBY & EXISTING BUILDING

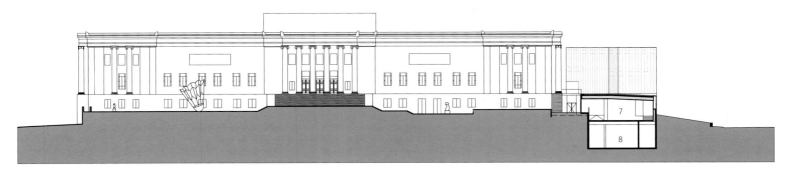

CROSS SECTION THROUGH MODERN & CONTEMPORARY GALLERIES

1 Parking Garage
2 Lobby
3 Museum Store
4 Library
5 Stacks
6 Mechanical
7 Modern & Contemporary Art
8 Collection Storage
9 Noguchi Court

10 Special Exhibition
11 Art Receiving
12 Existing Building
13 New Opening & Stair
14 European Art
15 Asian Art
16 American Art
17 Auditorium

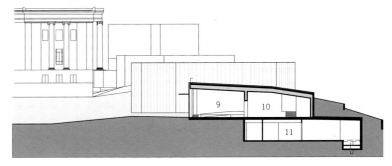

CROSS SECTION THROUGH NOGUCHI COURT & SPECIAL EXHIBITION

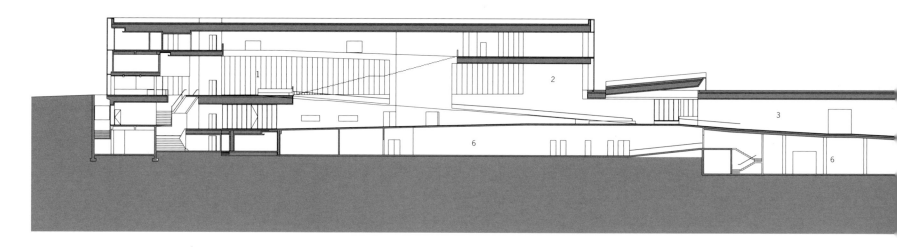

LONGINTUDINAL SECTION ⊢————————┐ 50'

1 Upper Lobby
2 Lower Lobby
3 Modern and Contemporary Art

4 Photography
5 Special Exhibitions
6 Basement

Below: Main ramp at the entry.

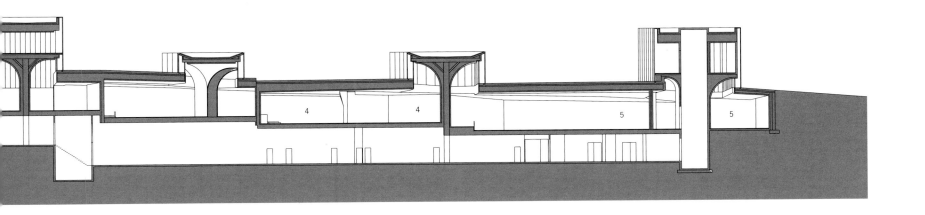

Below: A fluttering "T" mixes north and south light.

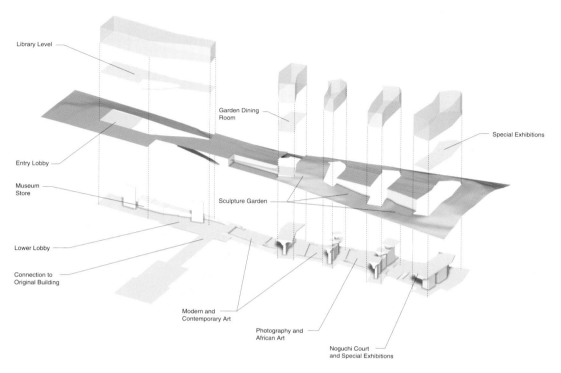

Library Level

Garden Dining
Room

Special Exhibitions

Entry Lobby

Museum
Store

Sculpture Garden

Lower Lobby

Connection to
Original Building

Modern and
Contemporary Art

Photography and
African Art

Noguchi Court
and Special Exhibitions

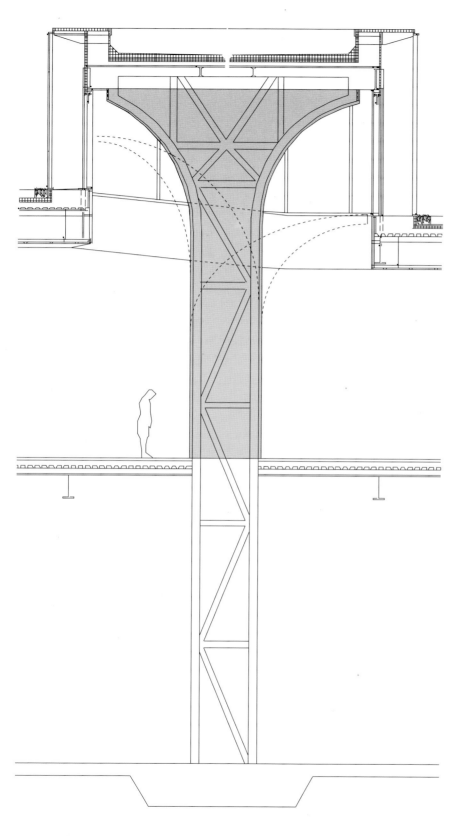

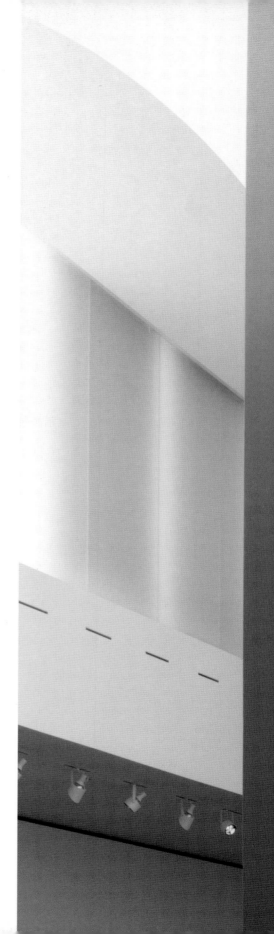

"T" SECTION AT LENS 3   5'

Right: A fluttering "T" mixes cool and warm light.

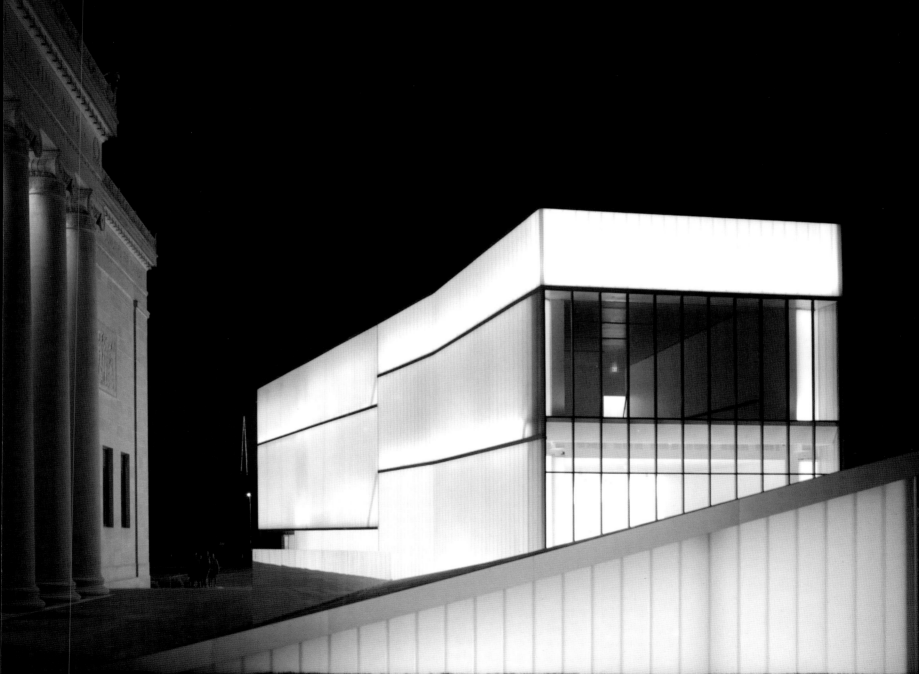

Left: Walter De Maria's One Sun and 34 Moons *fuses with the reflecting pool at the main entry court.*

Edge of a City (Parallax Towers), 1989–1990

1000' SITE PLAN

WORLD TRADE CENTER

New York, New York

2002

In collaboration with
Richard Meier and Partners,
Eisenman Architects,
and Gwathmey Siegel & Associates Architects

In the tradition of Rockefeller Center, we propose to build a great public space for New York City at the World Trade Center site. We call this place Memorial Square. While the 19th- and 20th-century precedents for urban plazas are contained spaces, our 21st-century Memorial Square is both contained and extended, symbolizing its connections to the community, the city, and the world.

Memorial Square will renew the spirit and the quality of life in Lower Manhattan. But the most visible sign of renewal for the city and the world will be the proposed hybrid buildings, which rise 1,111 feet to restore the Manhattan skyline with geometric clarity in glowing white glass. For all the activity that the buildings will sustain—from a hotel and apartments to offices, cultural spaces, and a memorial chapel—the image they project is one of dignity and calm. As the iconic pieces of Memorial Square, they will draw visitors from around the world, who will travel to the memorial observation terrace to once again view New York City from the top of Lower Manhattan.

Comprised of five vertical sections and interconnecting horizontal floor elements, the two buildings represent a new typology in skyscraper design. At ground level, these forms become ceremonial gateways into the site. In their quiet abstraction of solids and voids, the buildings appear as screens, suggesting both presence and absence, and encouraging reflection and imagination. Their cantilevered ends extend outward, like the fingers of the ground plan, reaching toward the city and each other. Nearly touching at the northeast corner of the site, they resemble the interlaced fingers of protective hands.

Opposite: Early scheme with sloped horizontal connections.

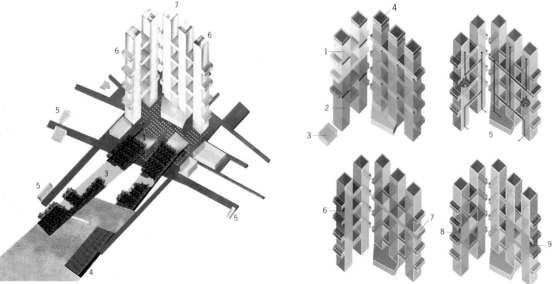

Far left: MULTIPLE MEMORIAL SITES AND CULTURAL FACILITIES
1 Tower Footprints / reflecting ponds
2 Volumes of the Towers' footprints below grade
3 Shadows marking last shadow of WTC with trees and memorial lights
4 Floating memorial plaza on the Hudson, largest gathering place, site for memorial competition
5 Multiple memorial sites at the tips of the fingers
6 Sky memorials at the top of the towers on the observation decks
7 Memorial chapel with meditation spaces

Left: BUILDINGS' FLEXIBILITY
1 Public levels (hotel, observation decks, conference centers, sky lobbies and memorials)
2 Office levels
3 Cultural levels
4 Restaurants, observation decks, sky memorial and chapel
5 Life safety program (multiple escape routes)
6 Vertical offices
7 Horizontal offices
8 Staggered offices
9 Courtyard offices

230

BUSAN CINEMA COMPLEX

Seoul, South Korea

2005

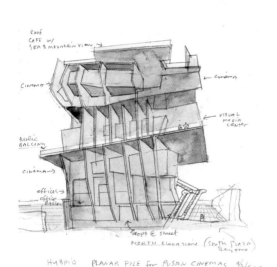

SITE PLAN

Stacked and expanded upward into a 75-meter-high (246-foot) tower, the new Busan Cinema Complex takes a unique form. Stretched like an accordion, the building section is analogous to "cinema time" expanding an action that took minutes into a one-hour-long film, or collapsing a 100-hundred-year span of time into an hour. The six cinemas are representative and comparable to collapsed time, and draw the surrounding plan elements inward to their planar interiors. The multifunctional character of the tower is invigorated by a "shuffled" program, creating lively spaces between the six cinemas, all with specific activities and functions.

The stacked cinema complex tower form allows for panoramic river and mountain views from the public spaces, including the rooftop and the cantilevered terraces adjacent to spaces throughout the section. As a consequence, the site is ordered as a true public plaza defined by a border of "cinema loft" residential condominiums, providing economic and social support by their proximity. The tower provides, in the tradition of the great urban cities of the world, a vital urban plaza energized by surrounding 24-hour-program Cinema Lofts.

Utilizing Korean ship building technology, the entire structure is a composite construction of Cor-Ten steel plates with concrete sandwich cores. At night, projected light illuminations expose the planes in space and the dynamic shade and shadow of this unique cinema tower. A computerized HVAC system connected to geothermal wells and threaded via plastic pipes throughout the wall system removes heat from the southern planes or cold from the northern planes.

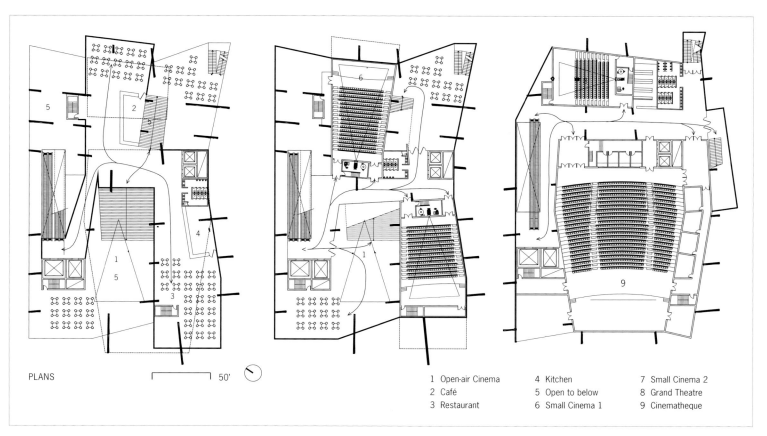

PLANS |⎯⎯⎯⎯⎯⎯| 50' ⊕

1   Open-air Cinema
2   Café
3   Restaurant
4   Kitchen
5   Open to below
6   Small Cinema 1
7   Small Cinema 2
8   Grand Theatre
9   Cinematheque

COMPOSITE STEEL AND CONCRETE PLANAR WALL "THERMAL WALLS"

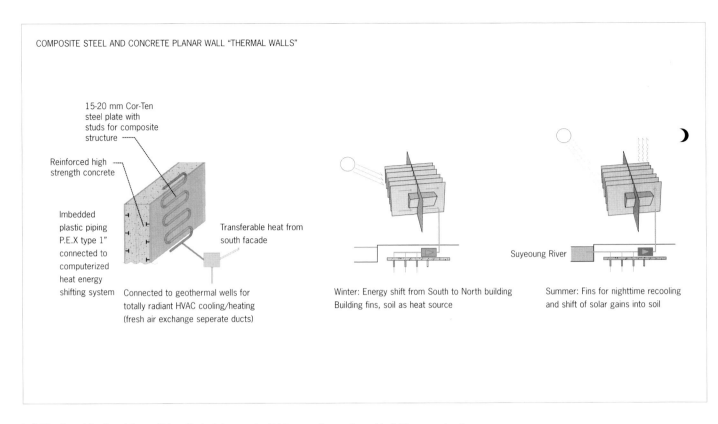

15-20 mm Cor-Ten steel plate with studs for composite structure

Reinforced high strength concrete

Imbedded plastic piping P.E.X type 1" connected to computerized heat energy shifting system

Transferable heat from south facade

Connected to geothermal wells for totally radiant HVAC cooling/heating (fresh air exchange seperate ducts)

Winter: Energy shift from South to North building Building fins, soil as heat source

Suyeoung River

Summer: Fins for nighttime recooling and shift of solar gains into soil

Left: View toward the Sea of Japan. Below: Stacked cinemas stand high among the ongoing residential tower constructions.

1 Concourse/Convention
2 Piff Center
3 Main Cinema Hall
4 Ticket Box
5 Snack Bar
6 Operating Office
7 Service
8 Midsize Theatre
9 Media Center
10 Small Theatre
11 Expansion Platform
12 Grand Theatre
13 Cinematheque
14 Roof Terrace
15 Public Rooftop
16 Bridge to Park
17 Working/Loft Units

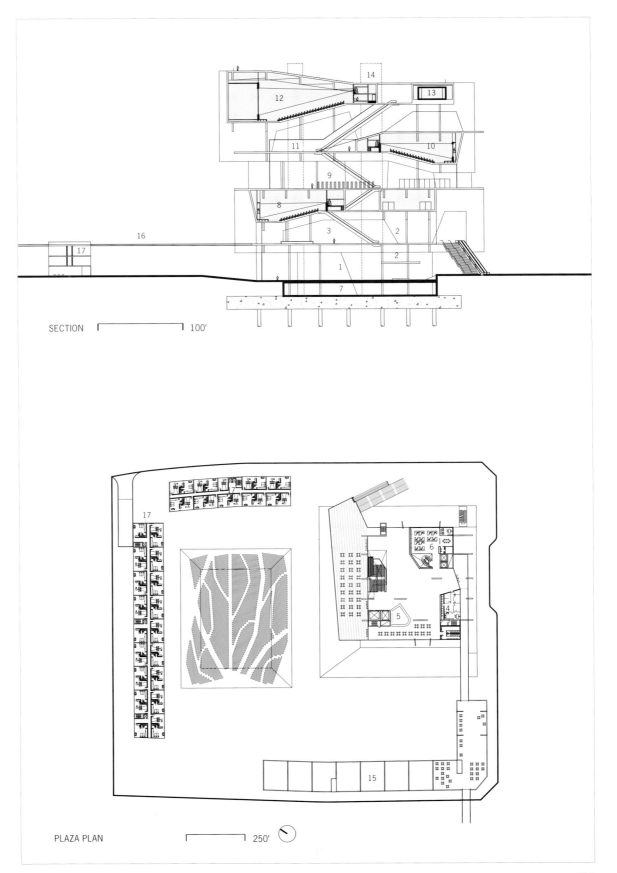

SECTION ⊢————⊣ 100'

PLAZA PLAN ⊢————⊣ 250'

One panel of the René Magritte mural in the existing Albert Place Casino.

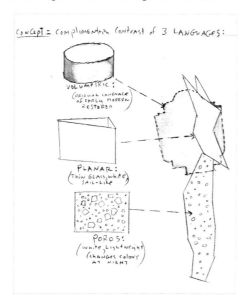

SAIL HYBRID

Knokke-Heist, Belgium

2005–

Located on the North Sea coast, the Belgian seaside resort town of Knokke-Heist required a renovation and transformation of their existing casino. With an enhanced program intended to provide an iconic landmark and bolster the town's stature and urban spaces, the project transforms the seaside resort into a premiere travel and architectonic destination.

The Sail Hybrid design was inspired by the René Magritte mural, *The Ship Which Tells the Story to the Mermaid*, one of eight original Surrealist masterpieces in the series called *Le Domaine Enchanté*, commissioned for the casino in 1953. The murals are housed in the Magritte Room, a protected monument located in the original Albert Place Casino built in 1930 by Leon Stynen. The Sail Hybrid concept expressly preserves the Magritte Room and restores the original casino facades. The mural inspired a hybrid transformation of the casino into three architectures: an early-modern restored volumetric architecture (the white, restored, and reprogrammed casino), a porous-bridge Hybrid Architecture (perforated congress hall), and a sail-like Planar Architecture (glass planes—hotel and apartment tower) to create a synergy of new functions.

The new three-part hybrid transformation rebuilds one of Belgium's great architect's fine works, becoming a glowing new beacon on the Atlantic wall and interconnecting the ensemble of city buildings in Knokke-Heist with new urban insertion.

SITE PLAN

Opposite: Pool in planar section, accessible by diving underneath the structural beam.

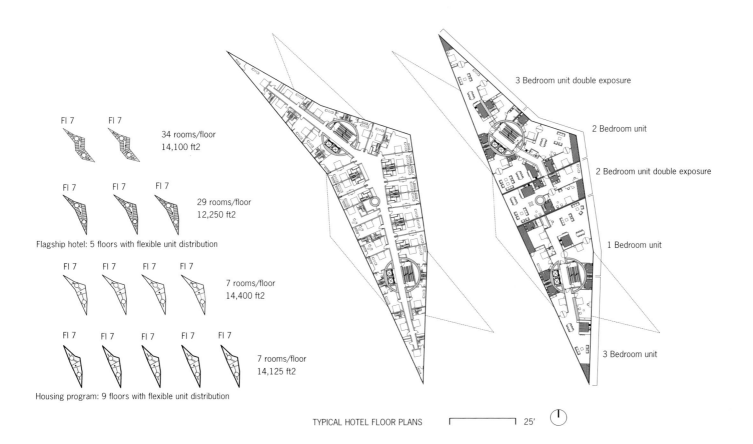

FI 7   FI 7   34 rooms/floor
                14,100 ft2

FI 7   FI 7   FI 7   29 rooms/floor
                        12,250 ft2

Flagship hotel: 5 floors with flexible unit distribution

FI 7   FI 7   FI 7   FI 7   7 rooms/floor
                                14,400 ft2

FI 7   FI 7   FI 7   FI 7   FI 7   7 rooms/floor
                                        14,125 ft2

Housing program: 9 floors with flexible unit distribution

3 Bedroom unit double exposure

2 Bedroom unit

2 Bedroom unit double exposure

1 Bedroom unit

3 Bedroom unit

TYPICAL HOTEL FLOOR PLANS   ⌐————⌐ 25'   ①

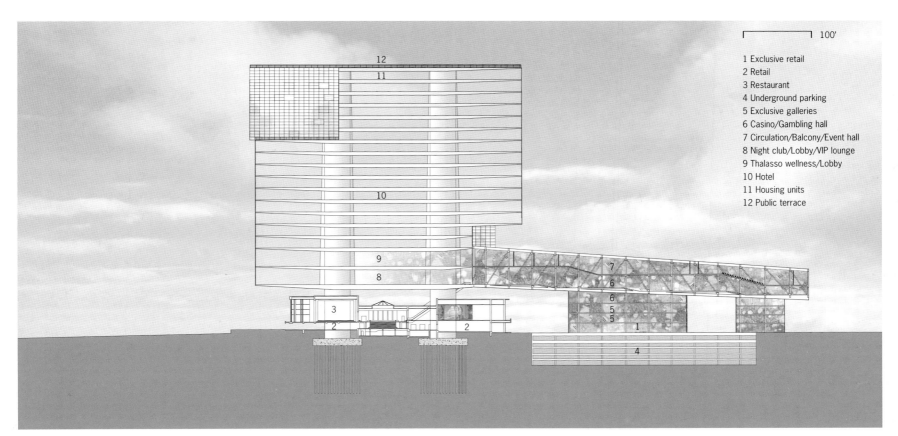

100'

1 Exclusive retail
2 Retail
3 Restaurant
4 Underground parking
5 Exclusive galleries
6 Casino/Gambling hall
7 Circulation/Balcony/Event hall
8 Night club/Lobby/VIP lounge
9 Thalasso wellness/Lobby
10 Hotel
11 Housing units
12 Public terrace

240

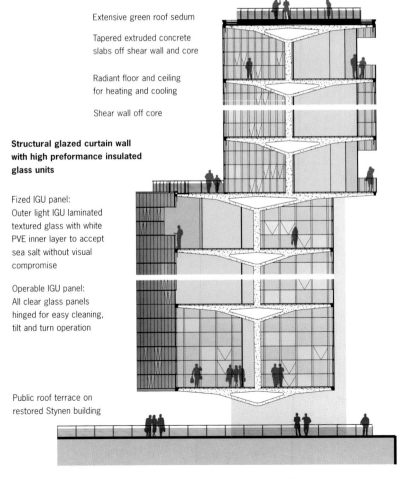

Extensive green roof sedum

Tapered extruded concrete
slabs off shear wall and core

Radiant floor and ceiling
for heating and cooling

Shear wall off core

**Structural glazed curtain wall
with high preformance insulated
glass units**

Fized IGU panel:
Outer light IGU laminated
textured glass with white
PVE inner layer to accept
sea salt without visual
compromise

Operable IGU panel:
All clear glass panels
hinged for easy cleaning,
tilt and turn operation

Public roof terrace on
restored Stynen building

HOTEL TOWER CROSS SECTION   25'

Right: The model showing the three parts of the design: the volumetric of the existing Casino, the planar hotel and apartment tower, and the porous conference center and bridge to parking.

Below: A visual break in the Atlantic wall marks the town's new center.

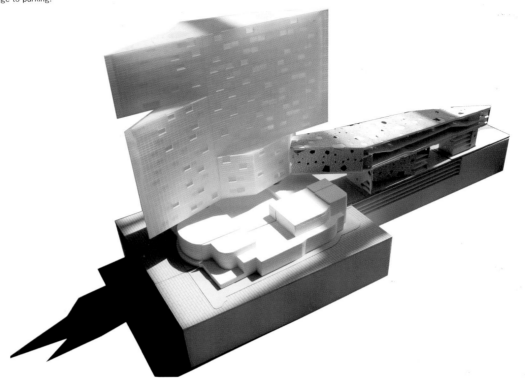

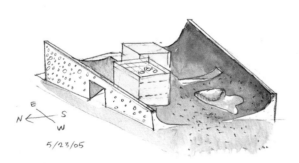

5/23/05

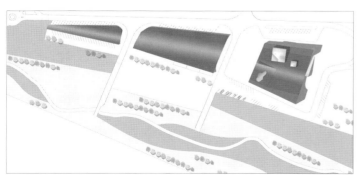

⓵ SITE PLAN

CITÉ DU SURF ET DE L'OCÉAN

Biarritz, France
2005–

In collaboration with Solange Fabião

This new museum intends to raise awareness of oceanic issues and to explore educational and scientific aspects of the surf and sea and their role upon our leisure, science, and ecology. The project is comprised of a museum building, exhibition areas, and a plaza, within a master plan site encompassing 22,600 meters (74,147 feet).

The design concept is based on the phrases "under the sky / under the sea." The building shape is intended to create a central gathering plaza, open to sky and sea, with the horizon in the distance. This "Place de l'Océan," with its curved under-the-sky shape, forms the character of the main exhibition space, while the convex structural ceiling forms the under-the-sea shape. Thus, the concept generates a unique profile and form for the building, and through its insertion and efficient site utilization, the project integrates into the surrounding landscape.

The building's inspiring spatial qualities are first experienced in the entrance space, where ramps pass along the dynamic curved surface on which filmed surf action are projected, animating the space with changing images and light. On axis with the ocean, toward the west, the site is slightly cupped on the edges, connecting the forms with the landscape while simultaneously concealing flanking parked cars. With its mix of fields and indigenous vegetation, the natural landscape extends the museum facility and provides a site for festivals and daily events.

Toward the south, the slab is peeled open from a covered area with space for indoor games and activities. Dedicated as a surfer's hangout, this area contains a skating rink and an open porch. The public mix of recreational surfing and scientific education focused on the ocean is a new laboratory, parallel to the experiment of fusing landscape with architecture.

Left, top: Café view of the Atlantic Ocean.

Left, bottom: Section at the entry stairs down to the main level.

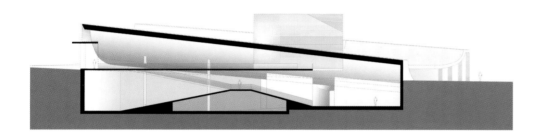

1 Entrance
2 Café
3 Shop
4 Foyer
5 Kiosk
6 Mechanical
7 Permanent Exhibition
8 Temporary Exhibition
9 Multipurpose Room
10 Porch

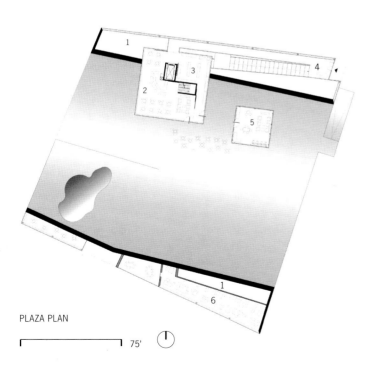

PLAZA PLAN

75'

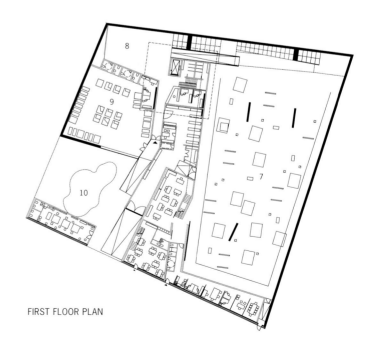

FIRST FLOOR PLAN

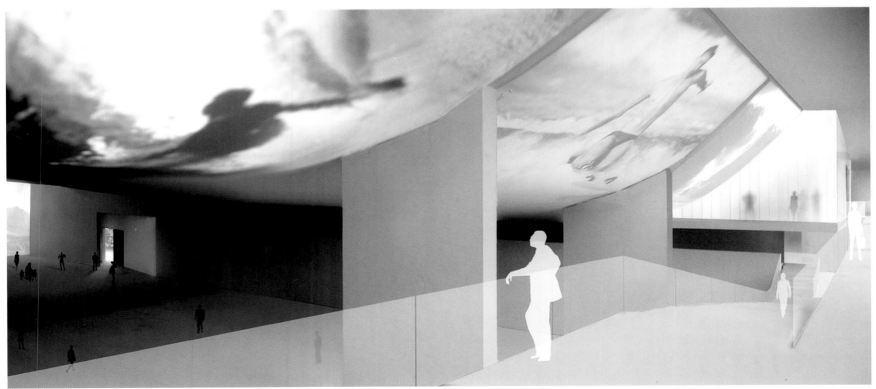

HERNING CENTER FOR THE ARTS

Herning, Denmark

2005–

A fusion of landscape and architecture, this proposal aims at "building the site." In transforming the flat field, a new landscape of grass mounds and pools conceals all the parking and service areas while shaping inspiring bermed landscape spaces that focus on reflecting pools positioned in the south sun. The curved green roof sections of the new one-level museum align with this new "built site." All gallery spaces are orthogonal and simple with fine proportions in respect to the art, while the curved roof sections overhead bring in natural light. The internal gallery walls in lightweight construction can be moved as per a curator's requirements.

The curved roofs are stress-skin structures in carbon fiber strands with a resin matrix. The textured surface of the structure painted white can be seen on the interior of the undersides. Like a see-saw tied down on each side, the roof is anchored by introducing thin rods within the window wall mullion as tension elements intended to counterbalance any uneven forces over the center support.

A fabric theme is carried throughout the project: in the fabric-formed texture of the white concrete walls of the elevation, in the sedum green rooftops that are very thin due to the fabric mesh rooftop-growing technology, and in an aerial view where the new building almost resembles a collection of shirtsleeves.

A geothermal HVAC system and gray-water recycling are among several green aspects that make this new museum an exemplary piece of 21st-century architecture.

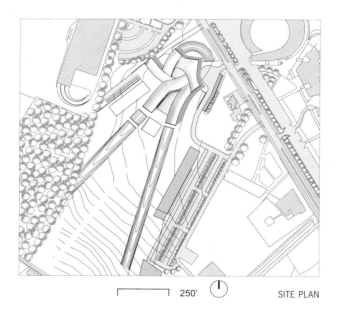

250'   SITE PLAN

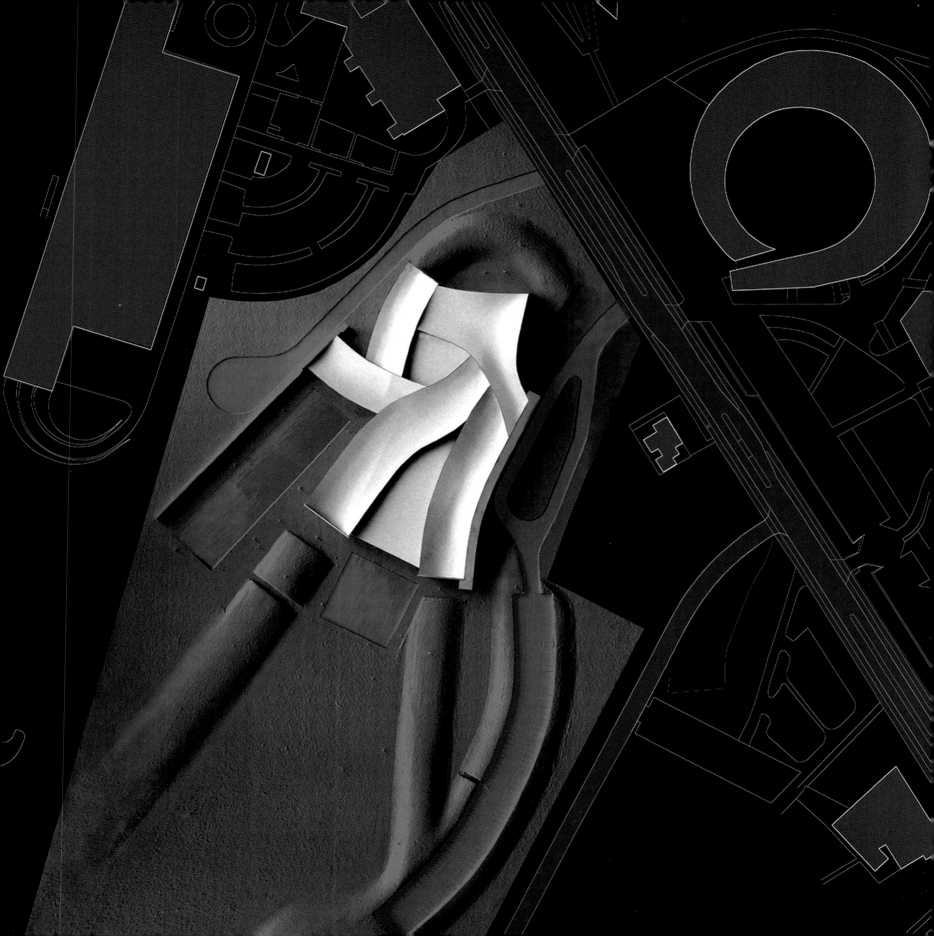

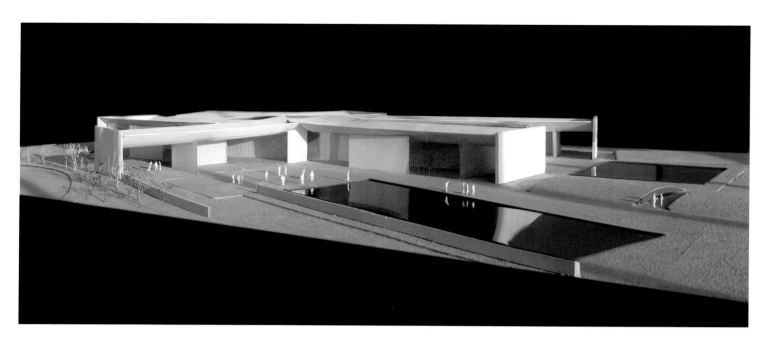

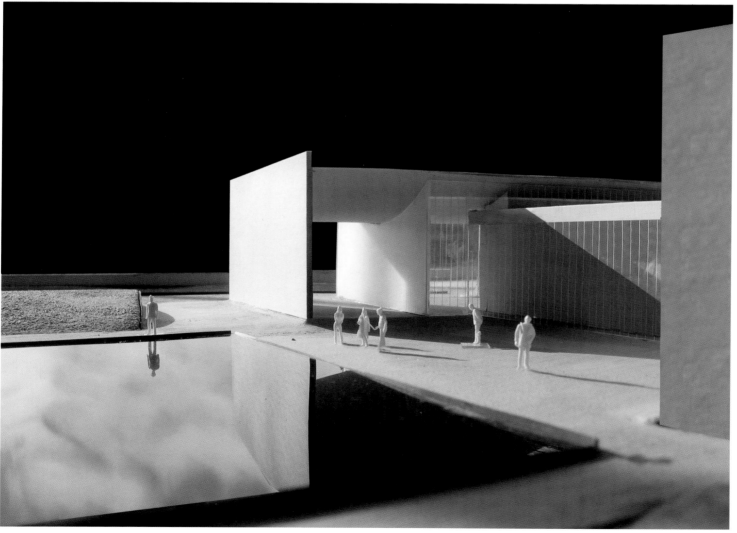

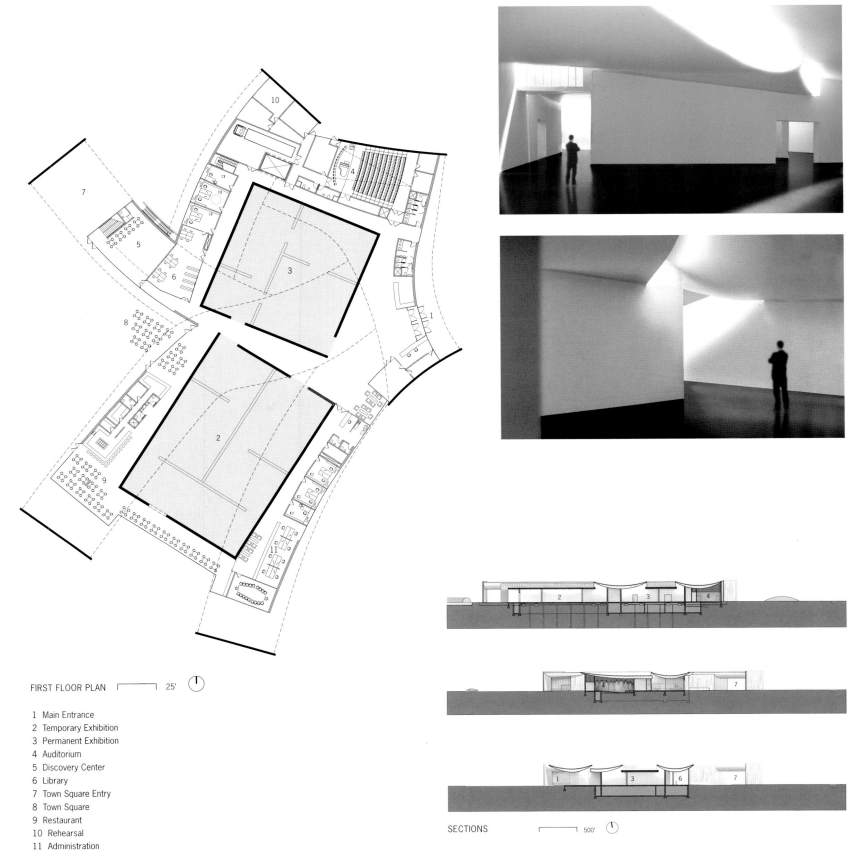

FIRST FLOOR PLAN ⊏───⊐ 25' ①

1 Main Entrance
2 Temporary Exhibition
3 Permanent Exhibition
4 Auditorium
5 Discovery Center
6 Library
7 Town Square Entry
8 Town Square
9 Restaurant
10 Rehearsal
11 Administration

SECTIONS ⊏───⊐ 500' ①

Whitney Water Purification Facility and Park, 1998–2005 (pp. 20–29)

The Whitney Water Purification Facility and Park is designed to purify the water from Lake Whitney and distribute 15 million gallons a day into the city. In 1998 we were chosen over five other firms at the interviews. It was a surprise that we got the project, because we had never done a water purification plant or anything like it. Later we learned that several Yale architecture professors live in that neighborhood. They weren't about to let the Water Authority build an ugly box covering up the tanks and functions of the treatment plant.

In the late '70s I worked on an Army Corps of Engineers flood control project for the city of Flint, Michigan, at Lawrence Halprin's office. We did some pumps, an Archimedes screw, and a water-lift pump to power some fountains, and we did a bridge across the river. I learned how it was working with engineers. When you were in a meeting, there were 30 engineers involved. It's interesting, because the discussion is about the budget, about the way the pipes flow, about gravity, about how high something is, and how the natural flow will be used, and where the shut-off valves are, or what is good for backwashing. The whole conversation is completely different from an architectural building committee meeting.

Usually, for treatment plants like this, engineers build big boxes, and try to make them look like something with applied architecture. We proposed to put all the functions (7/8ths of the total) below the ground, under a new park. They do not need light. The park would be divided into the 6 sectors of the main functions of the treatment plant. There's rapid mix, there's flocculation, dissolved air flotation, ozonation, GAC filtration, and a clear well. The first concept diagram showed six park sectors that would be equivalent to the functions that were below. The one part that would slip above would be the administration building, and it would be made like an upside-down water drop out of the same stainless steel that's in the plant below. The plant is computer automated. The administration "sliver" has a few windows, and there's an auditorium and a big glass window that looks at Eagle Rock. When you step out of the auditorium you can see Eagle Rock and the river in the distance. What started out as a shape that didn't have a functional meaning, took on a function in later development. This sort of teardrop shape started to get rationalized in accommodating pump-lifts for backwashing. It's really very exciting to be in the teardrop spaces. This is such a beautiful form for organizing spaces along a functional spine.

The notion of a chemical relation was suggested in the six sectors, and formally it was what I call a micro-macro reversal. These six sectors would take on characteristics of a shift from micro to macro scale. This geometric sketch is like a molecular diagram. We were looking at microscopic views of different chemical properties. For example, some shapes are like osmotic membranes, which is a little bit like what happens in the water filter treatment. There are many different kinds of filtrations and chemicals that are added to the water that allow solids to fall to the bottom.

This is really a water treatment plant with an educational aspect. The public groups can go through. Tours are arranged. But 15 million gallons a day run through there, which is a lot of water! This facility is in the public realm, and part of the community. The park will be an addition to the community as well. I like the fact that all the clients that are involved are very proud of it. Not only the Whitney Water Authority themselves, but the

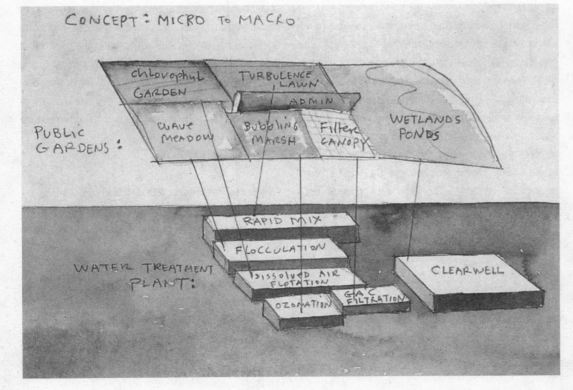

community group that guided them to choose architecture has followed it all the way through. One of the building's committee member's daughters asked to be married in the water treatment. A wedding, an unforeseen function, isn't that great?

Oceanic Retreat, 2001 (pp. 30–33)

We were being interviewed by Doctor Cheng from Hong Kong. He interviewed a number of architects and chose us because he said that I was the only architect that understood Feng Shui, the art of placement. And indeed I have read several books on Feng Shui when I had been working in Asia.

Not having ever been to Kaua'i, the first thing I did was read W.S. Merwin's *The Folding Cliffs*, which is an amazing piece of literature on Kaua'i. Solange and I flew to the site and spent a week there. What is interesting about it in relation to my philosophy of *Anchoring* is the specific character of site and circumstance and situation being at the birth of a project. This site is rare; these are the world's most isolated islands, lying 2,400 miles from any continent. They were one of the last places on earth to be occupied by humans around 100 AD. And yet there are more than 4300 species of animals and plants on the islands. Perhaps the strangest are these albatross birds that have nests on the part of the site that sticks out onto the ocean. It is a very windy site and the albatross birds walk around as if they are drunk. They were part of the character of our first studies and I read about the fact that they can soar around the ocean without touching land for four or five months. They are very strange birds.

The thing that I fixated on is the idea that Kaua'i moves on the tectonic plate northwest at 3.5 inches per year. So that became something obsessive. I wondered how I could engage that tectonic movement. The Hawaiian Islands are part of a volcanic formation at that tectonic plate. The geological time is really the core uniqueness of these islands and this site. After doing some watercolors we developed the project as two L-shapes which, like the continents on the tectonic plates, shift and separate. These two L-shapes—the guest house and the main house—would

be shifted apart from each other and it feels as if they could interlock with each other.

In the main house the stairs gradually go up at 3.5 inches, which is exactly the amount that Kaua'i moves each year. So every step is one year's movement of the tectonic plate, which pushes all land mass forward to the northwest. Everything on the island has a kind of wet, rainy, tropical feeling and that needed to be part of the architecture. The house would be in board-form green concrete, so it would get that mossy green texture of the site. And when you see the drawings and models you see that green.

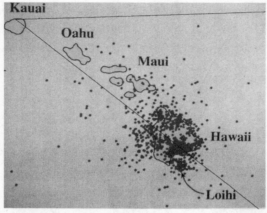

Site: North tip of the Kaua'i island.

Right now Hawai'i is running on coal-powered power plants, which are slightly disgusting for such a beautiful place. The house stands as an emblem of trying to move forward into the different value frameworks. Everything in the house would be designed with non-toxic materials: natural finishes, bamboo floor. There would be a water retaining system and all the gardens between the buildings would feature the natural plants of the island. The project employs the most efficient solar power systems. The main aspect would be a solar array on the roofs that would be so large that it would put power back into the grid. The panels would be placed horizontally on the roof of the guest house and the main house.

We were very enthusiastic about building this. The hardest part of building the house was finding the contractor, because there are only two or three contractors there and Dr. Cheng insisted that his house be

ready for his sixtieth birthday. We had almost finished the working drawings and I went down to Kaua'i trying to persuade various contractors, but I couldn't. So in the end I persuaded a contractor I knew from Seattle, a very good one, to move to Kaua'i with his family to build this house. He picked up his family and we gave him some financial assistance out of our architectural fee to make sure he could move there and that he would be able to build this. So we had our building permits, he was in place, his family moved, his kids were installed in the Kauaian school system, we were 98% complete with the working drawings, and I was trying to get the budget on target. And suddenly the house was cancelled in an e-mail from the client in Hong Kong. There was a downturn in the Hong Kong stock market and he cancelled in a one-paragraph e-mail!

This is the fragility of architecture. No matter how much effort you put in, it is so fragile. I was so taken into the process that if I would have had the money I would have purchased the site from him and built the house, but I didn't have the money. It all had to collapse.

I still think it is an important design, because it is exemplary in all kinds of environmental aspects, sustainability aspects, and in carrying on my philosophy of the specific idea of the site, being sort of giving the energy and particularity for a unique concept. The plate tectonic gave birth to the section and the plan. All of these aspects were coming directly from studying the site. The house was selected for the International Architectural Biennale in Venice and shown there with models and plans. So the project had a life, but it never got realized.

The Swiss Residence, 2001–2006 (pp. 34–43)

This project was a rather nice surprise for us to win. It was a competition that was suggested by Justin Rüssli, an old office colleague, now in Lucerne, who collaborated on the Kiasma Museum of Contemporary Art competition. He worked in my office from 1990 to 1992. In 1993 we won the Helsinki Kiasma competition. We had just computerized our office and Justin was instrumental in everything. In fact, I don't think we could have done those competition drawings without the computer, which for 1992 was advanced. In 2001 he called me and said the Swiss Embassy is initiating a competition for their residence next to the Lecasz Building in Washington, D.C. It was a limited competition, and the interesting thing was that a Swiss-American team was required. But in all the other nine chosen teams the American architect was just a working drawing side, but we would be true collaborators. I said fine, let's go ahead and try for it. In 1993 Justin and I did not only work on Helsinki but also Düsseldorf and Zollikerberg. He was working with me on those three competitions, the only time—except for this year—that we ever won three competitions in one year. So we were already a team and it was very easy to do this project. He also knew the Swiss standards left and right.

I went down to Washington, D.C. to view the building site and I noticed this incredible view of the Washington Monument on a diagonal axis across the site. So I made a simple diagram of what I call a "precinct," a little courtyard-like complex, inscribing in the center of it a masonry cruciform, with another element, which was the guest house. And we did this over e-mails and developed it back and forth. The model was built in Lucerne. As it turned out, the jury took place on the site in Washington, D.C., so the material had to be sent first to Bern and then they brought it all back to Washington, D.C. To make a long story short, we won this competition, and then immediately I became nervous. I thought, "Oh, when they find out an American designed it instead

of a Swiss they will be upset." But in fact in Bern they were not upset at all. They loved the ideas and the simplicity, the central thought of moving diagonally through orthogonal space, and I found that we won by an unanimous vote.

In fact, it isn't the first time I did a cruciform in a courtyard. In the Bridge of Houses project you can see, I think it's called the House of the Dreamer, there's a rectangle in which a cruciform plan body is inscribed, forming four courtyards. But certainly the way you experience the building isn't as a cruciform. You experience it in a series of spaces. Maybe the immediacy of that form made it easier for the jury to choose it but I doubt that, because it wasn't mentioned in the jury notes. You know, when the Swiss have a competition they give you a booklet afterward that shows you every entry and all the comments from the jury; very, very thorough.

The building has a green roof with sedam. I don't think any of the embassies in Washington have a green roof. It has a small pond on the south garden and an herb garden by the kitchen; the users can plant herbs and use them in the kitchen. That's up to the people who inhabit and cook and utilize the place, but I want to offer them the chance.

The interesting thing about building this project in America was that finding contractors who could do the

HVAC systems according to the required Swiss Minimum Energy Standards proved impossible. We brought most of the materials from Switzerland and the engineering was done in Switzerland for all our systems. It just shows you how different one culture is from another and how much more cognizant the Swiss and Europeans are (and the Chinese, for that matter) about our present energy predicament and how unbelievably awkwardly behind we are in America. But I'm hoping that will change.

Knut Hamsun Center, 1994– (pp. 50–55)

I was working on the Kiasma Museum in Helsinki when we were contacted by the chief curator at Kiasma about a center for Knut Hamsun in Hamarøy, which is north of the Arctic Circle. Hamsun was the first genuinely surrealist author from a Scandinavian country. His first important book was *Hunger*, published in 1890. Born in Norway, he lived in America for a while, based in Minnesota. He was diagnosed as having tuberculosis at a very young age, so he rode on top of a boxcar all the way from Minnesota to New York with his mouth open, breathing in the air, in order to cure himself of TB. Miraculously, somehow, he did, and he returned to Norway to write an amazing body of work, from *Hunger* to the novel *Mysteries*, and a much larger, ponderous work called *Growth of the Soil*. He was Norway's most inventive 20th-century writer, and was awarded the Nobel Prize for literature in 1920. In some ways, he was breaking new ground that everyone would follow later on. He was for Norway in literature what Alvar Aalto was for Finland in architecture. But there was a stain on Hamsun's reputation. During World War II, he was naively sympathetic to some of Hitler's activities; he actually went to visit him at the Wannsee Villa near Berlin. Many Norwegians tend only to look at that stain at the end of his life. He was already very old when those things were happening. It was a considerable blemish on a long career of creative writing. When they asked me if I would be interested in designing a museum at his longtime home in Hamarøy, I said that I would. I think that all those things, good and bad, can be shown in a museum dedicated to the life of one person. You can include that stain in the exhibitions. Life isn't all clean. It has some messy corners.

This museum was an assignment, not a competition. They didn't have any funding at all. They had only the town and a small group of people who tried to make this happen. They also had the desire for tourism. The building would be about the work and life of one person. There is a series of exhibitions, most of which would be films and digital projections. There will be some original biographical objects, like books and pens. There will be archival materials for people to work with; there's a meeting hall and a seating area that is multi-functional for the local community, with something like 200 seats. Every other year they have "Hamsun Days" on his birthday, the 4th of August. They have plays, dramatic enactments, and various celebrations of Knut Hamsun's life, his characters, his novels, and readings. Knut Hamsun Days attract scholars and interested laymen from all over Europe.

This is a place that is north of the Arctic Circle. We were checking the sun angles on the building when we were designing it. In June, the midnight sun lasts six weeks in Hamarøy. It just touches the horizon and goes back up. In winter, the sun does not come up between about December 20th and January 12th. The horizon gets red and the snow is white powder on the ground. It is one of the most spiritual times to be there.

I've been to Hamarøy during the midnight sun and seen a whole yard full of children playing at 4:30 in the morning; they just don't sleep. My grandfather was born in Tonsberg, Norway, and both my father's parents were Norwegian. So I have these connections to Scandinavia. When I was invited to come and make this sketch, I wasn't completely an alien American being brought into Scandinavia. The people who introduced me really liked the Kiasma Museum in Helsinki and suggested that I make drawings to try to launch this project.

The site is very far from Oslo. It's three or four hours to Bodø by plane, then you take a boat that brings you to Hamarøy and then you drive from where the Hamarøy ferry lets you off. So it's quite a long way to go. But the landscape is incredibly beautiful and there is almost nothing there. There's no spoiled, polluted anything. It's all wild and wonderful, with the mountain and the quality of the light, and the sunsets. When the sun sets behind the Lofoten Mountains that are just off the little coast, streams of light come through, like a celestial apparition.

During the design I read every Knut Hamsun book I could get my hands on. I went to the Museum of Modern Art, where there are a number of films about Hamsun's writings. There are 15 films based on the novel *Hunger*. We saw a couple of the famous ones, and in one of the films there was a character wearing a yellow suit and carrying an empty violin case. So in order to get more into this, I started to carry an empty violin case. I would go to Helsinki, and I carried furniture models for Kiasma in it. I would meet with the director, Tuula Arkio, in a restaurant near the museum, and she said, "What's that?" I'd put the violin case on the table, and then a little later on during the dinner I'd open it up and show her the furniture for her café. I still have that violin case. But no violin. I never got a yellow suit.

The first sketches I made, I called "buildings as a body, a battleground of invisible forces," like what Hamsun wrote about in the novel *Hunger*. There are forces at work inside the body that are passionate and invisible, and bursting to get out. There was an elevator that was like a spine, and the stair was like bone, and there was a big brown dog collar of Mexican silver over the

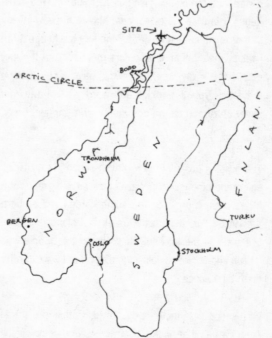

entranceway. The window was based on the passage "women, with two blue feathers in their hats," and a balcony was based on "girl with her sleeves rolled up polishing the glass." There were chunks of the novel that inspired the idiosyncratic activity, and intersect a warped black building.

The center evolved from the idea of connecting to the site and program, and also to the angle of light, with the low winter sun. The first sun that rises in February comes through almost horizontally. The sun never gets above 47 degrees on the horizon. We designed a concrete shear wall building covered with tarred boards. I used the same blackening technique as that of the stave churches of Norway. I traveled to Trondheim and visited a lot of the stave churches, which are absolutely amazing—thousand-year-old wooden buildings. They are still standing because the wood was treated with boiled peat. When they boil the peat they get a black oily substance—creosote—with which to paint the board staves. Unlike paint, which locks moisture into wood and causes it to rot, peat allows wood to breathe.

The Hamsun Center is a small building, probably 6,000 square feet. There's one element per floor. Visitors take the elevator to the top and walk down. The interesting thing for me is that even though the design will be years old when it's finished, it's brand new. I believe that architecture needs to be completely anchored in its program and site. Its meaning must be so deeply rooted in the conditions of its inception that it's unfazed by fashion. My first book was *Anchoring*, the relation of a building to a site, to its culture, to its metaphysical origins. If architecture's original concept can get deeper, rather than broader, it builds a meaning on the site. It fortifies a locus of thoughts and philosophical hopes, or even humor and stories, which are oblivious to whatever style it is. It's not postmodernism, it's not late Modernism. This is not a Gothic-period Norwegian church just because it is sheathed in black wood. The diaphragm of the building is concrete, and there are four inches or so of insulation on the outside of the concrete, then mounted in strips to the boards, which are treated with peat. So you have a texture that is very Norwegian in its origin, but in a very modern insulated

building. There's a long tradition in Norway of sod roofs. I didn't want to completely quote the sod roof, so I was thinking of a very wild kind of long grass. The grasses on the roof partially came from the idea of hair. My wife says, "The hairy guy! I love that building."

When this was designed, it won a *Progressive Architecture* award in the U.S. and generated more press about a piece of architecture than any recent building in Norway. The building had been published so much that some people thought it had been built. There's a story of a Norwegian friend of mine who was on the ferry to Hamarøy. Three Japanese architecture students were on the ferry on their way to see the building, asking for directions. They'd gone all that way—and they thought it was there, built… but it was only an idea. There are people who thought that the architecture was just completely over the top, so they made cartoons of the building as a body; they made a big picture of Hamsun's head. Someone built a big model of the building in a local tavern as a tap and poured beer out of it.

The building came back alive in 2005, exactly eight years after I designed it, and I am very excited to say that it appears to be going forward. Alf Einar, a Knut Hamsun scholar, believes so much in the Hamsun project that he is resurrecting it from the dead. How could it be that a building was killed or forgotten or not funded, and somebody would believe so much in the idea that somehow he would convince Parliament and people in the Norwegian Government to go forward with it? I think it's an extraordinary case. More commonly, if a 1996 project came to life in 2005, you would just hire another architect and create the Knut Hamsun Center in a different way. But they wanted this particular building. The idea of this project and its meaning are at stake here.

This underlines what I thought was the right track when I wrote *Anchoring* in 1989. At the time I was 41 years old and I had a show at the Museum of Modern Art in New York, and I felt I had to write a manifesto. I wasn't going to just show my work, pin my stuff up on the wall. I had to write what it was I believed in. And the text wasn't long; all the work I've done since then relates

directly to the thinking and the short philosophical texts in *Anchoring*. It's very different from a totally empirical work of architecture to work only in theory. It is driven by some hope for meaning that is extra-architectural, outside of the architecture.

The Knut Hamsun Museum is incredibly intense in every element, from its conception to the details; everything has a meaning in relationship to this problem. I think in the future, a cultural facility that is a museum for a single artwork or a museum for a writer—a single figure who had some importance to a place—may continue to be important for educational tours, and for bringing locals something positive about their heritage. Now we have the digital capacity to hold huge amounts of information. Everything a person ever wrote can be there, digitized and accessible, so I see that type of facility as an example of a future educational building type. The problem today is that there's so much information, so much thrown at you, that it's very hard to connect things that have plausible likenesses and tenuous connections. You need a certain solitude and silence and coalescence. It can happen in the authentic place… each unique site on earth.

Chapel of St. Ignatius, 1994–1997 (pp. 56–67)

At the beginning of the selection process for the Chapel of St. Ignatius the jury narrowed a group of thirty architects down to six. We were one of them. All six would be interviewed and were asked to give a lecture at the Seattle University the following night. During the interview I admitted that I had never done a chapel before and that I was not a Catholic, and in fact, if I was religious that maybe I would be a pagan. But I really wanted to contribute to the university in the form of this campus chapel that had this ideal stature, and I told them about my belief in the religiosity of architecture.

I don't know if the interview went that well, but the following day I gave the lecture "Questions of Perception," which described the phenomenology of architecture. It had just been published by *A+U* and I drew a full house. Father Cobb and Father Sullivan were shocked: "Why didn't the other five finalists draw a full house?" "What were all these people doing in the auditorium to hear him talk?"

So, we were selected and I started reading about St. Ignatius. In one of his books I read that he returns to the metaphor of light. It was about the notion of not being quite aware of where the light source is, but knowing it's coming down from above. It gave me the idea of making the whole chapel a collection of light vessels. So I called the key concept sketch "Seven Bottles of Light in a Stone Box." These seven bottles would refer to the different aspects of the liturgical program as the Blessed Sacrament, the Choir, the Narthex, and the Procession. The second part of the concept was the fact that students of 60 different nationalities attend Seattle University. By this gathering of different cultures a global thought in that one specific place is created. These two concepts were vibrating inside the rectangle of the site. I decided to make the site into three quadrants, one to the west, a future one to the east, and a new square to the south, which would have a reflecting pond, a bell tower, and a stone for the Easter fire coming from Mt. Rainier.

The project got off to a very good start. When I presented the concept, again a lot of people attended. The campus ministry really appreciated the conceptual

structure, just like they appreciated the tactile dimensions of my phenomenology lecture, which is in a way philosophically Jesuit. I saw parallels between my work and the spiritual exercises of St. Ignatius in teachings, and in the openness to phenomenological thinking. Father Sullivan became very enthusiastic about the whole project. He said: "Steven, make your whole plan and we'll see if we can raise the money." Initially we only had 2.2 million, but because of the architecture we raised 5.5 million and we could build the reflecting pond and the bell tower, everything necessary to create a centerpiece for the campus.

We had a liturgical consultant by the name of Bill Brown, who really told us how to put a chapel together in all the correct ways. I remember that during the process the Physical Planning Department wanted to make the building smaller and proposed getting rid of a couple of those bottles of light. The campus ministry said: "Absolutely not. There are seven days and there shall be seven bottles of light." So I can honestly say to my students now that they need to have a good concept that drives the design and that can help when defending the design against naysayers who may not have the same philosophical platform.

We couldn't afford the stone and together with the contractor I decided that tilt-up concrete is also a kind of stone, especially if you stain it with this penetrating ochre stain. And so the chapel became the largest figural tilt-up construction ever made on a university campus, with some of the tilts being 30 feet and weighing 70,000 pounds.

We had a great contractor, but Father Sullivan was the actual leader of the schedule of this building. I remember a very seminal meeting about when to open the building. The contractor pulled out a lot of schedules and diagrams and papers and this and that. Father Sullivan took his hand and just pushed them off to the side of the table and said: "It shall be open on Easter."

So they had to build it in nine months, and they did. I remember Father Sullivan and I watched the building go from lying horizontal to being totally tilted up in something like 18 hours' time. I think there is a mythical quality to making a tilt-up building. There is no scaffolding. The whole thing is flat, but the entire structure is there. The students would be riding their bicycles on the campus and then they would stop, frozen, by this apparition that had unexpectedly appeared on the campus. When the chapel opened it was a great celebration. There's a traditional ceremony of the consecra-

Opening Day Ceremony at the Chapel of St. Ignatius.

tion of the space. The architect hands the drawings to the Bishop, there's a procession, and they go into the space for a two-hour ceremony in which they take the sacred oils and make crosses, almost like graffiti, in the plaster. The building was no longer ours, it was theirs.

Years later it's one of the buildings that has given me a lot of joy. First of all because it is in my hometown and second because it is the center of the campus. The Museum of Modern Art purchased the model, which is now in their permanent collection and has won all kinds of awards. However, I have to say that for me all those awards don't mean as much as certain events that happen on the street. The public embraced the building: Two years later they put an image of the chapel on the student ID card that every student at Seattle University carries. In June 2006 the president of Seattle University presented me with an Honorary Doctorate degree. They wanted me to speak about the chapel and about my experience as an architect. In a way that is interesting. I have been teaching architecture at Columbia University for the last 20 years, but I don't even have the degree that I'm teaching the students to get (which is a Masters degree in architecture). I just have a Bachelor's in architecture. So finally I'm getting a degree in the field of making.

It is a building of only 6,000 square feet. Architecture isn't about the size, it's about meaning, intention; whatever kind of emotion that can be in it, embodied in it. It becomes a facility for others to enjoy. I think that is still the mystery of this particular place, as one can tell from some moving stories. For instance: Someone was having a very depressing moment in his life. He stopped his car in the rain and went into the chapel and just sat there for two hours. He photographed the light and the image was published in the *Seattle Times* in a very touching article. Another one happened to me personally a few years ago. I'll never forget that day. I was in a supermarket near Capitol Hill buying something with my credit card. The lady at the checkout read "architect" on my card and said: "You're an architect? You'd better go up there over the hill, there on that campus and look at that chapel. That's some building." To me her enthusiasm was better than an architectural award.

College of Architecture, Art and Planning, Cornell University, 2001 (pp. 68–71)

To design an architecture school? It is a little like a brain surgeon operating on his own head. Cornell's undergraduate architecture program had outgrown its home in Rand Hall and was in need of new facilities that could provide the necessary studio and office space. The budget was set at 25 million dollars; the program called for a structure of 57,000 square feet, including studios, group instructional spaces, faculty offices, and an auditorium. The competition organizers asked for a design that would meet these functional demands but that would also meet the need for a piece of significant design that would mark this entrance to the campus. All four offices in the competition were required to submit two models and eight boards and to make their final presentation to the public in an auditorium. In order to prepare for the presentation stage, the jurors were given the architects' written proposal 24 hours in advance. Given the proposed building's function as an undergraduate teaching building, the university decided to extend the pedagogical nature of the project to the competition itself, making the presentation stage a public event. Students were encouraged to attend, and they did. A crowd of 750—including students, faculty, and alumni—was present when we presented our cases on April 18. On April 20th the jurors made their recommendation. They were anonymous in their choice for Steven Holl Architects over the offices of Peter Zumthor, Morphosis (Thom Mayne), Tod Williams & Billie Tsien.

We proposed a building as a gateway pavilion to the campus. Sited on a busy pedestrian path, the building will have a 24-hour passage through the ground floor of the building. Three of the building facades will be clad in a recycled structural glass.

The prominent site at the northeast corner of the Arts Quad is in a gateway position because of the pedestrian traffic passing north over the Gorge Bridge onto campus. The traffic on this trajectory will only increase during the coming years due to the new residence hall construction on the northern part of the campus. At the ground level the building would function as a passage open to all and creating a new access to the architec-

ture school. We wanted to make that school more accessible not only to the architecture students but also to the other students. We were hoping that students from other faculties would stop by for an architecture lecture every once in a while. The passage would work like a social condenser. Architecture students have this night rhythm and we were hoping that this building would be occupied at night by students who would still be working. With the lights on in the studios the building would glow like a lantern.

Demonstrating a Tesseract

At first our scheme seemed to be a simple cube that sits high above one of the gorges that cut through the Cornell campus. The site had so much potential in view that we thought that a school of architecture should benefit from that. Cornell seemed to have turned its back on the natural beauty of Fall Creek Gorge. That is why we developed the stacked studio space for this new school of architecture. But we wanted to be sure to make a cube with four fronts instead of just one. So we started working with the mathematical idea of the tesseract. A tesseract is the four-dimensional analogue to a cube; a hyper cube. The building concept is further clarified in the simplicity of structural channel glass planks with translucent insulation on three façades and a foamed aluminum facade for the tesseract wall.

A square is to a cube what a cube is to a tesseract. This cube aims at non-Euclidean properties in overlapping internal perspectives. The review rooms, the heart of the studio experience, would be located in the central overlapping cubes. The three review rooms are not stacked neatly, not one above the other, but pushed in different directions. Openings in the floors and ceiling of each review space would allow daylight to reach even to the deepest one. Regular studio space would flank each review room on three sides, and all services and vertical circulation are pulled to the fourth, western side of the building: the tesseract facade of the building. That tesseract zone is embedded in the open-air bracket as a shifting irregular section. Here the large service elevator, a 9'x9' cube, and a 6'x6' passenger elevator are found with stairs connecting all floors with views to the lake and gorge. Seminar rooms, restrooms, and utility sink rooms would be collected there. Compared with the softly molded light from the white translucent insulation in planks around the studio the spaces in the tesseract zone would be darker and digitally interactive. The associations for the facade on the tesseract side are outside the cube in the landscape of the site: at the bottom of Fall Creek Gorge, the distant view of Lake Cayuga, or even the angle of the sun. In fact, the open bracket of loftlike studio spaces is made operative by the infrastructural tesseract zone, which is pulled inside out forming the west facade.

The simplicity of construction material and the exposure of all construction materials add to the didactic qualities of the teaching spaces. The tesseract wall's folding geometry would be directly translated from disk to engineered composite panel in the shop and bolted together on the site. The proportions of the building from the 3'x3' cube of the shadow box windows to the 13'x16' interior studio volumes to the 34'x34' review rooms are analogous to the Fibonacci series 3, 5, 8, 13, 21, 34, 55, 89.

Originally the jury including Kenneth Frampton, Terence Riley, Toshiko Mori, Carmen Pinós and Heinz Tesar, and James Stewart Polshek wrote: "If constructed as designed, this brilliant design will set a new standard of excellence for Cornell's architecture." We agreed in June 2001 to mutually end the relationship because we could not agree on changes in design, required by the faculty program and budget. The unanimous vote of a fine jury did not insure the realization of this project due to other factors that we could not control. Architecture is an incredibly fragile art.

Writing with Light House, 2001–2004 (pp. 72–79)
For Writing with Light House the clients came to me out of the blue. He's a brain surgeon and she is a former architect. I had been to the Hamptons many times, preparing to do houses there, but nothing materialized until this one. There was a little site, a postage-stamp site, less than a quarter of an acre, with a great view of Mecox Bay. There was a little house that they were going to tear down, and they had to build exactly on top of that space and fill the envelope to include their program. The site is not far from the Springs and Jackson Pollock's studio, and my first impulse was to relate to Pollock.

Right down the road from Jackson Pollock's studio lives Ruth Nivola, the wife of Nivola, the sculptor, who knew Le Corbusier. In her house are those incredible full wall murals that Le Corbusier painted in 1950. She still lives there. I went to see her one afternoon, and the work is amazing.

One inspiration from the Pollock studio is the light that you could see through the boards. The other was the notion of a free plan, just throwing the paint on; throwing the plan down. I took one painting from 1949 called *There was 7 in 8*. So I made 7 rooms below and 8 rooms above, and I made the whole plan just a paint-

inglike scatter. The front wall was to be latticed wood in a frame. The first scheme showed cedar wood; you could see through the slats. The site is right on the road and needed some privacy. The wall material behind the slats is wood. There's nothing behind the slats at the swimming pool, which is over the garage. They were hesitant about that, but I convinced them that over the garage is a great place to put the pool, because when you're up there, you can see the ocean. So this now works wonderfully.

Then I had a crisis. I started the plan, and it looked like a Jackson Pollock painting with a bracket around it and I had different colors and different forms—but I hated the model. And then I showed it to them, and they liked it! Now I had trouble. The design was just too scattered; it was all over the place. But they liked it. So I worked on it and reworked it. I wanted to contain it, bracket it more, bring it more into a frame. I was using all the colors that Jackson Pollock used in his painting. I used the same colors as the painting all over the scheme. It just didn't work. I decided to take all the colors out, and just make the scheme black and white. The sunlight would do the painting. When the light comes through the slats (now, here's the concept, "Writing with Light"), the linear strips bend and turn in space. It's dynamic, changing with the time of day and the seasons.

If they read this, the clients are going to remember that they liked the first house. Still, they're very happy with the final. It was a long design process, because I had started down the wrong road, and I couldn't see it until I saw the model. I've often been inspired by works of art, however, this process shows you that you just can't take a painting and try to make a house out of it. It doesn't work that way. An inspiration has to lead to something fundamentally different. It's a transformation. There are ways of making something so transformed that it becomes a new thing.

What was happening here is that the seeds of the Jackson Pollock are still there; still underlying deeply in this design. However, it's so transformed that it's not literal any more. The problem with the process was it took an enormous amount of time, because I had gone down the wrong road, and they liked that road. That's

not the first time that that's happened to me, where I'm not ready and the client must see something. (Now that I am 56 years old, I have finally, in the last four or five years, gotten enough behind me to know that if I don't get the concept right, I just don't show it.) I came to them with a new set of drawings. The idea of the plan was still there; this plan spins out, almost pinwheels out, these rooms start to fly off, centrifugally flying off, and giving you views across Mecox Bay. As you move up, there's another bedroom, there's the master bedroom, and finally, on top of the spiral space is the pool, which is over the garage, with a terrific view out to the ocean. It's wood slats; the white plaster inside gets shadow lines during the day, depending on the angle of the sun.

The neighbors said it looked like a boarded-up grange hall. They're getting used to it now. We did the landscape with wild grasses that were on the site before. We are trying not to have lawns but to landscape as naturally as possible and let the weathering take the cedar to silver. In some cases, the lines of the cedar slats go right over the windows. There are variations: There's a hole that the slats go into. There's a window that's just a window. There's a window that's completely behind slats. There's a window with half the slats over it. And there are slats with nothing behind them. Basically, you look at a rectangle and you're not sure what's behind what. There are five different variations that play a kind of musical game with whatever a window or an opening is, so that the slats read first. They're playing the predominant game, but it's not an arbitrary composition. The choice is very important.

The meaning here is deeper than the fact that this house has 7 bathrooms. There could be one, and I'd be happy. The reality of architecture is that in some cases, the program has a lot of meaning. In other cases, it doesn't. I would say that on this frame, in a site like this, in this particular situation, the program could be something in flux. The sequence of spaces and the fact that the pool is over the garage, and you arrive and see the ocean—that's important.

When I try to teach architecture, the hardest thing to communicate is the deepest and most subtle, subjec-tive part. Actually, it could be the most important. You can't make a recipe for architecture. A design has a relationship to a site, and it has meaning because of where it is. I wouldn't build the Nail Collector's House in the Hamptons! In the case of this house, this is really related to its site, not any other site. The light, the ocean, the spiral in space... it is very particular.

Nail Collector's House, 2001–2004 (pp. 80–85)
The client, writer Alan Wardle, came to me five years ago. He wanted a small house for himself, where he could write and view the lake nearby. He said, "I want a poetic utterance." He had read my 1989 manifesto *Anchoring*, and he remembered my sentence about the relationship of a building to its site: A building isn't so much an object on a site as it builds the site that it's on, and establishing a unique relationship to a site is the beginning point of architecture to me. That is what he wanted. Of course, I was very excited to do it, but then he proceeded to say that he didn't have any money, and he couldn't start any time soon. A year later, he came back to me and said that he now had a little money, and he wanted to start. He said the house didn't have to be very big. He goes there to write and will stay for a month or two, depending on what he's working on.

In October 2000, we went up to see the site in Essex, which is a historic town. I don't think they've built anything there since 1850. It's a little 19th-century American town, with all the trappings. Begg's Point, the site, has in an incredible view of Lake Champlain. The house is on the site of an old nail factory where they made square-headed nails by hand. Alan said, "the only thing I'm keeping there, beside myself and my books, is my nail collection." He has a bunch of square-headed nails that he found. He's had a little shack on that site for five years.

There is a flat ferry that goes across the lake with cars sitting on a platform with a pilothouse that the ferry master sits in. It comes back and forth every hour, directly in front of this little house. I had the feeling, watching this ferry, of being on a raft and being on a journey on a vast "wine-dark" sea. I was rereading Homer's *The Odyssey* at that moment, which was a fortunate coincidence, because when I went up to the site and saw the lake I thought, that's not a lake, it's like an ocean, it's so huge. This little house sits on a stone wall right on the lake's edge; the house itself was like a port, an end and beginning to a long journey. Homer's *The Odyssey* is an epic poem, a prehistoric literature. As I was reading, I noticed that both *The Iliad* and *The Odyssey* have 24 chapters. So right here, in my first sketch, you see "northeast 14, southeast 5, southwest 5, northwest 0, 24 windows, equal to chapters in the *The Odyssey*." I made the plan of this house as small as I could, by putting the bedroom above. The house spirals up in space, three levels reach the maximum height allowed. Then I floated the windows on the elevations according to the light, chapter by chapter.

I began to think about how Homer uses words in groups, and he uses them over and over again so you can't forget them. I read it in high school, and I never could forget the sentence about the wine-dark sea. I have a memory of reading it when I was about 13. I was supposedly mowing the lawn, working on my first job, making $1.25 an hour. I was staring at the sea across Puget Sound (this was in Manchester, Washington), and the sky was so blue that the sea was wine dark. The other phrase I'll never forget is "the rosy-fingered dawn." That's when there are bits of clouds on the horizon making the sunlight come down in streaks… that's what I imagine. I thought the 24 windows would be the perfect way—inside an otherwise white-walled, plaster-walled house—to read the time of day as it changed. From sunrise to sunset, the reading of light would always be different. Depending on the season; figures of light would be higher or lower. I thought that there could be a different feeling for every window in the house though they're all the same dimension—just the ends of "rosy fingers," projecting the light. There is a double meaning in the 24 chapters; as somebody else pointed out, there are 24 hours in the day.

The house interior developed as a spiral space. Then I twisted the volume. I made it fit better on the land by siting it into the corner. I pinched it so it fits better on the site, which is very tight, and then I pulled the edge of it out toward the lake.

In the Nail Collector's House, you come through the door and the whole space opens all the way to the top, which is 30 feet high. It spirals up, counterclockwise, to a small sleeping part in the tilted portion. When you're up there, you feel the whole space. Even these smaller, one-sided open areas partake of the feeling of the big space. It is hard to read this in plan. You look at the plan and you can't really understand; it seems you can barely fit a bed in there, but it doesn't feel small at all. With the hinged opening cut out from the wall, it is really quite enormous, spatially. The entire house is conventional wood-frame, except the exterior sheathing. I decided I wanted to do it in cartridge brass, which is the brass that gun shells are made of. It comes in rolls. So we rolled it out and put it up, allowing the nail-heads to be exposed so that you can see the nails holding on. The brass was made in a gun factory in Ohio. It's currently yellow, which complements the fall foliage, but it will turn. It will change in color with the trees and the seasons.

One man constructed this house practically by himself, Mitch Rabideau; he's a wonderful contractor from Plattsburgh. Ninety percent of the time he worked alone. He framed it up in the middle of winter; he put a kind of tarp around himself and worked in minus-10-degree weather. It is hopeful when there is a human factor of inspired energy that negates the general problems with U.S. craftsmanship.

There are some important details to the house. All the cabinet pulls are made of forged square-head nail-like elements from a local blacksmith. When you get into the top of the space, you can have privacy or not, and so the walls at the top of the space are on large hinges, like huge flaps. If Alan is there by himself, he can open the entire space. The kitchen is over against the wall. He owns a big 19th-century farm table, and he has a bunch of old chairs that he's going to put there. The flooring is all hickory, with a wonderful grain, as are the treads on the stair.

This has been a five-year process. My small fee was used up two years ago; and yet excitement continues. For me this is a very important work. It goes back to my feeling that it isn't about how big something is; it's about the meaning of what you're doing. In architecture, I think we get disillusioned into thinking that just because we're making something big, it has a lot of meaning. I don't think that's true. Meaning is scaleless.

Turbulence House, 2001–2004 (pp. 86–93)

The Turbulence House, in Abiquiu, is for the artist Richard Tuttle and the poet Mei-Mei Berssenbrugge. It is a guest house. Earlier, Richard Tuttle had built two buildings—one for her as a writing studio and one is their house—and then there's an old concrete building that is his studio. They spend about six months a year out there on the mesa. In the beginning, Mei-Mei said, "I would like to have something that's like an Airstream trailer, that could be built somewhere else and brought on-site, different from what we have here, something that isn't adobe." I said, "Oh, that's interesting; I'd like to try that. We'll get a local architect to oversee it and do the construction drawings, and I'll just trade you the design for a painting." That was 2001. I went out there, and I had a sketch idea for a little house that sits on the mesa with lines extending down into the earth referring to something much larger. The mesa comes up 80 feet from the valley floor and it is flat on the top. It's a really interesting blank desert horizon with different mountains. Tabletop Mountain in the distance is where the remains of Georgia O'Keeffe are buried.

The idea is to open a small void right through the house. The roof slope faces south for solar collectors. There's no air-conditioning. The wind blows through the opening; it's shadowy there, and the turbulence pulls the air through to make it cooler.

The stress-skin panel enclosure comes in 32 pieces, and it was prefabricated in Kansas City by the same Zahner company that makes Frank Gehry's work. I did something very different than Frank. He makes wavy things, but behind them there is a steel structure frame. I merged the structure and the skin. So these panels are skin, waterproofing, and structure combined. They are shipped, then bolted together and set on the concrete slab.

The Turbulence House has a very wonderful plaster interior, with a sleeping platform and a writer's table and a little kitchen. It's a very small house, 1,000 square feet. One bathroom, a little kitchenette, dining table, one sleeping platform. Richard Tuttle said from the beginning that he wanted the space to be sculptural; he didn't want to put sculpture in the space. He's a sculptor and a painter. Therefore, I didn't need any orthogonal walls in this house. That's part of its program.

When we were designing the house, I got a call from Francesco Dal Co in Vicenza to make an exhibition of my work in Palladio's Vicenza Basilica. There was an old 14th-century Basilica, and in 1500 Palladio built a new building around it. So I said, "We'll just make another house shell and send it to Vicenza; order 32 prefab pieces twice."

My manifesto for the exhibition was something like *Edge of the City: Protection of the Landscape*. This house shell is like a sentry dog protecting the landscape, and inside I had projections of the desert. Falvio Albanese helped get the funding for this. He sold this shell to his client, who resurrected it on a little concrete slab in Vicenza. It was funny, because I had the idea for the house enclosure, and I sent the sketch to them and said, "If anybody has $160,000, that's what this shell is going to cost," and they sent back, "Yes, we'll do it."

Then we were running out of time. The exhibition was to open on September 2nd. By June the four containers were just leaving Kansas City. They went to sea at Newport News, across the ocean, came into Genoa, went on four trucks, and those trucks arrived in Vicenza two days before the opening. If they had opened up the containers in the wrong sequence, this house would never have been done on time. The pieces were numbered, and they had to come out of the containers in the right sequence to get the thing to go up. But they did it. Opened it all together. It was a great effort.

Richard Tuttle doesn't mind that there are two houses. He was very happy about it, because it was to be a prefabricated house. So now we've finished his house, after what I call "the fallacy of the individual." The New Mexico slab was poured and the pieces were assembled in a week. The house exterior existed in one week, but it took two years to finish it on the inside. The guy who was doing the glazing was from Albuquerque, a 2- to 3-hour drive from the site. He was an alcoholic. He got the windows half-glazed and then he got a drunk driving citation, and was put in jail for six months. What are you

going to do? What's interesting is, you can put all your optimism and chutzpah in a project like a prefabricated house that's going to be created in a matter of weeks, but what you can't project is the human factor. And the human factor is always there.

A man approached me to do a series of these houses. He came and we had several meetings, and we had a contract. But right at the end of it, I backed out. I said to myself, "What am I doing?" My philosophy is about the relation of a building to its site. The idea that the greater meaning that you can bring as an architect is all bound up in a landscape, the weather, all these specific conditions. If someone starts putting these things up in a pasture in Chicago, I'm not going to be happy. This house was a concept for the desert mesa with the desert wind blowing through it. This was designed for the site.

There's a lot of publicity going on right now about prefabrication. *Dwell* magazine had a prefabricated house competition and the winner is being built. I think that modular construction and prefabricated houses

are inevitable because of the USA cost for construction labor. It's happening now. It's not happening with poise, but it's happening a lot. The percentage of mobile homes that are sold in America is higher than any other new house type. They're sprawling all over the country.

I think we should be building densely packed communities. I don't think we should be increasing suburban sprawl. Detached house subdivisions are not a way to occupy the landscape. A key factor for the future is a progressive transit system. We need transportation alternatives rather than the SUVs that everybody tries to jam the highways with. We need new concepts for housing built in such a way that it is integrated with the landscape, not sprawling and misusing the land. So yes, I would love to have that ideal community project. But who is the new client?

Richard Tuttle and I are still working together. He's done some furniture, and we collaborate on things. My philosophical writings speak about phenomenology and space and light, and the nice thing about working with Richard is that he understands all these things. We don't have theoretical arguments. We go right to the point. That's the way he sees the world so it is a very special collaboration. He understood the house...he helped tweak the design. He understood the process 100%. It was a pleasure.

Planar House, 2002–2005 (pp. 94–103)
The Planar House was designed for a couple who came to me from a recommendation via the Art Institute of Chicago. They said, "the main thing is our art collection; we have to have orthogonal walls." They have several Robert Rymans, a Kounellis, Bruce Nauman videos that they want to project, several Christopher Wool paintings, and many others. They're knowledgeable, and she'd seen a couple of my books. I started this project quite differently from the other houses we've talked about, because of the program; basically, it's one bedroom and gallery walls for art. They left Chicago, sold their apartment, and put the art in storage, while living in a condominium in Arizona, to build this house.

They bought a terrific little site that had a shabby 1950s house, which was removed. The site has a great view of Camelback Mountain. Saguaro cactus is right there in the wonderful desert landscape. I thought of a house that was orthogonal and planar in all ways, even in the way it is made. Instead of wood studs, we would make it in planes: pieces of tilt-up concrete.

The structural/material and planar ideas are integrated; the tilt-up concrete is the structure and the wall. There are cooling elements on the inside: cool-air, planar light traps that cut through the ceiling, and come down on the inside. The pool court is a rectangle inside the house composition. There are Cor-Ten steel doors that are digitally cut and rust to a reddish color. What's really wonderful is the way the windows are made. They're the result of the tilt-up planes that interlock and touch, creating gaps. Skylights are over the cool pools on the

Buster Keaton, *a Jeff Koons which was not for sale.*

inside, and there's a ramp to the roof for sculpture. From this roof the magical view of Camelback Mountain in the distance is revealed. We decided that the Camelback Mountain will be the sculpture; no other art is on the roof.

The planar language is like a game with big parts. We have worked with tilt-up a couple of times. The Chapel of St. Ignatius was a concrete tilt-up project. I've never realized it on a small house; but the client loves it. They're both retired, and he was worried about the money. I was honest with them. I said, "if we do it in tilt-up concrete, we'll have a presence and solidity that's not that visible, but you will always know. In the desert, it also has a mass that helps the cooling. The thermal mass is really productive as an ecological element, you won't worry about termites. But it's going to cost you more to do it in tilt-up. We can do the same house for less in wood and stucco. I don't want to fool you with that, before we go any further." And I added, "It seems to me that if you sell that Jeff Koons sculpture, you won't have any problem at all." She laughed. Anyway, just when we were trying to finish with the working drawings, she came to New York and sold two or three pieces and easily had enough to do the tilt-up. They love it now. During construction they went out there and put up folding chairs to watch the contractor. The contractor had to erect a chain-link fence around the site because of the architecture students coming around, bothering them.

The interior is a standard museum wall construction, flexible plaster over 3/4" plywood. There is just one bedroom. She has a little studio that is about 3,000 square feet though it looks much bigger because of the spatial scale. It's not large in floor area but it is tall. That's the economy of a tilt-up construction. The whole house is poured on a flat slab in pieces. When they tilt up the two walls, they weld a seam. There are clips embedded in the walls, steel angles, and then they weld the two together. In two days, the whole house is tilted up. That's what I love about it.

My father spent 1946 in Japan. He was on a secret mission. If the bomb didn't stop the war, they were going to invade Japan. Anyway, he was on a boat on his way over there when suddenly it was peacetime, so he

built buildings for the occupational forces. He had a Japanese crew. They were working for weeks, just cutting and cutting. He had an interpreter who explained what was going on. The officers were getting very upset and the interpreter kept saying, "Just be calm; in a couple of days, everything is going to change." They were cutting all the wooden pieces, and they didn't use nails. The building in wood was erected suddenly in a day and a half. They were whittling and cutting and marking, and then... magic! That was a bit like the apparition of a tilt-up building. It is exhilarating to see it appear.

This is my third tilt-up design. First we made the Chapel of St. Ignatius, and second is the design for a house in Long Island. I've been working on this house since 1997. When the client began the house, he ran a competition between Michael Graves, Robert Stern, and me. It was a house competition. He has five kids and dogs and horses. It is not a house, it's a city; it really is a city. I convinced him to collect architecture models, and since we began working together, he's purchased all these architecture models, so I added an architecture gallery. He bought models from Herzog & de Meuron, models from Mark Mack, and from Gisue Hariri.

He's a businessman who has a machine company that digitally cuts gears with computer-driven equipment. So if you have gear ratios like 5:1 and you are revamping your assembly line for a factory, he can make the gears on a 24-hour order out of solid aluminum blocks. At his factory the computers are in the front room, there is a glass wall, and all the cutters are in the big space beyond. The machines cost $200,000-$300,000 apiece, and they are made in Japan. He is a business genius, a Harvard graduate who came right out of school and immediately was a successful business man.

The last two houses we discussed are like night and day. They're as different as people are. You can't second-guess what people are going to be like or what they will do. So you do your best. I like Louis Kahn's statement that "Architecture does not exist. What exists is the spirit of architecture." Therefore, it doesn't matter how big something is. It can be very small. I think that inside of something very small can be quite a large spirit.

Sarphatistraat Offices, 1996–2000 (pp. 108–117)

The explorations in porosity began in 1996 with the project for the Het Oosten headquarters in Amsterdam on the Singel Canal. Het Oosten builds and manages both social and private-sector housing in Holland. The company purchased a turn-of-the-century u-shaped structure, originally built for military medical supplies. The company wanted a large space that could be readily converted for a variety of activities from meeting to informal receptions. It was for that reason that they asked us to develop an addition that would give the company a unique and visible identity. Het Oosten contacted us because of our eye for detail and expression. During one of our first visits to the projects I told them that the original building would need more light and space. We wanted to conceptually turn the building around so that it faced the canal. This company that employs 240 people is a developer of social housing. The pavilion is used for meetings, Christmas parties, or lunchtime activities; the question was how to design a building that had no singular program, no particular programmatic aspect.

Our scheme was exactly what Het Oosten was looking for. Before the scheme could be built we, together with Het Oosten, had to convince local authorities on two design-review panels that the pavilion would be a worthy replacement for the boiler plant and smokestack that originally dominated the waterfront elevation of the former warehouse. We designed the pavilion with a separate access, so that it, and its waterside, could be open for public use after hours. Eventually the city officials received the project very enthusiastically.

We took as an initial analogue something that is the same in plan, section, and elevation—a scientific object called the Menger Sponge, which has porosity within porosity. We combined this form with a musical concept from a piece called *Patterns in a Chromatic Field* by Morton Feldman, utilizing chance operations to define the color fields of the building. Feldman's experiments with random configurations of notes allowed beautiful things to occur in his music. The pavilion has the overall porosity of the Menger Sponge, with windows and color fields that were located by chance process, like throwing dice.

The Menger Sponge.

Our perforated screens are intentionally uneven to introduce random patterns of light that reflect off the canal, filter through the porous metal, and mix with the color applied where it extends beyond window openings. At night, lighting fixtures buried in the copper layer project the pavilion's colors outside to paint the canal in colors that slowly move in the rhythm of the water. We created this inner space in which the light can wander, and because of the colored patches you get the idea of the chromatic patterns in a field. Our ambition was to achieve a space of gossamer porosity with chance-located reflected colors that paint the Singel Canal in reflection.

The outer skin is perforated copper and all of the HVAC systems run in the zone between the inner and outer skins. Likewise, the interior finish is porous—perforated plywood backed by acoustic insulation so that the large space can be used by multiple groups simultaneously. It allows you to have a meeting in one corner and another meeting in the other corner. Without disturbing each other.

Under the building is a computer-activated parking garage for 48 cars, where no people are allowed. You put your hand in a scanner and the car goes down and is moved around on nylon wheels. The computer is so smart that if you typically leave work at 5 p.m., it anticipates this by starting to shuffle your car up to the surface so that when you put your hand in the scanner, the car comes up quickly. This parking garage is also

under water. If you were to propose this in America, the client would say you were crazy and throw you out of the room. In Holland, where the Dutch successfully hold back oceans with dikes, they built the parking garage without blinking and there are no leaks!

Simmons Hall, Massachusetts Institute of Technology, 1999–2002 (pp. 118–129)

When we started the interview process for the new dormitory at MIT in December of 1999 they already had a master plan which would yield a homogenous brick wall along Vassar Street. They invited five architects for the orientation session. After hearing about the master plan I made a sketch in my hotel room. I actually made a sketch of different types of porous buildings that open to the river and that connect to Cambridge Port, which is the blocked-off community across Briggs Field to the river. When I came back to the interview with that sketch I said: "I'm sorry, I would really love to work on this dormitory, but I think you have the wrong master plan and if we were going to work on it, we would have to redo the master plan. I think you need something permeable instead of a brick wall of seven stories. You need porosity." I asked them if it would be possible to do a one-month or a six-week master plan study and they agreed. We got the commission and it started with a master plan.

I have to say they had a great committee with Chancellor Larry Backow as a visionary leader. He was not afraid to take the chance to work with the most challenging of the architects, who said that they had to start over from scratch again. Their aspirations were very high. After Alvar Aalto's Baker House, no good dormitory had been built at MIT. For instance, at McGregor House all the windows are barred shut, there is no kitchen, and there are no real communal areas. The dormitories in the new master plan would have the same program as Alvar Aalto's Baker House, but the committee wanted even better architecture. So in six weeks we produced a master plan that had four buildings. Each would be a 350-bed dormitory; each one would have 25% porosity. MIT loves precision, so the idea of 25% porosity was received positively. They loved the design for the master plan and Larry Backow said: "Choose the building you want to develop and make it the most visionary project you can." Out of the four options (vertical porosity, horizontal porosity, diagonal porosity, and all-over porosity) we chose the most difficult one, which we called "The Folded Street."

Twenty-five percent porosity in four buildings.

After three and a half months of design development we had a very somber meeting with Chuck Vest and Larry Backow at MIT. They were advised by the local community not to exceed the 100-foot height limit. This meant we had to start all over, because we designed a 180-foot-high building. Originally we would have to finish the schematic design by August 20th and they could not give us any more time to develop a revised project. They knew what they were asking from us was unreasonable and they would even understand if we would need to decline. They were very gracious about it. I remember coming back to the office after that meeting and I realized that it was already June 1st. I happen to love the month of August. I like to use it for thinking, reading, and swimming. I could see that we were going to miss our summer, because we would be in charette. We had 15 people in the office at that time and I said to them: "We have this all-over sponge building. I think that we could develop that into a new scheme but we only have until the end of August. Look, if we decide to go forward, it means we're going to have no summer at all." So I went around for a silent vote. 14 people voted yes and 1 person voted no. I was that no. At that moment the energy of the office, and in particular of Tim Bade, really carried the project, not me. The young people in the office gave me a new boost of energy.

So we began to work on the building, making a seminal sectional diagram that brings the light and air down for ventilation and functions as social condenser. That notion of the social connection inside the building was the most important thing for me.

In the dormitory there would be 10 houses with their own unit master and a lounge. I wanted to make sure students wouldn't just sit in their individual cells, but that they would have the possibility to move through the building in all possible ways. By drilling these vertical sections and connecting the lounges vertically people easily meet each other. You open a door in one of the lounge spaces and you can either go up or down to another house, to another group of people. The spaces have really proven to be social condensers as we anticipated. Another kind of social condenser is the cafeteria on the first floor. We fought very hard for a great eating space to bring life to the street. Now that it is there, people from the dormitories without eating facilities come to the Simmons Hall and get their food and interact. There is always some presence at the base of the building at night. A lot of the ideas that we had were social, and they have proven to be something really positive in terms of making a dormitory.

Organizationally we took the overall notion of porosity first at an urban level and then at the scale of a wall, and divided each room into nine windows. All windows operate, so that each student has nine windows. We thought about a structure that would keep the sun out during the summertime and would allow it to penetrate deep into the space during the wintertime. It became a passive solar wall. Together with Guy Nordenson and Associates we developed a structure called perf-con. In each perf-con section the columns in the walls are merged with a set of 18 windows. The sections are made in a single mold and are all digitally manipulated to give them the necessary different structural capacities. It is perfect concrete in steel forms. It is just like stone, but it is more economic and faster. The 6,000 pieces were brought down on trucks from the manufacturer in Canada and delivered to the site so we could bypass the bad concrete you get here. The whole building is an experimental construction. It is an exoskeleton wall, where the concrete is bearing and taking up the lateral loads, and then insulation and aluminum skin over that. The structure was analyzed by Guy as one of the most efficient passive solar walls possible.

I thought it would be good to work with reflected color. I wanted color between the outside and the inside of the building. The ten different houses inspired me to develop a color code for the different sections. There would be ten different colors that you could read from the outside, but they would neither be on the outside face nor the inside face. The color would be on the micro section between the outside face and the inside face. Unfortunately the students didn't want to be identifiable from the outside. So I went back to the office a bit depressed: How was I going to get color for the building and what was it going to mean? Then I saw Nordenson's structural diagram of all the forces in the steel. It shows the rebar pattern with different colors for the different rebars, and I thought: "Aha, there is a structural and color correspondence. Number 4 bars are blue, number 9 bars are red, etc. There's a kind of color coding that could give us an engineering reading in the building." And so we adopted the structural diagram as the color scheme of the building. To this day the students say that it was somehow altered and manipulated, but it is not. They really are the colors of those different structural forces.

School of Art and Art History, University of Iowa, 1999–2006 (pp. 130–145)

This project began in 1999 as an interview, as often projects do. We were up against a number of very established architects. The art faculty and Dorothy Johnson, who is the director of the school and a wonderful person to work with, all attended. When I ended my interview they said, "Is there anything that you can say in conclusion?" I said, "Well, I notice that when you added on to the school in 1968, you blocked the old facade of the original building, whose inscription is 'ars longa vita brevis est'—'art is long and life is brief.'" I said, "I hope you won't make that kind of a mistake when you do this addition. In fact, I would like to tear that piece of the building away and reveal that inscription."

Perhaps that anecdote brought us the job. Dorothy Johnson said the committee vote was unanimous. So we began the design research. The Physical Planning Department gave us a site, a large piece of lawn across the street from the original building, on which to build a 70,000 square-foot building. We spent six months on some studies. I came back and told them that I thought they were building on the wrong site, that they should build adjacent to the lagoon; it would be closer to the original school and they could save the green lawn area and use it for another academic building or as part of campus landscaping. I remember Dick Gibson, the Physical Plant director, said, "Steven, stay away from the lagoon; we gave you the site." He said, "There's a utility line running on the road next to the lagoon, and I don't think you can possibly put the building in between the utility line and the lagoon. I went back, and I worked for another six months, and they were very calm. Then I came with a presentation; I really took a chance. I didn't put the building on the first site. I came with a building that has a bridge element over the lagoon, cantilevering over the it, and I said, "Dick, let me show you something; I'm not on your utility line. Look at that. The building has 70,000 square feet, and I'm not on your utility line." He looked at the plans, just a schematic design, and he said, "Fine. Keep going."

So when I presented this to the school, I described a new campus building that had fuzzy edges. It was porous around the edges, it was integrated with the landscape, it reaches out over the lagoon, it engages those great views of the old quarry. There was an old limestone quarry in the 18th and 19th centuries, and they removed enough limestone to cause the water to collect there, in a little forgotten lagoon. It was a wasted piece of the campus until our building engaged it.

In order to make the library cantilever work, we ran some tension rods over the top of the building. At a certain moment, I was looking at the models of what we were working on, and I said to one of the architects in the office, "Do me a favor; build me Picasso's 1912 guitar at the same scale; I'm just curious how close the geometry is"—and it was very close. It was a comparison.

The geometry we had developed was close to the Picasso. There was the planar aspect and the red rusty steel. I have not been directly inspired by works of art before, at least not overtly. When I revealed this comparison to the faculty, they loved it. They under-

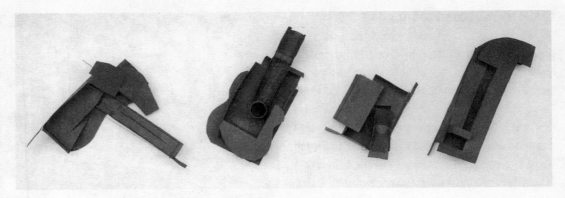

stood why I wanted it to be planes, why I wanted it to be loose, not symmetrical, open at the edges, and what the cantilever was about, and how the lagoon was being incorporated into the design. By moving the building off that big lawn and putting it on the lagoon, we bring the new building about 150 feet closer to the original building. You can circulate through the building and walk along the deck, which is also a café that over-hangs the lagoon. The conceptual artist, Richard Artschwager, has been commissioned to create a outdoor work for the site.

The use of fuzzy edges to embrace the natural phenomena, and the notion of sunlight hitting the water and shining on the undersides of the ceilings, are exciting phenomenal aspects of this building. It isn't just the space inside, but how the spaces engage the landscape and become part of the campus—a struc-ture of the campus; that is important. A walk through the spaces connects to campus and lagoon. It is a very economical building in Cor-Ten steel construction. We knew the project budget was tight, so we decided to expose all the raw elements of the structure. The precast concrete planks were exposed, just like the raw steel of the beams and the trusses. The stairway is made up of steel plates that form the railings, but also function as the structure that holds up the stairs. The auditorium shapes the way the building turns the corner on the street, so as the street slightly bends, the auditorium bends. The building is really a very loose assemblage of planes. From the inside looking out is where this architecture is really special. I had a professor who said, "Architecture should always be much more after you go into it and experience it than it is from the outside."

We had to go to the state legislature to present this building, because it is a state project. We had exactly five minutes to present the building. The legislature would immediately take a vote, "yea" or "nay." I worked on this project for two years! So the crisis was, this is Cor-Ten steel, a rusty steel building. I was concerned that the representatives would not understand what that meant. Mary Sue Coleman, who was then President of the University, loved the building, but she knew it wasn't just an average building. I mean, how many buildings are made out of exposed rusty steel sheets cantilevered over a lagoon?

She introduced the project, and that took about three minutes. So I had two minutes left. I showed the proposed building, and I showed the image of the original building, and I said, "Our building is in a light-weight material, it is metal, and it is red, just like the red brick of the 1937 building." That's what I said. And it was true. My time was up, and they took the vote, and it passed, unanimously. So the money was appropriated.

This building is economical because all the finishes are natural and exposed material; there's no second layer. There are concrete floors, exposed concrete on the ceilings. All the HVAC system runs through the concrete floor planks, which have holes in them, so all the heat and cooling comes through the structural planks of the floor. It is a complicated thing to do, but it means there's no exposed ductwork. The few addi-tions include a kind of felt for sound reasons in the auditorium, and some of the lecture rooms are walled in exposed plywood.

Linked Hybrid, 2003–2008 (pp. 146–155)

Our Beijing project was not a competition; we were directly contacted by Modern Group to design the housing. I want to be clear in these stories about architecture. I never went to China to look for work. Corporate architects are all going to China because they read in the newspaper that it's booming. Anyway, I was in Nanjing and got invited to come over to Beijing: Would I be interested in coming to Beijing to look at a project for eight towers with 800 apartments? I said, "What? If you're serious, send me a plane ticket from Nanjing." So a plane ticket was there. This is all happening within a day. We change plans and we fly to Beijing, we arrive at 10 o'clock on a Sunday night. A white Mercedes pulls up with two drivers, one with white gloves. They pick us up and they take us to the big hotel that overlooks the Forbidden City.

Groundbreaking ceremony, December 28, 2005.

They said, "We'll be back to pick you up at 9 a.m." So we're in the hotel, wondering, "God, what is this, anyway?" The next morning they came back in the same Mercedes and they bring us to the Modern Group. The name of the project that they're building is called MOMA. They use this name because they want prestige. So on the billboards on the way into the project there's Le Corbusier, a big picture, big as a wall, with one of his buildings; Mies van der Rohe, with one of his buildings. And you won't believe it; they have the Steven Holl picture up already! It's strange. You can't believe the thing. They built a little pavilion on the site, a rounded glass cylinder, and there's a model of half the whole city, their area of Beijing, floating above white rocks on a glass platform. In the middle of this, all the old buildings are torn down, and there are little buildings all over the place! The brown ones are theirs. I'm thinking this is like *Blade Runner*. This has got to be a movie. Right around this time, I'm really feeling that this can't be real, this is just too weird, I hear this cheering: RUNH-RUNH. A whole group of people, like a football team, cheer. RUNH-RUNH. I'm saying, "What's that?" The guy translates it for me. That's the sales staff doing their morning pep talk. When they all come out from behind they look like stewardesses. They are the sales staff selling the condominiums.

After the cheers of the sales staff, they take us over to the main building, where there's an L.E.D. screen that says, "Welcome, Steven Holl and his assistant Li." Then we go up to the conference room. There are long black leather tables, and each leather chair has a little microphone. Even though there may be only ten people in the room, they all talk into these microphones. I sat with the people and they showed me a really difficult site, with the zoning envelope of these eight towers, and they tell me that they want to keep that old factory and turn it into a museum. It was an ugly building, and certainly a building that wouldn't be nice to look down on from above. So already, as I'm sitting there in the first meeting, I'm thinking to myself, "No way am I going to keep that; I can't keep that; that's not going to work." I said to them: "For X amount of money and two months, I'm going to do a brilliant scheme for this project. I'll fit it into your zoning envelope. But it's not going to be what you think. You've got to give me the freedom to really make excellent architecture." So we make the agreement.

We proceeded to work very hard. There are a lot of models in the office. In the end, we had a huge model. We had torn down the factory and created a giant reflecting pond with two floating cinemas with gardens on top that make this whole centerpiece, like cinematic architecture of the future. There is also a round hotel that was never in the program. We connected all the towers by a zig-zag of bridges with spas; there's a swimming pool in one of the bridges; there are cafés, there's a deli; there's a kindergarten and there are schools nearby; we envision all sorts of different functions. I insist on having all the basic needs on-site so that one doesn't need to drive for essentials. There is a place for bicycles but this will be a pedestrian-oriented community. They do not have to get into their cars and drive away to do anything. The looped hybrid buildings relate to the MIT dormitory as the perf-con structure is in the exterior wall. In Beijing I said: "What happens if you just blow it up in scale completely so you keep the horizontals and the verticals the same?" So the scale in this possibility is just transferred to the height of a floor. That was an experiment, and it works.

Two months later we returned to Beijing with our design. At the end of my presentation on the 3rd of March last year, the president takes his little microphone and he says, "What's important here is the spiritual aspect. We know we can sell all of these apartments." That's his statement. I mean, I'm thinking to myself, "they're going to build all of this?!" Then I thought: "Okay, I can imagine…" They got excited about it, I can imagine. But it's possible. So everything keeps going and going. I said, "Li, we've got to get a budget." So we settle the drawings, and then they did this big analysis, which took two weeks, and then came an e-mail with two sentences. It said, "Your project considerably exceeds our budget. However, we're adjusting our budget to meet your project."

Beijing is a little colder than New York. It has this terrible dust in March that comes from the Gobi desert. It last for six weeks. You can't see. It's really dense. It's due to deforestation, and to the desert and the wind. That's a continuing problem there. The city is also going to have a problem with water. They don't have enough water. It's like Los Angeles. The Linked Hybrid is an example of making architecture out of a piece of infrastructure that I believe in the next fifty years is going to become much more urgent and dominant in our minds. Water is a tremendous piece of phenomenological potential in terms of the weather. Water reflects the rain in a positive way. It reflects the rising sun, the setting sun, the ripples of the wind. So you can just take two inches of water, and you've got a piece of landscape. So we are all doing that. I'm using recycled water. This water court that these two cinemas float on in Beijing is going to be recycled water from the plumbing systems of the apartments. It's going to freeze in the winter to become an ice-skating rink. The water in the whole project is divided into sewage, solid waste from the toilets, and gray water, which is water from the sinks and the showers. It will be piped down in a separate system, run through an ultraviolet filter, put into the big reflecting pond, with vegetation like water lilies and grasses. It will be a major piece of green recycling. All the cooling and heating will be done by drilling geothermal wells. There will be 600 wells drilled below this project, five meters around the center; they are 100 meters deep.

Beijing, for years, was a low city because you were not allowed to see over the thirty-five-foot high walls into the Forbidden City. P'u Yi, the last emperor of China, was forced to leave in 1924, and it would not be before the mid-30s when it was possible to construct buildings taller than those surrounding the Forbidden City. But with the Communist government in place they followed the Soviet model. After Mao died in 1976, there was a gradual opening up, and real changes began to occur in the mid-1980s. Now they are trying to slow it down. To give you a scale: We have 300

million people in America. There are 1.3 billion people in China. Now, imagine that suddenly they get to own their apartments. For a long time, they haven't been able to do that, so everybody wants apartments, just like suddenly everybody wants a car. Our scheme is going against what's currently being built in China. What is being built now are point towers, isolated at the base. Gated communities with no services—that is what's being built. I realize I'm going out on a limb with this project. So far, Modern Group keeps saying yes but they are exceptional clients. Most of these corporate firms have no urban aspirations at all, and some of them I don't even call corporate firms—they're just businesses. They're building the maximum 30-story buildings with the maximum number of apartments, the biggest marble-floor-kind-of-brass-doorknob apartments. At the base there's a fence, and there are two guards, and you drive your car in. Right across the street from our project there are three of these buildings. Isolated, antiurban.

I believe we have to make a project that has a vision for urban interaction, one that has services and is open to the public. (It has to be, in order for the shops to survive.) I said, "Look, it is semi-public." They had a

wonderful groundbreaking ceremony on December 28, 2005, with golden shovels, jumping Chinese dragons, and fireworks that exploded in multi-colored confetti blown through the air.

College of Architecture and Landscape Architecture, University of Minnesota, 1990–2002 (pp. 160–169)

I worked on the University of Minnesota School of Architecture for thirteen years. Harrison Fraker was the dean when we started in 1988. I'd never done a building bigger than a house at that time. But he loved my work. I had just gotten a project for Fukuoka Housing in Japan, which was a pretty good-sized building. He said, "We're adding onto the School of Architecture, it's a big state project, but WE WANT architecture. And Steven, I just called you to tell you, you were number six, and we only chose five for the short list. Steven, I just wish you could have teamed up with someone to get on the list." He told me that Ellerbe Becket, the big Minnesota firm of a thousand people, was on the short list. He said, "If you could team up with them, with your philosophical bent and their production capacity, you guys could get the job. Why don't you call them and ask if you could team up?"

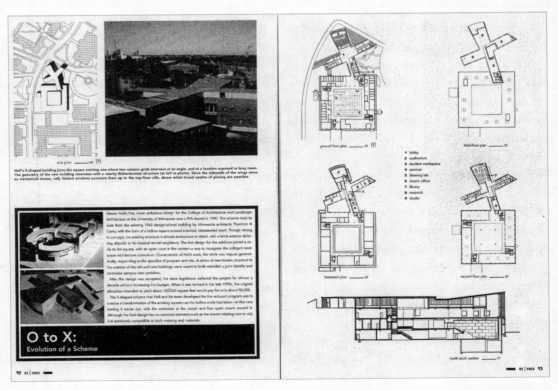

So I called Ellerbe. They listened to me, but they didn't reply. A few more days passed, and they didn't reply. Time was running out. The interview was going to be on Friday. A week before the interview, I called them again. They said, "We're considering it, but we're not sure. We are considering it." On Thursday night, the night before the interview, they called to tell me that they wanted to join forces to get the job. I had to fly at 7 o'clock in the morning to cold Minneapolis and do the interview. The client was a large university and state group. Now, one of the good things about a state group is that as soon as the teams present, they vote. And they don't meet again, because they never get together again. So I flew out there on an evening's notice and I got to Minneapolis at 10:30 or 11:00 a.m. We went into the interview at 2 p.m. that afternoon. Then I flew back to New York. I arrived at my office at 10:00 p.m. to receive the notice that we got the job! They took the vote right after the interview. They voted at 5 o'clock while I was going back. However, Ellerbe never wanted us, so they organized an internal competition: us against their team. They invited Harrison to come to New York, and Harrison called me up and said, "Steven, do you know I'm coming to see the scheme for the design?" I said, "What? What are you talking about?" He said, "I'm coming to see the scheme for the design of the school of architecture. They invited me to come out and see it." I said, "But we haven't even met! What is going on here?" He said, "Well, I guess they're trying to run this as an internal competition." I immediately had to start working on a scheme. We did a scheme, and they did a scheme. We were working on ours and developing ours, and they were developing theirs. We had to go and present to the Physical Planning Department, the faculty of Architecture, and the Landscape School, and they voted on which scheme to take. So there was a really awful day when this unplanned competition jury took place, and an embarrassing presentation between me and our scheme, and them and their scheme. And the faculty voted for our scheme. Now, our partner Ellerbe was bitter, because their scheme was eliminated.

We proceeded and the scheme developed, but the Ellerbe firm was making our lives miserable. They would be paid by the university, and they wouldn't pay us for six months. After many months of work and expense—money I didn't have—the project went up to the state legislature and it failed to pass. So then Harrison said, "We're going to get in line next year. Don't worry. We'll try to get it through next year." After three tries, Harrison told the university, "If they don't put this on the top priority next year, I am going to resign as dean." And he did. He went to Berkeley.

The following year, longtime faculty member Garth Rockcastle went into the legislative meeting and asked them how to get this thing passed, and they said, "If you cut the budget in half, we'll pass it." So they cut the budget in half, and passed it.

Now, this is 1996, I believe, or 1995. I get a phone call from Garth, who says, "The building has been passed." I said, "Are you kidding me?" It's been sitting in the drawer for six years. And then he told me that the budget is half. I said, "then we have to cut the project in half." He says, "Yes; can you do this in two months?" Now the dean is Tom Fisher. Tom wanted us to prevail. I said "We have to turn it around, and we have to turn it inside-out. It's a new building. It's a different building. It's the inside-out of the other building." We chose the local architect Vince James, removed Ellerbe, and had a great working team.

When that building opened, I had worked on it for thirteen years. It was a lesson on how difficult things can be. You know what's interesting? If you just stay the course, keep your integrity, other things drop away, and they come back in another form. In the end, when we opened the building in 2002, everybody originally involved had changed. The dean was different, the president of the university was different, the Physical Planning people were new, every single person was different. I was the only one remaining to the end of the project, after 13 years.

Kiasma Museum of Contemporary Art, 1992–1998
(pp. 170–183) The competition for the Helsinki Museum of Contemporary Art began in 1992. I remember that we visited the site in October and interviewed the people who were in charge of the project. It made me realize that the project was real, with a real

Mannerheim Statue Controversy.

budget. I made some initial drawings in the hotel room after the first night of the visit and parallel to that process I was reading Maurice Merleau-Ponty's *The Visible and the Invisible*. One of the chapters was called "The Chiasm," which is about criss-crossing in space. It is like the crossing of the nerves behind the eye. Soon "chiasm" became the concept of the building.

Coming back to New York we worked very hard for six months. And I remember how eager I was to try to connect spaces in a building to the notions in Merleau-Ponty's writings. This building could somehow be a vehicle of the body moving through space and of the notion of natural light. The building would have 25 galleries, all of which have some degree of natural light, and like a piece of music, you could understand them in a sequence. And as you move through there would be an overlapping of space and light, and finally you would reach the kind of crescendo, which is the top gallery.

So the building really took off from this philosophical concept, and proceeded along the lines of meeting the program. We created a rectangular section as an ideal line of galleries, and a curved section, which responded to a line of culture and a line of history in the morphology of the city. In Finnish competitions it is required to choose a project name that identifies you anonymously on your presentation boards. I used chiasm and I spelled it c-h-i-a-s-m, the way the Greeks spell it, the way Merleau-Ponty spelled it. But there is no "c-h" in Finish, so they changed it to a K: Kiasma. We won the competition and the project adopted this mysterious title that related to the interlocking of the building shape. After years of development they became so deeply attached to the name that they called the museum officially "Kiasma."

The process of developing the building was facilitated by Juhani Pallasmaa's office in Helsinki. He's one of the great Finnish architects. When we won the competition I asked him to be my partner architect. It was such an important site in the center of the city, right next to the train station, that he realized how important this building could be to Helsinki. To my surprise he agreed to join us. It is really through his political awareness and acumen that we have been able to realize this project and not through my naiveté. I was completely unaware of the subtleties in the Finnish culture and history. At a certain moment 10,000 signatures against the building were collected. It turned out that the building was defacing the site of the statue of Marshall Mannerheim. I didn't realize that Marshall Mannerheim was the Abraham Lincoln of Finnish history. As soon as Juhani told me about him and got me to read about him, I realized how important that statue was. I went to Mannerheim's house, which is now a museum, and studied the paintings that he collected (some of which were the most radical modern paintings of the day). I went to his favorite restaurants, I ate his food and drank his Schnapps. I tried to become Marshall Mannerheim so I could understand who he was. Then I got interviewed on television about the whole situation. I argued persuasively that this new museum would provide a better backdrop for the statue. The museum would function as a blank backdrop creating a new vantage point to see that important statue. We convinced them.

It was a project of very curious and almost surrealistic events, such as the decision-making process for the scale of the drawings. You would expect that this would be decided together with the officials of the building department in an anonymous boardroom. In Helsinki even decisions like that are only made in the sauna,

where all major Finnish decisions are historically made. So I'm sitting in a sauna with about five building officials, all of whom have enormous bodies, some of them with hairy backs. We are sitting in the painful heat and I can't take it. I'm a little skinny New Yorker sitting on the floor, begging them to make the decision. They go out and jump through holes in the ice and they come back. I would just go out to cool off. And finally the decision was made: the scale of 1:50 for the construction drawings.

They had a groundbreaking in the snow with fire marking the edges of the building. It was a great dance event. After that they began to construct the building in the freezing January weather. And everything after that was done at an absolute speed and with an amazing observation of workers. The building needed to be built for an absolute price of $40 million, not a penny more, and they really rose to that challenge.

For me as an architect the project was a real turning point. Until that time I was mostly a teacher. I had built some houses and a 30-unit apartment building in Fukuoka, Japan. But to do this museum my office suddenly had to grow from four people to at least ten people. The fact that it was a competition between 516 others and that the jury voted unanimously for our design gave a gigantic boost to our presence as international architects. Ever since, a lot of projects have come to us, such as the buildings in Langenlois (Austria). I can say now that there is one building in an architect's life that can change everything; and for me it was the Helsinki Museum of Contemporary Art, which is now with a K, Kiasma.

Higgins Hall Center Section, Pratt Institute, 1997–2005 (pp. 184–191)

It is great to have good architects as clients. I've known Tom Hanrahan for years and I taught with him at Columbia. Tom had just become the dean of the School of Architecture at Pratt. In July of 1997 there was a fire that was started by a Coke machine in the center section of the Pratt architecture building and it burned down. In fact, I lectured a few months before in the very room that burned down. After the fire there was insurance money — if I remember right it was $4 million —

to rebuild the center section, but they needed to put the whole thing in the pipeline by the end of the year. So they conducted an interview process with four architects. I went to the interview, and having had already done a school of architecture at the University of Minnesota, we got the commission. Then the requirement was that you had to do the whole design within six weeks and get it through the administrative process. I remember that it was a very hot summer and I was sweating in the office!

We had this very simple idea of taking the floor plates from the 1850 building on the left and the the 1860 building on the right, and because they didn't align, drawing them through into rebuilt space to create a "dissonance zone" at the center and forming a new entrance to the building. When the center section burned down, it presented an opportunity. For years these two old buildings were not properly joined. There was a little piece of asphalt roof instead of a courtyard. There was no real great entranceway to the school. So by this building burning down you had the first chance to make a proper entranceway at the center point of the school, to make an entrance courtyard and to make a proper auditorium that they never had. All of these opportunities present themselves but everything had to be done very quickly and inexpensively.

This notion of these floor plates coming through and the notion that the whole composition sits on a plinth that's made out of bricks recycled from the burned-down center section was really a two-part idea. The tectonics were to be didactic; to make the whole new section come down on just six columns, which could be precast so they could be very fine material—

Pratt's burned-out site, July 2007.

precast beams, planks, and columns. There are six columns supporting the whole center section. These ideas came rather quickly — they had to — and I presented them in the first week of September, right after being selected as the architect, and people on the committee liked the ideas; they were straightforward, they were easy to understand, and the design was approved. We started working away but the project got delayed. It's a long story, but it got diverted and delayed and funds were diverted and delayed and years went by. Around 2003 the school said they were ready to start so we did the working drawings with Rogers Marvel Architects, who did the restoration and renovation of the other two sections. The builder was Sciame Construction — Frank Sciame is really a good contractor who cared about architecture, they built it really well — it's a tough building with everything exposed. When we cut the ribbon on September 22nd this year, it was a very happy moment because it brought forth a new architecture link that unites the school in a way that it didn't have before: we made a new social aspect for the school. We are very proud of the new interaction and gathering activities.

The building does present a kind of tectonics of the minimum because all the materials of the building are exposed. Nothing is covered up. You see the exposed concrete beams and planks, the steel channel that receives the glass planks. You can see through the glass planks and see the insulation. I see this building as a kind of "zero ground" of architectural elements to make up this simple concept. At the school of architecture we did at University of Minnesota, there was also an effort to make a didactic structure with tectonic clarity. Probably more important here at Pratt are the social possibilities of the new space. Pratt is nearly the largest school of architecture by volume in America. There was never an entrance court to this complex. In the front court we sculpted the brick and made benches and places to sit, places to tie your bike; you can see students congregating there in the morning, in the afternoon. Then there is a rear section that looks out on the green spaces of all the brownstones beyond and that's the perfect place to hold class when it is warm enough. So there are two outdoor spaces that are created by the building.

When the floors cross over from one building to the other, the glass planks of the elevation are obscure except for at the dissonance zone, facing west and facing east. The floor turns into a ramp right at the dissonance zone; as your body is moving north and south you suddenly turn east and west at the dissonance zone. You are turned to look east at the green in the back or west at the courtyard in the front. Even though it is a minimal idea, it has a maximum impact because it has a way of grabbing hold of your body and turning it. The building has spatial consequences, which are also social consequences because, after all, it's people mixing up, making them meet each other, and giving a place for that to happen. It's a bit like our MIT dormitory. It has spatial concept, which is a formal concept, but that concept has a social mixing potential. That is a very interesting thing, that architecture isn't just an exterior envelope, but has real sectional, interior, and social consequences. How a building is put together is one thing, but how you experience it, how you move through it, how those spaces have some consequence socially in the use of the building, is very important to me.

Loisium Visitor Center and Hotel, 2001–2005

(pp. 192–205) This wine center and hotel & spa in Langenlois, Austria, began as a strange coincidence. I was working on an exhibition for the Arkitectur Zentrum in Vienna, around my topic "Idea and Phenomenon." The directo,r Dietmar Steiner, who is an impresario of architecture in Vienna, came for one of the exhibition's organization meetings. This was early 2001, a year before the exhibition. He said that he'd been contacted by a group of four families that make very fine wine in that region. They wanted to make a new wine center, and they wanted a really interesting building; they didn't know how to do that—and would he oversee a competition?

While they were having the first meeting, one of the family members, Tuula, asked, "Do you think we could invite Steven Holl to do this competition?" Tuula grew up in Helsinki, and she goes back to Finland every summer with her husband, and so they know our museum Kiasma. Steiner said, "Well, I'm on my way to

New York next week; why don't we ask him if he'll make a design for it?" So he came, and I said, "Of course, I'd like to make a scheme for a building in Austrian wine country."

The date of the first sketch is June 11, 2001. I was on the site, and I was attracted to the old vault system, which is an ancient morphology. Some of the vaults are 900 years old. I thought that the wine center could be a simple cube punctured by a morphology exactly like the old vault system. The second phase would be a hotel, which would be a translation of that language in some way, so that the old vault system is "under the ground" the new wine center is "in the ground," and the hotel would be "above the ground."

These vaults are storage areas for wine and compose the families' main storage cellar system. They are carved of local tufa stone, which is very soft. Some of the vaults are directly beneath buildings; they dig them out as you'd dig out for a subway. Then they line the inside with stone.

Langenlois hasn't had a new building in 100 years. It's a wonderful, old, conservative place, a very small town that has a main street, a church, two or three restaurants. The town exemplifies very conservative Austrian culture yet they said they wanted an interesting, modern building for the new wine center. I started making watercolors and drawings and models with the slightly skeptical feeling that they're never going to be built. I thought, "You really can't connect to the old tile-roofed, yellow stucco medieval and 19th-century buildings typical of the town. This must be a completely different project."

My initial concept sketch was followed by schematic design drawings. We made a model, and we made a collage that showed the old town in the foreground. It showed the wine center, which is a tilted cube sitting in the ground surrounded by the vineyards, and it shows the hotel as the second phase in the back. There was a presentation meeting to discuss the idea in Langenlois, and only five people there: four people from the wine center families, and the mayor of the town. After I presented, the mayor said, "We're going to build that,

and we're going to build the hotel as well." Little did I know, the town is so small that there is no building department! It was the mayor's decision; he would issue the building permit.

The first phase, the wine center, was finished and opened in September 2003, and it's been published many times. It was so popular that 90,000 people visited this building in the first year. So the next year they decided that they definitely wanted to build a hotel and they wanted it to open in October 2005. In one year. The construction went on seven days a week and at night. It opened on time in October 2005. There are 82 hotel rooms, an Aveda spa, a restaurant with our furniture.

This project is a case where architecture is a prime catalyst for its realization. They have several very fine Gruner Veltliner wines, and they sat me down on one of my visits and said, "Would you choose your favorite Gruner Veltliner?" I tasted 30 different Gruner Veltliners. I picked the one I liked and then they made the wine label. They chose my very first watercolor for the project as the wine label; on the label you can see the vaults, the wine center, and the hotel: UNDER, IN AND ABOVE THE GROUND.

It is surprising that they built this building in Langenlois; its quite radical compared to everything else in their town. They had no 20th-century architecture at all; suddenly they built this and they love it. For me, what is exciting is the possibility that architecture can be a catalyst for a lot of other things that are unpredictable, and that people you would never imagine would go along

with a radical modern design—not only go along with it, but embrace it wholeheartedly. People of all ages visit the center but often there is a group of retirees on a wine tour, a whole bus full. There are 40 people, and they are all over 75. One day, such a group pulled up to the wine center, some got out, and then they turned around and went back to their bus and drove away. They must have picked up some literature because 30 minutes later they returned and stayed the rest of the day. They decided to like this strange architecture.

The Austrians have been suffering from a wine scandal since the late '80s. There was an accusation of fortifying the wine, and some vineyards were closed. It tarnished the reputation of Austrian wine. I heard from some people that this building has resurrected and reestablished the reputation of Austrian wine, which is a very good wine and very well made. Austria even issued a stamp with the wine center on it.

The architectural idea is a simple cube that's tilted toward the vaults. The vault system morphology punctures the walls and brings the light in. Every workman understood the relation of the main idea and the old vaults. Even though it's a unique building, they could articulate why it was this way. The workmen could take ownership in creating the architecture. I also think when architecture is imaginative and interesting, more people want to work on it and, in doing so, become inspired by it.

The whole building is lined in cork. It's a concrete structure with a sanded aluminum skin. For the interior acoustics and the warmth of the color of the cork, we found big sheets of cork from Portugal, mounted on plywood. You can smell the cork. The ceiling is concrete; there are no columns. The cube building is self-supported with very thin concrete and it's tilted 5 degrees toward the vaults. Rather than just sitting there like a static cube, the whole building tilts 5 degrees leading visitors down the ramp toward the 900-year-old vault system.

Before this building they had a very nondescript shop in the town and there was no hotel; you couldn't stay overnight there. Most of the project funding came from the four families that came together. There's a funding

program in Austria that involves quasi-cultural and community facilities. Loisium can host community meetings, concerts, and speeches, and the hotel will provide meeting rooms; therefore, it received 30% of the project's funding from the state. The client's enthusiasm to realize architecture really gives back a lot of energy.

Nelson-Atkins Museum of Art, 1999–2007

(pp. 206–227) The Nelson-Atkins Museum project was a competition in 1999. You first had to submit qualifications, and I think they had some 200 applicants. It came down to six competitors, which included Christian de Portzamparc from Paris, Tadao Ando from Japan, Machado/Silvetti from Boston, and Gigon/Guyer from Switzerland. We were visiting the site for the first time, and my first impulse was not to follow the rules, which proscribed building on the north side of the existing museum and blocking that north elevation. Okay, that would be the most pragmatic way to add to the building, but I said no, we want to make landscape and architecture merge, we want to restore the existing building facades, and our project would really take a completely different route. One of the ways I defended our approach was to read an inscription on the limestone façade of the existing building. So when I'm presenting to the jury, including J. Carter Brown, Ada Louise Huxtable, and the museum director, Mark Wilson, I said right at the beginning of my presentation, "Excuse me, but I broke the rules and I was very nervous about coming down here today because I spent all this time on a scheme which basically is going against where we're supposed to be adding on. The way I got the courage to break the rules was I read an inscription on the elevation of the old building: 'The Soul Has More Need for the Ideal Than the Real.' Even though we'll probably be disqualified, I'm going to present what I think is the 'ideal addition' to this 1937 building.

"Ideally, you would not block any of the elevations of the original building; you would restore all four elevations. Ideally, you would have a wonderful entrance court, which wouldn't be full of cars; the cars would be below grade, there would be a reflecting pond, and one would have the feeling of a real public space, something that

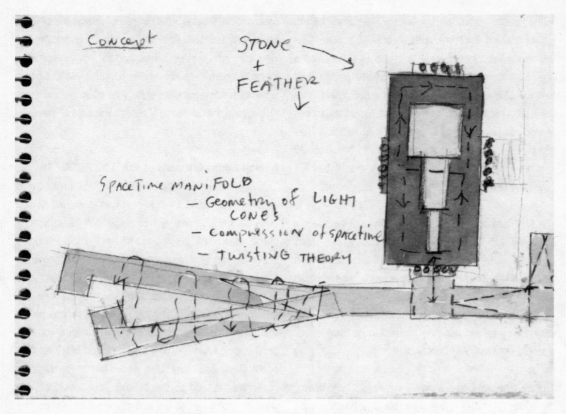

Concept

STONE
+
FEATHER

SPACETIME MANIFOLD
— Geometry of LIGHT CONES
— compression of spacetime
— TWISTING THEORY

was made special for the new building as well as the old building. Ideally, the old building is in multiple levels and it's heavy in stone; the new building would have a single level—the single level is the best way to circulate—and it would be light like a feather in the landscape."

Then I presented this drawing that shows what I called the "stone" and the "feather"—the stone being the original building, and the addition as this light element, the feather, going into the landscape—I even went so far as to show them a bunch of what I would consider "failed schemes." What's interesting about doing a competition is that there are only so many ways to solve the problem and when you can show them rejected alternatives, you can convincingly argue for something else. That was a good strategy, actually, in the presentation.

Here's that key drawing, "The Soul Has More Need for the Ideal Than the Rea,l" and then you can see the stone and the feather. The stone is heavy, the feather is light. The stone was 1933, the feather is 2002. The stone has directed circulation, the feather open circulation. The stone is bounded, the feather unbounded. Stone, inward views, feather, outward views into the

landscape. Hermetic, meshing. Imported, indigenous. So there are all these aspects that are very, very different about the new thing that complement the old thing: it gives you experiences in the new that you couldn't get in the old.

One of the first drawings was the view into the landscape garden from the new building. I had this notion of looking out into the great sculpture garden—they have a tremendously large outdoor sculpture collection, one of the largest in America. I made this drawing before I made the drawing of the plan from which this is viewed. A lot of times with a watercolor I'll have an idea, a basic thrust, then I work from the inside out. Like in Helsinki, I made the drawings of the inside of the Kiasma Museum before I knew what the outside would be; I hadn't resolved the outside, I was drawing the galleries first. It isn't just to make the concept diagram or the basic schematic diagram, it's to work experientially. Once you've got a concept and a strategy, you work your way from the main interior spaces out to the building, because the inside is always more important than the outside. So you're conceiving complete spaces, complete sequences

that have all the implications of light, view, and the direction of movement. The psychological need for natural light, the way that natural light characterizes the horizontal extension of the 850-foot long gallery sequence is a key aspect. The idea of fusing the building with the landscape of the sculpture garden took the form of "lenses" in the gardens, or as some critics have said, "Shards of glass flung across the landscape." They define and separate the sculpture gardens above, while bringing spatial excitement of natural light developed in perspectives below. It is as if the building defines a new field of senses to be experienced on different levels. So the glass pavilion-like elements are not just light monitors, but serve in many spatial ways, top and bottom, with different qualities of diffused natural light. I even imagine them related to the physics of art and light from particles to waves... from monocular images to binocular vision. Of course the whole light and space idea is activated by the body moving through it—by perception and contact with the overlapping perspectives and contact of staff to visitor, staff to staff, staff to student, student to visitor.

The building is created from structural glass made in Munich. Between structural glass planks is the Okalux [light diffusing] installation. Channel glass had been used for parking garages in Europe. This is white glass that has to be specially made because normal glass has a soda content that turns it green. To properly get a batch of pure German optical glass means closing down the entire operation, cleaning out the soda glass and running the German optical glass through the system. We first used this glass technique in '94 in Helsinki with the mockup that was built outside the city. That was beautiful, this quality of white light and the Okalux. And it's been a technique of glazing that we've used in a number of buildings, and because it's structural glass and you don't have the vertical mullions, you save all that money in the system. There's also this energy aspect to it with the Okalux because you can cut down to 18% sunlight transmission; it's almost like a different material. It's like a shoji screen, like a durable version of what a shoji screen's light is like. It's not expensive; it's an economical, industrial material. There are now manufacturers that are doing the white glass, but in our case this is still a special installation, as this is 16-inches-wide glass, custom-made for Kansas City. It's wider and it can span a little farther.

I call them lenses because they're bringing light down below and as you move through the landscape they shape the sculpture gardens up above, so they're really about the parallax of movement and light, which are all related to something like a lens. Whenever you move through a series of spaces, when you change your body's location you change the perspective of what you see. If you turn, you have changed the perspective, so it's like moving through a colonnade in ancient architecture. The space glides. You move your body, and the space opens up and closes and opens up and closes. As you move through the double rows of columns you can see the parallax of space opening and closing and changing. And for me that's a central measure of architecture, the body moving in space.

In the 21st-century city, the vertical dimension is much stronger than it ever was. Diagonal movement through the vertical dimension is an exhilarating potential, and it can happen at any point in the section of a building. You could go up elevators, arrive at some floor 30 floors above the city, and mount a series of escalators that take you up to another series of spaces, but suddenly those views that you have from those escalators are 30 floors in the air. So, if you can open up the city views to that experience, you really have something unique that's going on with the way the body feels and the way the space feels, the way the city's experienced, the way the perspective is. So this notion of the parallax of movement in the urban space of the 21st-century cities is really an exciting dimension.

The Nelson Atkins is horizontal but it's moving down, the section gently, gently drops. This goes 850 feet so it's like a 40-story skyscraper laying down in the grass and you're walking through it. We studied perspectives at every shift and change and every drop. And any time I drop a floor to another floor I never raise that more than three feet, three and a half feet, so when I'm standing in this space, and that space is a little higher, I can see across the floor of that space. That draws you through. You never block the spatial overlap by

shifting the floor too far. You always have the continuity of one space overlapping another one. If you don't work it out in perspectives or in your brain ahead of time, or if you just try to draw a bunch of plans or sections and don't think about spatial overlap it doesn't work. And it's also something that's very hard to convey in photographs. You really need to move through it with your body. Only the people who visit the Nelson Atkins and actually go down through the spaces will know what I'm really talking about. From that point, by the way, books can never convey architectural experience.

If I wrote a piece of music that I'm going to describe to you, I can read the score, I can tell you that I'm using 7/8ths time and I'm working with a pentatonic scale and I'm going to use instruments that have never been joined together in a single proposition before, and I can say anything I want. But the real success of the piece is when you listen to the music or when you walk through the spaces. It's going to succeed or it isn't. That's the true measure of the architecture. You have to feel it. These ideas don't photograph or hardly photograph, so this is a very difficult dimension of the problem of architecture.

In the Chapel of St. Ignatius there's this moment when you walk in through the door, you enter the building at the corner, not at the front. And you can see the narthex but in order to arrive in the main gathering

space I needed eight inches of rise in the floor. I had to have that. I need to lift the body and I need to drop the narthex down and I fought the physical planning director, who didn't want it. He says, "There's no need for that. You're just doing that." I said, "I know I'm doing it. I need that, we need that." "There's no need." I mean, you need to move the body through the space and you have to elevate and drop and turn and shift the body in the trajectory of movement according to the overlapping perspectives that are in the conception. That is like what happens at Pratt: a very simple idea of sectional change but then when you change movement to this direction you see it's also connected one to one. So this notion of moving the body through the space is connected one to one with the concept.

The movement through the spaces and the way the light works are both connected and central to the feeling and the concept. When they're really working these spatial aspects are powerful, that's the music, that's the melody, that's the core. You have a concept, you have a conceptual drawing—that's the seed that drives the design. Then the design is measured in the experience, and the success comes from the experiential nature. I'm very excited that the few people who have gotten into the Nelson Atkins to drop down through that series of perspectives have been exhilarated. You know, one reporter said, "Wow, it was like the space had been blown up into billowing sails from which light cascaded in." The building doesn't reveal that from the outside, which I really enjoy. I enjoy the fact that held in this series of lenses that apparently sit in the grass is a whole exhilarating realm that has to be experienced, and in a way it's the secret of the place. You don't have to wear everything on your sleeve. Just because you have some swirling spaces outside doesn't mean you have to have swirling spaces inside. I really like the muteness of the outside, when it comes with the exhilaration of the spaces inside. That's the right proportion with emphasis and the interior experience. I wouldn't want it the other way.

The parking garage is unique. Instead of your double tees of precast concrete, we connected two bottom flanges and formed it into a curve, and then the whole parking garage feels like an undulated vault. These "wave tees" span 65 feet and then they come down in a series of columns. The space has a unique feeling because these wave tees are connected but there's no horizontal beams, just the wave tee going in the transverse direction.

The building is just being finished. It was a long process; although we had a unanimous vote from the jury, there was a stalling process because the building committee didn't believe the glass would work. The glass had to be ultra tested in Florida in a testing lab that uses jet props blasting at 200 miles an hour at these glass wall sections that are spanning their maximum spans. Architecture is not easy. But I can say that I'm very enthusiastic that basically what's being built here doesn't have any compromises, but it took a long time to convince them and a long time to reassure and study and test and everything. We built the whole thing in phases so the parking garage and the pond opened two years ago. There are 500 cars underneath that reflecting pond with a great artwork by Walter De Maria, *One Sun of 34 Moons*. It is a serene and inviting forecourt joining both the new and the old with a vast artwork by De Maria.

World Trade Center, 2002 (pp. 228–231)
On September 11 I was here in my office at 31st and 10th. I arrived after the first plane hit and I was coming up the elevator when the second hit. I watched the entire collapse of the towers in real time, which was a horrific experience.

It goes beyond words.

I sent all the staff home. I was watching with binoculars, and I could see people jumping off the towers. This is a tragic event that etched deep.

After 9/11 I made drawings of a memorial spontaneously, because I make drawings every day. When Max Protech asked for ideas in an ideas exhibition I continued to work on that. My first proposal developed into an idea called the *Floating Memorial/Folded Street*. That project was an armature for grief, for public space, and for some public amenities, but there were

no programmatic functions as offices yet. Six months later there was the official competition and five teams where to be chosen. Peter Eisenman called me and said: "Steven, we want you on our team." I told him that I didn't really want to do it. I was on my way to Europe; in fact I was literally going out the door and he called me again to ask me whether he could put my name on the submission papers. I agreed.

So now I had the stress of collaboration with Peter Eisenman, Richard Meier, and Gwathmey Siegel to come up with a scheme. Our meetings were endless and enormously confrontational. My main argument was that we should come together and make a project in the spirit of Rockefeller Center: a 21st-century armature to frame urban space and create a new skyscraper typology.

I had been working on a vision called *Parallax Towers* years before, in which I envisioned horizontal linkage of vertical thin towers. The notion of these was as hybrid buildings, meaning that they had offices, living, commercial aspects and they were linked in section, orchestrating what is normally known as a vertical typology into a horizontally one. The flexibility of that idea would work for the program we were given for this new project. Peter Eisenman and I fought until the end on how the horizontal should meet the verticals. I always wanted them to move, as my original project from the early nineties, but he wanted them straight.

The compromise was to keep them straight. Basically we came up with an idea of a memorial square and a new type of skyscraper: horizontally and vertically balanced and developed in section as well as in plan.

What is curious is the feeling of anxiousness about that place in Manhattan. What haunts me about it is an e-mail from a Feng Shui expert I got. A year after 9/11 she sent me an e-mail describing the Asian concept of unburied souls. When they don't know where to go they haunt the site hovering over it and exist in that place. I can't get that out of my mind. Every time I go down to that area of the city I feel uncomfortable. Perhaps all of this bad karma is inevitable; perhaps it is some kind of Feng Shui hovering in that area.

Looking back now, the competition unraveled, the winner was basically pushed out of the picture, and there still is this enormous sense of national tragedy. Now nothing seems to be idealistic as it was in the six months of effort we put into it. However I still think that architectural project and visions have validity afterward. I feel proud that four very egotistical architects collaborated without making the project a signature. We proposed something in the spirit of Rockefeller Center that would frame public space. It was a new skyscraper typology and a new type of living for the city. When time moves on this project even looks more interesting to me than before.

Busan Cinema Complex, 2005 (pp. 232–237)
I never wanted to win this competition. I wanted to participate and to use that moment as research, an exciting delve into what architecture could be at that place. Yes, if we could have won that would have been

great, but you don't have to win them all. The second jury would choose the final winner of the Busan Cinema competition in South Korea. There were fifty original architects, they whittled it down to seven, gave us six weeks and $30,000 to compete. We all built models. This is supposed to be the Cinema Festival Building, which is to me a radical possibility for this new town. We stacked the cinemas; we built the building vertically with all these public spaces, a composite steel structure with cantilevered terraces, views to the sea. We were the only one of the seven finalists that stacked all the cinemas on top of each other in a way that created a new kind of composite architecture for that place.

Since 1988 we have done 56 competitions and we won 21 (from 2005 to April 2006 we won six competitions in seven). The upside of doing competitions is that they are vehicles of research; you continue to challenge yourself intellectually, about everything that architecture stand for or could stands for, could mean, or might achieve. Usually in a competition there is some notion that the organizers want the highest possible level of design for a project. Usually when we lose it's to a much more conservative design (which doesn't hurt my feelings). More than anything is this notion of new ideas that one hopes to experience in the process of an architectural competition. In competitions an idea strategy, a new strategy and perhaps multiple meanings are explored.

When entering the competition for the Busan Cinema we studied our competition for the Pallazo del Cinema for Venice in 1990. In that cinema competition the notion of cinematic time was explored as a kind of accordion in which you could take an event that lasts 40 years and collapse it into two minutes, or you could take an event that lasted a minute and stretch it into three hours. The scheme explored three kinds of time: diaphanous time, absolute time, and accordion time. We lost the competition but you don't lose when you have developed an idea. To be invited and to have a little bit of funding to work is an honor; that is making architecture. I don't believe that you must build an idea to make it meaningful. If you wrote an incredible symphony and no one played it, that doesn't mean it

wasn't conceived. I remember a story about Louis Sullivan lying in his death bed. He was on this cot in a small room with a light bulb hanging over him and someone came to him and said: "Mr. Sullivan they are tearing down the Schiller Theater." Sullivan sat up and said: "I am not surprised, it doesn't matter. If I live long enough I'll probably see all my buildings torn down, it's only the idea that counts." In Busan the jurors got in such a fight they came at loggerheads to one another. For this competition Coop Himmelbau was finally chosen the winner. Our scheme was second place— fine for radical ideas.

Sail Hybrid, 2005– (pp. 238–243)
The Ship Which Tells the Story to the Mermaid
We were invited to participate in this competition among a few other international architects and I remember the day we began to work on it. Hendrik Vermoortel, our co-architect, came for a full day of brainstorming. There was an existing casino and it was not in very good shape because it had been renovated over and over again. When I looked carefully at the site plan and the defaced building I suddenly remembered my book on Leon Stynen. I had done an exhibition at the Singel in Antwerp in 1992 and the director gave me this wonderful book on Leon Stynen as a gift. I pulled it off the shelf and realized that this casino was done by him. He was the only great modernist Belgian architect. So my first impulse was not to tear down this casino but to develop a scheme that would be in three parts, three architectures—one of which would be the restoration of the casino.

So that all happened during the first half of the day brainstorming, and then we started to study together the great Magritte murals from 1953 that are in the existing casino. It is probably the greatest collection of giant murals ever executed by René Magritte, who for sure is the most important 20th-century Belgian artist. I thought, "this is a very particular site. It is not just Knokke-Heist, but it is the site where Magritte made this great mural room. And this room is enormous. This can be the core value of what the whole project would be." When we were looking at the murals more carefully I found one in particular that I thought was pregnant with

a possible concept. That is a mural called *The Ship Which Tells the Story to the Mermaid*. It has three elements: there is a big planar sailing-ship made out of fragments of the ocean, and there is a upside-down mermaid that has an inverted condition, and then there is a rock. That mural was the inspiration to make a building in three parts, a hybrid building that could accommodate the many different functions: hotel, apartments, casino, congress hall, etcetera.

This hybrid building would have three distinct parts like the mural. I had the idea of saving the casino in three compositional types of architecture: volumetric, planar and porous, coexisting in this composition. The planar element rises out of the building, the volumetric rock, on masts, like the ship has two masts. They are two cylindrical cores that puncture the existing Leon Stynen building and rise up in this planar architecture flapping as sails can do in the wind. That part would be connected by a porous bridgelike element that would contain the congress hall.

Where the two triangular sections flap like sails in the wind and split apart, there is a swimming pool. From the interior you dive down below a beam and swim out into this pool that has no guardrail, just a rim of water that reaches out to the horizon. The building only has two elevations, because it comes to a point on the east and west. The planar construction only has a north and south elevation. I went to attend the great meeting of the announcement and we got some wonderful articles in the Belgian press stating that Magritte inspired the new hotel-casino project.

It is the center of the town: there is a building rule of ten or eleven stories that has created this Atlantic sea wall that is a monotonous repetition running down in both north and south directions. This new building is located centrally. And by going up above and by allowing it to be iconic it becomes a centerpiece for the town, bridging back to the lagoon on its eastern side.

The building is preserving and restoring the original casino. It forms a bridge and becomes a centerpiece for the town of Knokke-Heist. This notion of the hybrid building was developed in a single day, and then we had a couple of months to develop the program and the structure. Together with a very good team we prevailed. I remember they brought the competition down to two: Neutelings Riedijk and us. They asked us to put apartments in the sails, because they didn't believe these would fit into the sail form. And we made these apartments fit into the forms, which work wonderfully with these great triangles and views to the sea. Right now it has been through the environmental commission and it is almost sure that it is going to be built. But like every piece of architecture, you just hold your breath and cross your fingers and wonder.

Cité du Surf et de l'Océan, 2005– (pp. 244–247)
Biarritz was a competition that we won this summer and I did it as a collaboration with my wife, Solange Fabião. Because we have had so many invited competitions this year, our office was not going to do this one, but I said to Solange, "The only way we're going to do this competition is if you and I do it together on weekends, and if you go see the site." We were together at the Milan Furniture Fair to put up our experimental "Porosity" exhibit. Afterward I had to be in Austria for site meetings for the Loisium hotel, then under construction; Solange flew to Biarritz, saw the site, understood everything about the site, met the local architect, and began to think about it. We then

Surfing from Washington state south to the California coast, 1966.

came back and together came up with the design, which was based on a simple idea of "under the sky and under the sea"; the principle idea of fusing landscape and architecture, and extending the project beyond the rectangular site that they gave us to go all the way to the ocean's edge. We made a landscape composition that went all the way to the sea where you surf. There are two famous Biarritz rocks out there that we pulled into the composition as two "glass rocks." One is the surfer's kiosk and one is the café. It's an utterly simple scheme of fusing architecture and landscape into this inverted wave where the projections of the surf museum collection would be projected on the underside of this shape.

Going into the presentation there were six competitors and the technical jury already had put in a ranking order based on the models and the drawings that we submitted. The presentations were made in one day,

all six presentations, and our turn was toward the end of the day, around 5 o'clock. I got up in front of the mayor and the 18 advisors, and Solange was with me. It was like some sort of Parliament: the mayor sat in the middle, everyone had microphones, and it was all simultaneously translated into French. I said I have to tell a story before I start this presentation: "When I graduated from high school in Bremerton, Washington, in June 1966, my best friend and I surfed every beach from Washington State down to the end of California. Three months later I began architecture school at the University of Washington. And this is the first time in my life I've been able to unite these two events, these two activities. My wife grew up on a surfing beach in Rio de Janeiro, being very close to all the surfing culture there, and we believe that your center at Biarritz needs to be an international center for surfing. Therefore, she represents South America and I represent North America."

We hadn't even presented the project but the mayor began to laugh about our connection to surfing. And then we presented the ideas of the project, which they didn't understand from the drawings and the boards. They were trying to understand what this shape was, how it is made out of little stones and grass, and how it is a place of gathering, how you enter the building along this wave of space and go down and get glimpses of the large exhibition center. As they asked questions I said, "You know, probably all your other entries in this competition have four elevations. This has a fifth elevation and that fifth elevation is the center of the scheme: the idea is that the project doesn't stop at the building. It connects through two more sections down the landscape to the ocean: under the sky, under the sea." I said, "If any of your other schemes don't connect directly to the ocean you should have them revise their project because a center of surf that doesn't connect to the ocean isn't a great scheme. You have to connect to the ocean. It's right there. It's two parcels away." So I was very arrogant in the presentation and argued that they needed to extend the site another two blocks. At the end of the day the mayor told our local architect that we had been ranked last by the technical jury, but now we were ranked first at the end of the presentations. So they didn't know what to do. I found out the next day that I would have to return to make another presentation ten days later. So I decided to stay in Europe and go to the south of Sicily to visit the island of Pantelleria and return to Biarritz on the 9th of August. I made the presentation directly to the mayor again, and in another ten days we were told that we won the competition. The program has been revised to include emphasis on the science of the ocean, allowing the educational aspect to be as important as the surfing culture aspects.

Herning Center of the Arts, 2005– (pp. 248–251)
Drawing is one of the things that I love doing; I can just sit there and draw forever. When I go on vacation I take all my watercolor pads and different kinds of drawing equipment and just draw because that is what I love to do. When something appears in the drawings that is really exciting, that is even more energizing, and then the energy feeds the energy.

For example, this competition that we have won for the Herning Center of the Arts. We weren't going to do the competition because we had done too many competitions at the time, seven competitions in six months. But I was trying to take a week off and I was up at the Lake Hut near Rhinebeck. It was August 23rd and I didn't want to read the paper because it was full of news of the current Bush administration and I just can't stand getting myself in that mood. I just threw away the paper. I was listening to some music and I was making some curvilinear sketches, and I had the material for the Herning competition sitting there. So I thought why not make these sketches to scale because this approach is kind of interesting. I am happiest when I am drawing. I was making this drawing, which was just a curvilinear drawing about nothing. There's an existing building from 1975 across the street for the site in the shape of a shirt collar. In approximately 1955 the director of the shirt factory drew this shape and asked an architect to make it into a factory. Those were very good architects, two young architects in Denmark, who made a perfect structure, with perfect lighting. I happened to be drawing this shirt-pattern-like shape, probably inspired from the Diderot's *Encyclopedia,* which I have a copy of in my studio up there. I was making these yellow curved things with blue between, and then I thought to arrange some of these "shirt sleeve" elements and fuse them with the landscape to make water gardens. I made watercolors the next two mornings, which were really the beginning of this project. This is a case study in a subjective beginning and the reason why I do all these watercolors. It comes out of the desire for architecture out of this love of beginning…

I came back down to the office on a Tuesday and I said, "Hey look, what if we develop these shapes, merge them with the landscape, and these curves are reversed so they bring light into the orthogonal spaces below." Martin, Noah, and Alessandro said: "Yeah, we can develop this in two and half weeks to do the competition boards." Two of these people haven't even worked here a year. I had to get far enough into the design that they could build a model and do the plans and sections. And they did it. I said: "Let's make the presentation all in black and white. This is not about

color. Light and space are the focus here. Let's just make the presentation black and white and our project will stand out."

In the competition, there were basically eight schemes, and then it came down to two. One was a matchbox, very rectangular, very early Arne Jacobsen; and our scheme, which is completely flowing, merging with the landscape, fusing landscape and architecture. The architects on the jury voted for the matchbox and the director of the museum and all the curators voted for our project. The director called me on Halloween saying that we won. This is an example of a project that merges effortlessly from my own desire to draw. I am just sitting up there, supposedly going swimming in the lake, but finding myself drawing and drawing.

Project Chronology *1974–2006*

1974
Residence
location: Manchester, Washington, USA
program: private residence
design architect: Steven Holl

1975
Manila Housing Competition
location: Manila, Philippines
program: international housing competition
design architect: Steven Holl
project team: John Cropper, James Tanner

1975
Flint Fountain and Arcemedies Screw
location: Flint, Michigan, USA
program: public promenade and fountain
design architect: Steven Holl at the office of
Lawrence Haprin
project team: John Cropper

1976
St. Paul Capitol (competition)
location: St. Paul, Minnesota, USA
program: competition for state Capitol, governing
functions, and a museum
design architect: Steven Holl
project team: James Tanner, William Zimmerman

1976
House for an Intersection (competition: third place)
location: London, United Kingdom
program: competition for residential community
design architect: Steven Holl
project team: Joseph Fenton

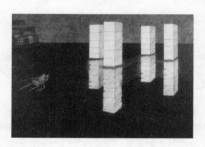

1976
Sokolov Retreat
location: St. Tropez, France
program: residence
design architect: Steven Holl

1977
Bronx Gymnasium Bridge
location: South Bronx, New York, USA
program: bridge to Randall's Island
design architect: Steven Holl

1978
Telescope House
location: Still Pond, Maryland, USA
program: private residence
design architect: Steven Holl
project team: Joseph Fenton

1978–1979
Millville Courtyard
location: Millville, New Jersey, USA
design architect: Steven Holl
project team: Joseph Fenton

1980
Metz House
location: Staten Island, New York, USA
program: residence for two artists
design architect: Steven Holl
project team: Paola Iacucci, Mark Janson, Melita Prieto, James Rosen

1979
Les Halles (competition)
location: Paris, France
program: competition for housing
and meeting place on the site of the
Les Halles Pavillions
design architect: Steven Holl
project team: Stuart Diston, Joseph Fenton, Ron Steiner

1980
Pool House and Sculpture Studio
location: Scarsdale, New York, USA
program: sculpture studio and bathhouse
design architect: Steven Holl
project team: Mark Janson, James Rosen

1979
Bridges of Melbourne (competition)
location: Melbourne, Australia
program: 7 bridge plans including residential, commercial, and recreational facilities
design architect: Steven Holl
project team: Joseph Fenton, Mark Janson, Suzanne Powadiuk, James Rosen

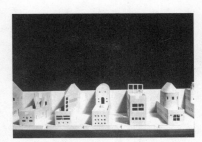

1980–1984
Autonomous Artisan's Housing
location: Staten Island, New York, USA
program: residences and artist studios
design architect: Steven Holl
project team: Paola Iacucci, Mark Janson, David Kessler

1980–1982
Bridge of Houses on Elevated Rail
location: New York, New York, USA
program: housing, elevated public promenade, convention center designed for the abandoned elevated railroad on Manhattan's west side
design architect: Steven Holl
project team: Mark Janson, Joseph Fenton, Suzanne Powadiuk, James Rosen

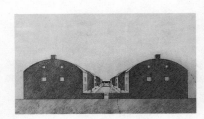

1981
Minimum Houses
location: Hastings-on-Hudson, New York, USA
program: alternative to high-rise housing
design architect: Steven Holl
project team: Rick Bottino

1983–1983
Guardian Safe Depository
location: Fairlawn, New Jersey, USA
program: renovation of existing
concrete building including face, lobby,
security system
design architect: Steven Holl
project team: Jospeh Fenton, James Rosen

1984–1988
House at Martha's Vineyard
location: Martha's Vineyard, Massachusetts, USA
program: private residence
design architect: Steven Holl
project architect: Peter Lynch
project team: Stephen Cassell, Ralph Nelson, Peter
Shinoda

1982–1983
Van Zandt House
location: East Hampton, New York, USA
program: private residence
design architect: Steven Holl
project team: Charles Anderson, Joseph Fenton,
Mark Janson, Peter Shinoda

1984–1988
Hybrid Building
location: Seaside, Florida, USA
program: hotel suites, shops, and offices
design architect: Steven Holl
project team: Laurie Beckerman, Stephen Cassell,
Peter Lynch, Lorcan O'Herlihy, Philip Theft, Richard
Warner

1982–1983
Cohen Apartment
location: New York, New York, USA
program: interior renovation
design architect: Steven Holl
project team: Joseph Fenton, Mark Janson

1985
Kurtz Apartment
location: New York, New York, USA
program: interior renovation
design architect: Steven Holl
project team: Mark Janson

1984
Ocean Front House
location: Leucadia, California, USA
program: private residence
design architect: Steven Holl
project team: Mark Janson, Peter Lynch, Suzanne
Powadiuk

1986
Pace Collection Showroom
location: New York, New York, USA
program: commercial showroom
design architect: Steven Holl
project team: Paola Iacucci, Peter Lynch, Donna
Seftel, Tom van den Bout

1986
Porta Vittoria Project
location: Milan, Italy
program: urban planning proposal
including park and botanical gardens
design architect: Steven Holl
project team: Jacob Allerdice, Laurie Beckerman,
Meta Brunzema, Stephen Cassel, Gisue Hariri, Paola
Iacucci, Peter Lynch, Ralph Nelson, Ron Peterson,
Darius Sollohub, Lynnette Widder

1986–1987
MoMA Tower Apartment (XYZ Apartment)
location: New York, New York, USA
program: interior renovation
design architect: Steven Holl
project team: Peter Lynch, Stephen Cassell, Ralph
Nelson

1987
Giada Shop
location: New York, New York, USA
program: retail showroom
design architect: Steven Holl
project team: Peter Lynch, Stephen Cassell, Darius
Sollohub

1987–1988
45 Christopher Street Apartment
location: New York, New York, USA
program: interior renovation
design architect: Steven Holl
project team: Peter Lynch, Adam Yarinsky

1988
Oxnard House
location: Oxnard, California, USA
program: private residence
design architect: Steven Holl
project team: Patricia Bosch, Pier Copat, Thomas
Gardner, Kent Hikida, Elizabeth Lere, Peter Lynch,
Lorcan O'Herlihy, Richard Warner

1988
Freedman House
location: Cleveland, Ohio, USA
program: private residence
design architect: Steven Holl
project team: Stephen Cassell, Pier Copat, Lawrence
Davis, Thomas Gardner, Kent Hidika, Peter Lynch

1989
Met Tower Apartment
location: New York, New York, USA
program: interior renovation
design architect: Steven Holl
project team: Atsushi Aiba, Stephen Cassell, Lorcan
O'Herlihy

1988
Amerika-Gedenkbibliothek (competition: first place)
location: Berlin, Germany
program: competition for renovation and
addition to the Amerika-Gedenkbibliothek
design architect: Steven Holl
project team: Bryan Bell, Stephen Cassell, Pier
Copat, Thomas Gardner, Friederike Grosspietsche,
Stephan Schroth Architects

1989
Paris Tolbiac (competition)
location: Paris, France
program: urban planning competition for the re-use of
the Tolbiac Railyards
design architect: Steven Holl
project team: Peter Lynch, William Wilson

1989–1990
Edge of a City (Parallax Towers)
location: New York, New York, USA
program: alternative proposal for Manhattan's 72nd
street rail yards, including offices, apartment, hotel
rooms, and the extension of Riverside Park
design architect: Steven Holl
project team: Peter Lynch, Romain Ruther

1989–1991
Void Space/Hinged Space Housing
location: Fukuoka, Japan
Program: mixed-use complex with
28 residential apartments
design architect: Steven Holl
project team: Hideaki Ariizumi, Pier Copat

1989–1990
Edge of a City (Spatial Retaining Bars)
location: Phoenix, Arizona, USA
program: proposal for a new city edge,
buildings providing residential, office, and
cultural facilities
design architect: Steven Holl
project team: Pier Copat, Janet Cross,
Ben Frombgen, Peter Lynch

1989–1990
Edge of the City (Stitch Plan)
location: Cleveland, Ohio, USA
program: urban planning project
providing living, working, recreational
and cultural facilities
design architect: Steven Holl
project team: Bryan Bell, Patricia Botsch,
Pier Copat, Janet Cross, Ben Frombgen,
Peter Lynch

**1989–1990 Edge of a City
(Spiroid Sectors)**
location: Dallas, Texas, USA
program: proposal for a hybrid building sited in the
partly settled area between Dallas and Fort Worth
design architect: Steven Holl
project team: Laura Briggs, Janet Cross, Scott Enge,
Tod Fouser, Hal Goldstein, Peter Lynch, Chris
Otterbine

1989–1990
Edge of a City (Erie Canal Houses)
location: Rochester, New York, USA
program: new urban sector at canal edge, providing
housing and retail
design architect: Steven Holl
project team: Bryan Bell, Pier Copat, Ben Frombgen

1989–1991
Stretto House
location: Dallas, Texas, USA
program: private residence for art collectors
design architect: Steven Holl
project team: Stephen Cassell, Kent Hikida, Terry
Surjan

1990
Palazzo del Cinema (competition)
location: Venice, Italy
program: Venice Film Festival Building
design architect: Steven Holl
project architect: Peter Lynch
project team: Stephen Cassell, Janet Cross, Thomas Jenkinson, Jun Kim, Lucinda Know, William Wilson

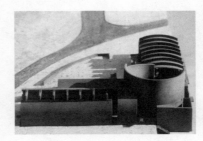

1991
Kemper Museum (competition)
location: Kansas City, Missouri, USA
program: art museum
design architect: Steven Holl
project team: Stephen Cassell, Janet Cross, Chris Otterbine

1990–2002 (first scheme 1998)
College of Architecture & Landscape Architecture, University of Minnesota
location: Minneapolis, Minnesota, USA
program: library, auditorium, offices, classrooms
client: University of Minnesota
design architect: Steven Holl
project architect: Pablo Castro-Estévez
project team: Gabriela Barman-Kramer, Molly Blieden, Sabina Cachero, Yoh Hanaoka, Jennifer Lee, Andy Lin, Stephen O'Dell

1991
D.E. Shaw & Co Offices
location: New York, New York, USA
program: reception area, offices, conference rooms, and trading area for digital trading company
design architect: Steven Holl
project architect: Thomas Jenkinson
project team: Scott Enge, Todd Fouser, Hideaki Ariizumi, Adam Yarinsky, Annette Goderbauer

1990
World Expo 95 (competition)
location: Vienna, Austria
program: exhibits, shops, hotels, public services for a World Expo
design architect: Steven Holl
project team: Peter Lynch, Romain Ruther

1991
Chapel and Town Square
location: Port Ludlow, Washington, USA
program: chapel, meeting hall, 4 multi-family housing units, town square
design architect: Steven Holl
project team: Janet Cross, Scott Enge, Todd Fouser, Thomas Jenkinson, Adam Yarinsky

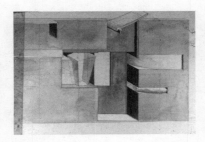

1990–1991
Experimental Glass Workshop
location: Brooklyn, New York, USA
program: facade renovation for workshop studio
design architect: Steven Holl
project team: Janet Cross, Peter Lynch, Hideaki Ariizumi

1991–1992
Shop and Office
location: Langley, Washington, USA
program: shop and office
design architect: Steven Holl
project team: Janet Cross, Terry Surjan, Adam Yarinsky

1992
Tower of Silence
location: Manchester, Washington, USA
program: architectural retreat
design architect: Steven Holl
project team: Janet Cross, Todd Fouser

1992–1996
Makuhari Housing
location: Chiba, Japan
program: 190 units of housing, retail and public facilities
design architect: Steven Holl
project architect: Tomoaki Tanaka
project team: Janet Cross, Lisina Fingerhuth, Mario Gooden, Thomas Jenkinson, Brad Kelley, Jan Kinsbergen, Justin Korhammer, Anderson Lee, Anna Muller, S. Schulze, G. Sohn, Terry Surjan, S. Takasina

1992
Villa Den Haag (1st version)**, Implosion Villa**
location: The Hague, The Netherlands
program: private residence
design architect: Steven Holl
project team: Janet Cross, Mario Gooden, Terry Surjan, Tomoaki Tanaka

1992–1998
Kiasma Museum of Contemporary Art
(competition: first place)
location: Helsinki, Finland
program: art museum including galleries, theater, café, shop, artist workshop
design architect: Steven Holl
project architect: Vesa Honkonen
project team: Tim Bade, Molly Blieden, Stephen Cassell, Pablo Castro-Estevez, Janet Cross, Brad Kelley, Justin Korhammer, Anderson Lee, Chris McVoy, Anna Muller, Justin Rüssli, Tomoaki Tanaka, Tapani Talo (with the office of Juhani Pallasmaa)

1992
Andrews University Architecture Building Addition
location: Barrien Springs, Michigan, USA
program: extension to school of architecture
design architect: Steven Holl
project architect: Thomas Jenkinson
project team: Stephen Cassell, Annette Goderbauer, Mario Gooden, Terry Surjan, Tomoaki Tanaka, Adam Yarinsky

1992–1993
Storefront for Art and Architecture
location: New York, New York, USA
program: facade renovation for small architecture gallery
design architects Steven Holl, Vito Acconci
project team: Chris Otterbine

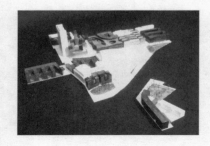

1992
Friedrichstraße (competition)
location: Berlin, Germany
program: urban planning competition including theater, hotel, health club, parks, and public gardens
design architect: Steven Holl
project team: Stephen Cassell, Annette Goderbauer, Justin Rüssli

1993–1998
Zollikerberg Housing (competition: first place)
location: Zollikerberg, Switzerland
program: 38 units of mixed housing types
design architect: Steven Holl
project architect: Justin Rüssli
project team: Timothy Bade, Stephen Cassell, Lisina Fingerhuth, Justin Korhammer

1993–1998
Cranbrook Institute of Science
location: Bloomfield Hills, Michigan, USA
program: addition and renovation to
existing science museum, new central
science garden courtyard
design architect: Steven Holl
project architect: Chris McVoy
project team: Tim Bade, Stephen Cassell, Pablo
Castro-Estevez, Martin Cox, Janet Cross, Yoh
Hanaoka, Brad Kelly, Jan Kinsbergen, Justin
Korhammer, Anna Muller, Tomoaki Tanaka

1994
Hypo-Bank and Art Hall (competition)
location: Munich, Germany
program: bank headquarters with offices, banking
hall, shopping facilities, apartments, and art hall
design architect: Steven Holl
project team: Tim Bade, Marie-Therese Harnoncourt,
Justin Korhammer, Anderson Lee, Justin Rüssli,
Tomoaki Tanaka

1994
Manifold Hybrid
location: Amsterdam, The Netherlands
program: 182 unit housing block
design architect: Steven Holl
project architect: Justin Korhammer
project team: Martin Cox, Anderson Lee

1994–1997
Chapel of St. Ignatius
location: Seattle, Washington, USA
program: Jesuit chapel for Seattle University
design architect: Steven Holl
project architect: Tim Bade
project team: Jan Kinsbergen, Justin Korhammer,
Audra Tuskes

1994
Z-House
location: Millbrook, New York
program: prefabricated private residence
design architect: Steven Holl
project team: Bradford Kelly

1994
Hypo-Bank (competition)
location: Frankfurt, Germany
program: mixed-use facility including banking hall and
residences
design architect: Steven Holl
project architect: Justin Rüssli
project team: Martin Cox, Anderson Lee, Tomoaki
Tanaka

1994–
Hamsun Center
location: Hamarøy, Norway
program: historical museum for writer Knut Hamsun,
including exhibition areas, library, reading room, café
and 230-seat auditorium
design architect: Steven Holl
project architect: Erik Langdalen
project team: Gabriele Barman, Yoh Hanaoka, Justin
Korhammer, Anna Muller, Audra Tuskes

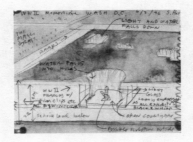

1995
World War II Memorial
location: Washington, D.C., USA
program: competition for new memorial on
Washington lawn
design architect: Steven Holl
project team: Tomoaki Tanaka, Martin Cox

1995
Villa The Hague
location: The Hague, The Netherlands
program: residence
design architect: Steven Holl
project team: Justin Korhammer

1996–2000
Sarphatistraat Offices
location: Amsterdam, The Netherlands
program: new headquarters for housing developer
design architect: Steven Holl
project architect: Justin Korhammer
project team: Hideaki Ariizumi, Martin Cox, Annette
Goderbauer, Yoh Hanaoka, Heleen van Heel

1995
I Project
location: Seoul, Korea
program: residential, office, family, recreational, and
banquet facilities
design architect: Steven Holl
project team: Brad Kelly, Justin Rüssli, Tomoaki
Tanaka

1996
UCSF Mission Bay Master Plan (competition)
location: San Francisco, California, USA
program: invited master plan competition for new
biomedical research campus
design architect: Steven Holl
project architect: Martin Cox
project team: Pablo Castro-Estévez, Annette
Goderbauer, Katharina Hahnle

1996
Nursing & Biomedical Sciences Building
(competition)
Location: Houston, Texas, USA
Program: new nursing school for
the University of Texas
design architect: Steven Holl
project team: Martin Cox, Yoh Hanaoka, Brad Kelly,
Tomoaki Tanaka

1997
UVA School of Architecture
location: Charlottesville, Virginia, USA
program: addition to the architecture school
design architect: Steven Holl
project architect: Tim Bade
project team: Martin Cox, Annette Goderbauer

1996
Museum of the City
Location: Cassino, Italy
Program: historical and contemporary art museum
design architect: Steven Holl
project team: Cory Clarke, Michael Hofmann, Paola
Iacucci, Brad Kelley

1997
Museum of Modern Art Expansion
location: New York, New York, USA
program: invited competition for expansion and renovation of the museum
design architect: Steven Holl
project team: Julia Barnes Mandle, Molly Blieden,
Solange Fabião, Annette Goderbauer, Michael
Hofmann, James Holl, Jan Kinsbergen, Chris McVoy,
Justin Rüssli

1997–2001
Bellevue Art Museum
(reopened as an arts, craft, and design museum in 2005)
location: Bellevue, Washington, USA
program: galleries, classrooms, café, auditorium
design architect: Steven Holl
project architects: Martin Cox, Tim Bade
project team: Elsa Chryssochoides, Annette Goderbauer, Yoh Hanaoka, Jennifer Lee, Stephen O'Dell, Justin Korhammer

1998
Residence
location: Long Island, New York, USA
program: residence for a family
design architect: Steven Holl
project team: Martin Cox, Gabriela Barman-Kramer, Pablo Castro-Estévez, Annette Goderbauer, Stephen O'Dell

1997–2005
Higgins Hall Center Section, Pratt Institute
location: Brooklyn, New York, USA
program: lobby gallery, studios, auditorium, digital resource center, review room, gallery terrace, workshops
design architect: Steven Holl
project architect: Tim Bade
assistant project architect: Makram el Kadi
project team: Martin Cox, Annette Goderbauer, Erik Langdalen

1999
Centro JVD
location: Guadalajara, Mexico
program: hotel and housing
design architect: Steven Holl
project team: Gabriela Barman-Kramer, Annette Goderbauer, Stephen O'Dell

1997–1999
Y House
location: Catskills, New York, USA
program: weekend retreat
design architect: Steven Holl
project architect: Erik Langdalen
project team: Annette Goderbauer, Yoh Hanaoka, Brad Kelley, Justin Korhammer, Jennifer Lee, Chris McVoy

1999
Swiss Expo 2002 (competition)
location: Biel, Switzerland
program: lakeside floating expo pavilion and facilities
design architect: Steven Holl
project team: Jan Kinsbergen, Justin Korhammer, Justin Rüssli

1998–2005
Whitney Water Purification Facility and Park
location: Southern Connecticut, USA
program: water treatment facility and public park
design architects: Steven Holl, Chris McVoy
associates in charge: Anderson Lee, Urs Vogt
project architects: Arnault Biou, Annette Goderbauer
project team: Justin Korhammer, Linda Lee, Rong-hui Lin, Susi Sanchez, Urs Vogt

1999–2006
School of Art & Art History, University of Iowa
location: Iowa City, Iowa, USA
program: facilities for fine art studios, administrative offices, gallery, library
design architects: Steven Holl, Chris McVoy, Martin Cox
project team: Li Hu, Gabriela Barman-Kramer; Arnault Biou, Regina Chow, Elsa Chryssochoides, Hideki Hirahara, Brian Melcher, Chris Otterbein, Susi Sanchez, Irene Vogt, Urs Vogt

1999
Center for Contemporary Art (competition)
location: Rome, Italy
program: art galleries, auditorium, library, café, offices
design architect: Steven Holl
project architect: Erik Langdalen
project team: Gabriela Barman-Kramer, Annette Goderbauer

1999
Centro de Culture Galicia
location: Santiago, Spain
program: competition for museum and cultural center, including café, galleries, opera house
design architects: Steven Holl, Solange Fabião
project architect: Pablo Castro-Estévez
project team: Gabriela Barman-Kramer, Sabina Cachero, Annette Goderbauer, Mimi Hoang, Stephen O'Dell

1999–2002
Simmons Hall, Massachusetts Institute of Technology
location: Cambridge, Massachusetts, USA
program: 350-bed dormitory including dining hall, auditorium, and other shared facilities
design architects: Steven Holl, Tim Bade
project architect: Tim Bade; assistant project architects: Ziad Jameleddine, Anderson Lee; project team: Gabriela Barman-Kramer, Peter Burns, Annette Goderbauer, Mimi Hoang, Ziad Jameleddine, Matt Johnson, Makram el Kadi, Erik Langdalen, Anderson Lee, Ron-Hui Lin, Stephen O'Dell, Christian Wassmann

1999
Morgan Library (competition)
location: New York, New York, USA
program: competition for addition to library
design architect: Steven Holl
project team: Gabriela Barman-Kramer, Matthias Blass, Sabina Cachero, Emmy Chow, Martin Cox, Chris McVoy, Susi Sanchez

1999
xky xcraper (competition)
location: Vuosaari, Finland
program: residential, retail facilities, public observation deck
design architect: Steven Holl, Solange Fabião
project architect: Justin Korhammer
project team: Annette Goderbauer, Vesa Honkonen Architects

1999
Museum for African Art/Edison School (competition)
location: New York, New York, USA
program: new headquarters for Edison School Corporation with elementary school and museum
design architect: Steven Holl
project team: Gisela Barman, Aaron Cattani, Emmy Chow, Martin Cox, Susi Sanchez

1999–2007
Nelson-Atkins Museum of Art, Addition & Renovation
(competition: first place)
location: Kansas City, Missouri, USA
program: museum addition & renovation
design architects: Steven Holl, Chris McVoy
partner-in-charge: Chris McVoy
project architects: Martin Cox, Richard Tobias
project team: Masao Akiyoshi, Gabriela Barman-Kraemer, Matthias Blass, Molly Blieden, Elsa Chryssochoides, Robert Edmonds, Simone Giostra, Annette Goderbauer, Mimi Hoang, Makram el Kadi, Edward Lalonde, Li Hu, Justin Korhammer, Linda Lee, Fabian Llonch, Stephen O'Dell, Susi Sanchez, Irene Vogt, Urs Vogt, Christian Wassmann

2000
Zachary Scott Theater
location: Austin, Texas, USA
program: theater
design architect: Steven Holl
project architect: Stephen O'Dell
project team: Ziad Jamaleddine

2000
Cinema & Toy Museum
location: Deventer, The Netherlands
program: cinemas, toy museum, retail
design architect: Steven Holl
project team: Martin Cox, Makram el Kadi, Li Hu,
Ziad Jamaleddine, Chris McVoy

2001
Paris 2008 Olympic Housing (competition)
location: Paris, France
program: housing for athletes
design architect: Steven Holl
project architect: Tim Bade
project team: Emmy Chow, Makram el Kadi, Ziad
Jamaleddine

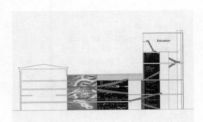

2000
American Museum of Natural History
location: New York, New York, USA
program: genome pavilion proposal
design architect: Steven Holl
project team: Li Hu, Mathew Johnson, Chris McVoy

2001
Musee des Confluences (competition)
location: Lyon, France
program: museum, auditorium, educational facilities,
workshop, cafe
design architect: Steven Holl
project architect: Tim Bade
project team: Makram el Kadi, Annette Goderbauer,
Ziad Jamaleddine, Mathew Johnson, Christian
Wassmann

2000
Museum of Human Evolution (competition)
location: Burgos, Spain
program: galleries, conference hall, auditorium
design architect: Steven Holl
project team: Aaron Cattani, Martin Cox, Makram el
Kadi, Paola Iacucci, Ziad Jammaleddine, Fabian
Llonch, Ben Tranel

2001
Monument for Religious Freedom (competition)
location: Richmond, Virginia, USA
program: competition for new monument
design architect: Steven Holl
project team: Makram el Kadi

2001–2004
Nail Collector's House
location: upstate New York, USA
program: private residence
design architect: Steven Holl
project architect: Stephen O'Dell

2001
College of Architecture, Cornell University
(competition: first place)
location: Ithaca, New York, USA
program: building for College of Architecture, Art &
Planning
design architect: Steven Holl
project architect: Stephen O'Dell
project team: Tim Bade, Jason Frantzen, Annette
Goderbauer, Hideki Hirahara, Li Hu, Paola Iacucci,
Matt Johnson, Chris McVoy, Chris Otterbein, Christian
Wassmann, Aislinn Weidele

2001
Oceanic Retreat
location: Kaua'i, Hawaii, USA
program: private residence
design architect: Steven Holl
project architect: Martin Cox
project team: Arnault Biou, Jason Frantzen, Steve O'Dell, Olaf Schmidt

2001–2005
Loisium
location: Langenlois, Austria
program: visitor center, hotel, and spa for winery
design architect: Steven Holl
project architect: Christian Wassmann
project team: Garrick Ambrose, Dominik Bachmann, Rodolfo Dias, Peter Englaender, Johan van Lierop, Chris McVoy, Ernest Ng, Olaf Schmidt, Brett Snyder, Irene Vogt

2001–2004
Writing with Light House
location: Long Island, New York, USA
program: private residence
design architect: Steven Holl
project architect: Annette Goderbauer
project team: Martin Cox, Irene Vogt, Christian Wassmann

2001
Copper Don
location: Copenhagen, Denmark
program: offices and retail
design architect: Steven Holl
project architect: Martin Cox
project team: Olaf Schmidt, Anna Müller

2001
Toolenburg-Zuid (competition: first place)
location: Schiphol, The Netherlands
program: planning competition for new residential community
design architect: Steven Holl
project architects: Gabriela Barman-Kramer, Martin Cox
project team: Molly Blieden, Makram el Kadi, Jason Frantzen, Mathew Johnson, Chris Otterbine

2001
Little Tesseract
location: Rhinebeck, New York, USA
program: solarstack prototype
design architect: Steven Holl, Solange Fabião
project architect: Chris Otterbine, Laura Sansone
project team: Makram el Kadi, Anderson Lee, Christian Wassmann, Urs Vogt

2001
Ile Seguin (competition)
location: Paris, France
program: invited competition for the Foundation Francois Pinault including galleries, university, cafés and public amenities
design architect: Steven Holl
project architect: Annette Goderbauer
project team: Asako Akazawa, Jason Frantzen, Li Hu, Mathew Johnson, Chris McVoy, Brian Melcher, Ayslinn Weidele

2001
Round Lake Hut
location: Rhinebeck, New York, USA
program: watercolor retreat
design architect: Steven Holl

2001
Los Angeles County Museum of Art (competition)
location: Los Angeles, California, USA
program: invited competition for museum expansion
design architect: Steven Holl
project architects: Chris McVoy, Li Hu
project team: Asako Akazawa, Martin Cox, Makram el
Kadi, Jason Frantzen, Brian Melcher, Olaf Schmidt,
Christian Wassmann

2002
New Town (competition)
location: Nanning, China
program: 9,000 residences, schools, shops, anthro-
pology museum
design architect: Steven Holl
project architects: Anderson Lee, Makram el Kadi
project team: Li Hu, Ziad Jamalledine

2001–2005
Turbulence House
location: New Mexico, USA
program: guest house
design architect: Steven Holl
project architects: Anderson Lee, Richard Tobias
project team: Arnault Biou, Matt Johnson

2002–
Beirut Marina (competition)
location: Beirut, Lebanon
program: apartments, restaurants, outdoor public
spaces with site-specific art installations, specialty
stores, harbormaster, yacht club, and public facilities
design architect: Steven Holl
associate in charge: Tim Bade
project architects: Ziad Jamaleddine, Makram el Kadi
project team: Brett Snyder, Masao Akiyoshi

2001–2006
The Swiss Residence (competition: first place)
location: Washington, D.C., USA
program: residence including living spaces for ambassador, staff quarters, and representational spaces
design architects: Steven Holl (SHA) and Justin
Rüssli (Rüssli Architekten AG)
associates in charge: Stephen O'Dell, Tim Bade (SHA)
project architects: Olaf Schmidt (SHA) and Mimi Kueh
(RA); project team: Arnault Biou, Peter Englaender,
Annette Goderbauer, Li Hu, Irene Vogt (SHA) and
Andreas Gervasi, Phillip Röösli, Rafael Schnyder, Urs
Zuercher (RA)

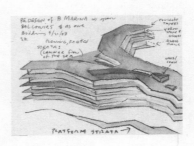

2002
Fifth Avenue and 42nd Street
location: New York, New York, USA
program: retail, offices, restaurant, café, sky space,
art room
design architect: Steven Holl, Solange Fabião
project architect: Simone Giostra
project team: Ziad Jamalledine, Irene Vogt

2002
World Trade Center (competition)
location: New York, New York, USA
program: proposal for World Trade Center site,
offices, mixed use, retail
design architect: Steven Holl
project team: Makram el Kadi, Simone Giostra, Ziad
Jamaleddine, Irene Vogt, Christian Wassmann
collaborators: Richard Meier and Partners, Eisenman
Architects, and Gwathmey Siegel & Associates
Architects

2002–
Los Angeles County Museum of Natural History
(competition: first place)
location: Los Angeles, California, USA
program: permanent and temporary exhibition space,
research and collection, educational facilities, exhibition gardens
design architect: Steven Holl
partner-in-charge: Chris McVoy
project architects: Makram el Kadi, Olaf Schmidt
project team: Tim Bade, Noah Yaffe, Masao Akiyoshi,
Ziad Jamaleddine

2002–
Nanjing Museum of Architecture
location: Nanjing, China
program: galleries, tea room, bookstore, and a
curator's residence
design architects: Steven Holl, Li Hu
partner-in-charge: Li Hu
project team: Clark Manning, Jongseo Lee,
Richard Liu

2003
Casa di Risparma di Firenze (competition)
location: Firenze, Italy
program: bank building including offices, public
spaces, bar, restaurant, and auditorium
design architect: Steven Holl and Solange Fabião
project architect: Annette Goderbauer
project team: Christiane Deptolla, Makram el Kadi,
Peter Englaender, Marcello Pontiggia, Irene Vogt,
Urs Vogt

2003
**Musée des Civilisations de l'Europe et
de la Méditerranée** (competition)
location: Marseille, France
program: galleries, auditorium, café and restaurants,
offices, support facilities
design architect: Steven Holl
project architect: Annette Goderbauer
project team: Masao Akiyoshi, Makram el Kadi,
Hideki Hirahara, Brett Snyder, Irene Vogt

2003–2008
Linked Hybrid
location: Beijing, China
program: 750 apartments, commercial zones, hotel,
cinemateque, kindergarten, underground parking
design architects: Steven Holl, Li Hu
partner-in-charge: Li Hu; project architect: Hideki Hirahara;
project designers: Garrick Ambrose, Yenling Chen, Rodolfo
Dias, Guido Guscianna, Young Jang, Edward Lalonde, James
Macgillivray, Matthew Uselman; project team: Christian Beerli
Johnna Cressica Brazier, Shih-I Chow, Cosimo Caggiula, Kefei
Cai, Frank Cottier, Christiane Deptolla, Matthew Jull, Jongseo
Lee, Eric Li, Richard Liu, Giorgos Mitroulas, Olaf Schmidt,
Judith Tse, Clark Manning, Kitty Wang, Li Wang, Ariane
Wiegner, Noah Yaffe, Liang Zhao

2002–2005
Planar House
location: Arizona, USA
program: private residence
design architect: Steven Holl
project architect: Martin Cox (Tim Bade, schematic
design)
project team: Robert Edmonds, Annette Goderbauer,
Hideki Hirahara, Clark Manning

2004
Lombardia Regional Government Center
(competition)
location: Milan, Italy
program: offices, public plaza, press conference and
exhibition and debate facilities, cafes, public observation deck
design architect: Steven Holl
project architect: Martin Cox
project team: Garrick Ambrose, Guido Cuscianna,
Makram el Kadi, Gian Carlo Floridi, Simone Giostra,
Young Jang, Ariane Weigner

2003
New National Library of Luxembourg (competition)
location: Luxembourg, Luxembourg
program: library including exhibition space,
amphitheater, meeting rooms, restaurant, café,
shop, offices
design architect: Steven Holl
project architect: Arnault Biou
project team: Chris McVoy, Jongseo Lee,
Makram el Kadi, Irene Vogt, Christiane Deptolla,
Urs Vogt, Annette Goderbauer, Peter Englaender,
Ziad Jamaleddine

2004
Saint Etienne City of Design (competition)
location: Saint Etienne, France
program: cultural complex, with exhibition spaces,
ateliers, workshops, artists living spaces, shops, conference spaces
design architect: Steven Holl
project architect: Arnault Biou
project team: Makram el Kadi, Nicolas Laisne

2004
The High Line (competition)
location: New York, New York, USA
program: proposal for renovation and transformation of the High Line into public space
design architect: Steven Holl, Solange Fabião
project architect: Martin Cox
project team: Brett Snyder, Garrick Ambrose, Olga Drobinina, Johan van Lierop, Young Jang, Priscilla Fraser, Molly Blieden, Andrew MacNair, Lara Shihab-Eldin, Connie Lee, Heather Waters, Roberto Requejo

2004–
NYU School of Philosophy
location: New York, New York, USA
program: school of philosophy
design architect: Steven Holl
partner in charge: Tim Bade
project architect: Edward Lalonde
project team: Lesley Chang, Jongseo Lee, Clark Manning, Ernest Ng, Irene Vogt, Ebbie Wisecarver

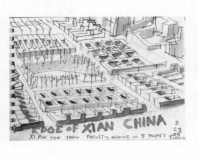

2005
Xian New Town (competition)
location: Xian, China
program: urban planning project including housing, cultural spaces, offices, public services, school, and commercial spaces
design architect: Steven Holl
project architects: Li Hu, James Macgillivray
project team: Garrick Ambrose, Nick Gelpi, Giorgos Mitroulias, Wu Lan

2005
Busan Cinema Complex (competition)
location: Busan, Korea
program: 6 cinemas (including one open-air cinema), conference rooms, event spaces, exhibition galleries, retail, restaurant, café, working loft, cinematheque, grand theater, visual media center
design architect: Steven Holl
partner-in-charge: Li Hu
project architect: Jongseo Lee
project team: Cosimo Caggiula, Frank O. Cottier, Nick Gelpi, Alessandro Orsini, Ernest Ng, Noah Yaffe

2005–
Sail Hybrid (competition: first place)
location: Knokke-Heist, Belgium
program: 3 architectures: Sail-Like Planar (hotel and apartment tower), Volumetric (restored, repro-grammed casino), Porous (congress hall)
design architect: Steven Holl
partner-in-charge: Chris McVoy
project architect: Nick Gelpi
assistant project architect: Noah Yaffe
project team: Young Jang, Richard Liu, Edward Lalonde, Alessandro Orsini

2005–
Cité du Surf et de l'Océan (competition: first place)
location: Biarritz, France
program: museum, plaza, and exhibition areas
design architects: Solange Fabião and Steven Holl
project architect: Rodolfo Reis Dias
assistant project architect: Ebbie Wisecarver
project advisor: Chris McVoy
project team: Ernest Ng, Cosimo Caggiula, Florence Guiraud, Richard Liu, Alessandro Orsini, Lan Wu

2005
Nanjing Massacre Memorial (competition)
location: Nanjing, China
program: memorial including exhibition hall
design architect: Steven Holl
project team: Dong Gong, Jongseo Lee, Wu Lan, Cosimo Caggiula, Zhao Liang

2005
Louvre Lens (competition)
location: Lens, France
program: galleries, auditorium, restaurant, exhibition garden
design architect: Steven Holl
partner-in-charge: Chris McVoy
project architect: Garrick Ambrose
project team: Nick Gelpi, Cosimo Caggiula, Frank O. Cottier, Rodolfo Dias, Jongseo Lee, Richard Liu, Young Jang, Irene Vogt, Lan Wu, Noah Yaffe

2005–
Herning Center of the Arts (competition: first place)
location: Herning, Denmark
program: temporary exhibition galleries, 150-seat auditorium, music rehearsal rooms, restaurant, media library, and administrative offices
design architect: Steven Holl
project architect: Noah Yaffe
project advisor: Chris McVoy
project team: Martin Cox, Cosimo Caggiula, Alessandro Orsini, Jongseo Lee, Filipe Taboada, Julia Radcliffe

2005–
Porosity House
location: Long Island, New York, USA
program: weekend house
design architect: Steven Holl
project architect: Rodolfo Reis Dias
project team: Cosimo Caggiula, Ernest Ng

2005–
Denver Justice Center (competition: first place)
location: Denver, Colorado, USA
program: 35 courtrooms, offices, and public spaces
design architect: Steven Holl
partner-in-charge: Chris McVoy
project architect: Olaf Schmidt
project team: Justin Allen, Lesley Chang; Gyoung Nam Kwon, Jackie Luk, Rashid Satti

2005
Friends Without a Border
Angkor Hospital for Children's Visitor Center
location: Siem Reap, Cambodia
program: visitor center for non-profit children's hospital
design architect: Steven Holl
project architect: Noah Yaffe

2005–
Highline Hybrid Tower
location: New York, New York, USA
program: mixed use/offices, hotel, and condominiums
design architect: Steven Holl
partner-in-charge: Chris McVoy
project team: Tim Bade, Frank O. Cottier, Peter Englaender, Nick Gelpi, Ernest Ng, Rodolfo Reis Dias, Ebbie Wisecarver, Noah Yaffe

2006–
Meander (competition: first place)
location: Helsinki, Finland
program: 49 apartments, 500-square-meter rental space, garage, rooftop sauna, and running track
design architects: Steven Holl, Vesa Honkonen
project architect: Jongseo Lee

2006–
Orestad
location: Copenhagen, Denmark
program: residential and commercial building
design architect: Steven Holl
project architect: Haiko Cornelissen
project advisor: Chris McVoy
project team: Garrick Ambrose, Francesco Bartolozzi, Christiane Deptolla, Julia Radcliffe, Rashid Satti, Filipe Taboada

2006–
Vanke Center
location: Shenzhen, China
program: mixed-use building including hotel, service apartments, and offices
design architect: Steven Holl
partner-in-charge: Li Hu
project architects: Gong Dong, Garrick Ambrose
project team: Justin Allen, Cressida Brazier, Kefei Cai, Yenling Chen, Hideki Hirahara, Eric Li, Filipe Taoada

Monographs and Published Writings

Holl, Steven. *Hybrid Instrument*. Iowa City: The University of Iowa School of Art and Art History, 2006.

———. *Luminosity/Porosity*. Tokyo: Toto Shuppan, 2006.

———. "Alvar Aalto: Villa Mairea, Noormarkku /Porosity to Fusion." *Entrez Lentement*. Ed. Lorenzo Gaetani. Milan: Lotus Eventi, 2005. 186–207.

———. *Steven Holl*. Ed. Ji-seong Jeong. Spec. issue of *Contemporary Architecture* 62. Korea: CA Press, 2005.

———. *Experiments in Porosity*. Ed. Brian Carter and Annette W. LeCuyer. Buffalo: University at Buffalo, School of Architecture and Planning, 2005.

———. *Simmons Hall*. Ed. Todd Gannon. *Source Books in Architecture* 5. New York: Princeton Architectural Press, 2004.

———. *Steven Holl: Competitions*. Ed. Yoshio Futugawa. *GA Document* 82. Japan: A.D.A. Edita Tokyo, 2004.

———. *Steven Holl*. Ed. Francesco Garofolo. New York: Universe-Rizzoli, 2003.

———. *Steven Holl 1986–2003*. Eds. Fernando Marquez Cecilia and Richard Levene. Madrid: El Croquis Editorial, 2003.

———. *Steven Holl Architect*. Intro. Kenneth Frampton. Milan: Electa Architecture, 2002.

———. *Idea and Phenomena*. Ed. Architekturzentrum Wien. Baden: Lars Muller Publishers, 2002.

———. *Written in Water*. Baden: Lars Muller Publishers, 2002.

———. *Steven Holl 1998–2002: thought, matter and experience* [*El Croquis* 108]. Madrid: El Croquis Editorial, 2001.

———. "Density in the Landscape." *City Fragments: Seven Strategies for Making an Urban Fragment in the Hudson Valley*. [*Columbia Books of Architecture*]. New York: Columbia University Press, 2001.

———. *Parallax*. New York: Princeton Architectural Press, 2000.

———. *The Chapel of St. Ignatius*. Intro. Gerald T. Cobb, S.J. New York: Princeton Architectural Press, 1999.

———. *Steven Holl 1996–1999*. Eds. Fernando Marquez Cecilia and Richard Levene [*El Croquis* 93]. Madrid: El Croquis Editorial, 1999.

———. "Intertwining with the City: Museum of Contemporary Art in Helsinki." *Harvard Architectural Review* 10 (1998).

———. *Kiasma*. Helsinki: The Finnish Building Center, 1998.

———. "Exactness of Doubt." *Pamphlet Architecture 1-10*. New York: Princeton Architectural Press, 1998.

———. "Twofold Meaning." *Kenchiku Bunka* 52 Aug. 1997.

———. *Intertwining: Selected Projects 1989–1995*. New York: Princeton Architectural Press, 1996.

———. *Steven Holl 1986–1996*. Eds. Fernando Marquez Cecilia and Richard Levine [*El Croquis* 78]. Madrid: El Croquis Editorial, 1996.

———. Stretto House: Steven Holl Architects. New York: Monacelli Press, 1996.

———. *Steven Holl*. Interview with Yushio Futagawa. Ed. Yukio Futagawa. *GA Document Extra*. Japan: A.D.A. Edita Tokyo, 1996.

———. "Pre-Theoretical Ground." *D: Columbia Documents of Architecture and Theory* 4. Ed. Bernard Tschumi. New York: Columbia University Graduate School of Architecture, Planning and Preservation, 1995. 27–59.

———. "Questions of Perception." *Archithese* 2.94 [Zurich] Apr. 1994: 25–28.

———. "Intertwining / Verweben." *Color of an Architect*. Intro. Dirk Meyhofer. Hamburg: Galerie Fur Architektur, 1994. 12–57.

———. *Steven Holl*. Intro. Kenneth Frampton. Zurich: Artemis Zurich and Bordeaux: arc en reve centre d'architecture, 1993. 21–115.

———. "Edge of a City." *Pamphlet Architecture* 13. New York: Princeton Architectural Press, 1991.

———. *Anchoring: Selected Projects 1975–1988*. Intro. Kenneth Frampton. New York: Princeton Architectural Press, 1989.

———. "Within the City: Phenomena of Relations." *Design Quarterly* 139. Cambridge, Massachusetts: MIT Press, 1988.

———. "Teeter Totter Principles." *Perspecta* 21. New Haven: Yale University Press, 1984.

———. "Foundations: American House Types." *Precis* IV. Eds. Sheryl Kolasinski and P.A. Morton. New York: Columbia University Press, 1983.

———. "Rural and Urban House Types." *Pamphlet Architecture* 9. New York: William Stout Architectural Books, 1982.

———. Anatomy of a Skyscraper: Cities, the Forces that Shape Them. Ed. Liza Taylor. New York: Cooper-Hewitt Musuem, 1982.

———. "Conversation with Alberto Sartoris." *Archetype* Fall 1982.

———. "Bridge of Houses." *Pamphlet Architecture* 7. New York: William Stout Architectural Books, 1981.

———. "The Alphabetical City." *Pamphlet Architecture* 5. New York: Pamphlet Architecture Press, 1980.

———. "USSR in the USA." *Skyline* May 1979.

———. "The Desert De Retz." *Student Quarterly Syracuse*. New York: Syracuse School of Architecture, 1978.

———. Rev. of *The Blue Mountain Conference*. *Skyline* Nov. 1978.

———. "Bridges." *Pamphlet Architecture* 1. New York: Pamphlet Architecture Press, 1977.

Photography Credits

2x4: 47 (bottom), 105 (top); Abaco Architettura: left end sheet (left middle 1); Dee Breger/Drexel University: 107 (bottom); Blikk: 257 (left); The Central House of Architects: left end sheet (middle bottom); Alice Chung (Omnivore): left end sheet (middle bottom); Gallery MA: right end sheet (right middle); Glenn Goluska: left end sheet (right top); Roland Halbe: 226; Steven Holl: 20 (top), 30 (top), 49 (top), 50 (top), 54 (bottom left, bottom right), 56 (top), 72 (top), 80 (top), 86 (top), 94 (top), 118, 120, 130 (top), 170 (top), 184 (top), 192 (top), 206 (top), 228 (middle), 231 (bottom), 232 (top), 238 (middle), 244 (top, middle), 248 (top), 253, 256, 260, 274, 280 (left 1, left 2, left 3, left 4, right 1, right 2, right 3), 281 (right 4), 282 (left 4, right 1), 283 (left 1, left 2), 290 (left 1), 290 (left 3), 293 (right 2), 295 (left 4), 296 (left 3); Iowa State University, School of Architecture: left end sheet (right, bottom); Michelle W. Lee (Division of Institutional Advancement): right end sheet (right middle 2); National Building Museum: right end sheet (middle, middle 1); Rene Magritte: 238 (top); Chris McVoy (SHA): 26, 27, 275; Voitto Niemula: 177; Robert Paz / SCI-Arc: 2, 12, 44, 45 (top), 104; Peking University Graduate Center of Architecture: left end sheet (left top); Christian Richters: 193, 196, 198, 200, 203, 204, 205 (left); Andy Ryan: 21, 28, 29, 34 (top), 35, 37, 38, 39, 40, 41, 42, 43, 73, 76 (left), 78, 79, 81, 83, 84, 89, 93, 119, 121, 122 (top), 123, 125 (left), 128 (top), 131, 132, 133, 135, 136, 137, 138, 139, 140, 142, 143, 144, 145, 154, 155, 156, 186, 187, 188, 191, 207, 209, 210, 213, 214, 216, 217, 218, 219, 220, 221, 223, 224, 225, 255 (left), 289 (left 2), 289 (right 4), 290 (left 2, left 4), 291 (left 4), 293 (left 2, left 3); SCI-Arc (Fall 2003 Lectures): left end sheet (right middle 1); School of Architecture & Planning, University at Buffalo: right end sheet (left bottom); Margherita Spiluttini: 195, 292 (right 1); Reino Tapaninen: 173 ; Bill Timmerman: 95, 97, 98, 100, 101, 102, 103, 264, 294 (left 3); Vassar College Publications Office: left end sheet (left bottom); Paul Warchol: 17 (top and middle), 22, 25, 57, 58 (bottom), 59, 60, 61, 62, 66, 74, 75, 76 (right), 77, 82, 87, 88, 90 (top right), 91, 92, 109, 110, 111, 112, 114 (top), 115, 116, 117, 125 (right), 126, 161, 162, 163, 164, 167, 168, 169, 171, 173, 178 179 (right), 181, 182, 183, 185, 282 (right 2, right 4), 283, (left 3, right 3), 284 (left 2), 285 (right 2), 286 (right 1, right 2, right 3), 287 (left 1, right 2), 288 (right 1), 289 (left 1), 289 (left 3, left 4), 292 (left 2); Washington University: left end sheet (left middle 2); all other images © Steven Holl Architects.

Acknowledgments

These works depended on great collaboration of all the energetic and creative individuals listed with each of the projects in this book.

Special thanks to:

Solange Fabião (for everything).

The *Architecture Spoken* team: David van der Leer with Christina Yessios, Alessandro Orsini and Priscilla Fraser (SHA); Dung Ngo, Diana Lind, and Alexandra Tart (Rizzoli).

And to: Molly Blieden, Mildred Friedman, Roland Halbe, Li Hu, Hollyamber Kennedy, Gyoung Nam Kwon, Ruth W. Lo, Chris McVoy, Christian Richters, Andy Ryan, SCI-Arc, Brett Snyder, Bill Timmerman, Paul Warchol, Lebbeus Woods.

First published in
the United States of America
in 2007 by

Rizzoli International Publications, Inc.
300 Park Avenue South
New York, NY 10010
www.rizzoliusa.com

ISBN-10: 0-8478-2920-0
ISBN-13: 978-0-8478-2920-0
LCCN: 2006931174

Distributed to the U.S. trade by
Random House, New York

Printed in China
2007 2008 2009 2010 2011
10 9 8 7 6 5 4 3 2 1

Designed by NGO Studio / www.NGOstudio.com

architecture. Strongly influenced by the philosophical movement of phenomenology, each project defines a distinctive process of investigation. Holl takes particular problems of function and represents them architecturally in ways that become universal. Often called "poetic," Holl's architecture is exquisitely detailed, richly textured, and strikingly lit. He will speak about his recent buildings in Japan, where he has worked extensively, and about the responsibilities of the architect post 9/11.

McGill University's
School of Architecture
Lecture Series

David J. Azrieli Lecture in Architecture

Steven Holl

Steven Holl

Architect, will deliver
the 2002 Agnes Rindge Claflin Lecture:

Pro Kyoto

Monday
25 February
6:00pm
Taylor Hall 203

Sponsored by the Department of Art
with the Support of the Friends of the
Lehman Loeb Art Center

PRESENTS

003 LECTURE

featuring

STEVEN HOLL

STEVEN HOLL

pro kyoto

COMUNE DI VICENZA
SCADE IL
20 OTT 2001
Ufficio Affissioni

conferenza all'auditorium Canneti di Vicenza, Levà degli Angeli 11

sabato 20 ottobre 2001 ore 17,00

ingresso libero fino ad esaurimento dei posti disponibili

COMUNE DI VICENZA   PROVINCIA DI VICENZA   REGIONE DEL VENETO

ISTITUTO UNIVERSITARIO DI ARCHITETTURA DI VENEZIA

ABACO ASSOCIAZIONE CULTURALE PER L'ARCHITETTURA

In occasione della mostra "Toyo Ito architetto" Basilica Palladiana di Vicenza
fino al 2 dicembre 2001 Informazioni: www.abacoarchitettura.org

18 FEBRUARY 6:00PM
COMPRESSION / ST
EVEN HOLL, AIA, AR
CHITECT, STEVEN HO
LL ARCHITECTS, NEW
YORK

ALL LECTURES TAKE PLACE AT 6:00 PM IN BETTS AUDITORIUM, ARCHITECTURE BUILDING,
UNLESS OTHERWISE NOTED.
FOR ADDITIONAL INFORMATION PLEASE CALL 609-258-3741. LECTURES MADE POSSIBLE BY
THE JEAN LABATUT MEMORIAL LECTURE FUND.
THE SCHOOL OF ARCHITECTURE, PRINCETON UNIVERSITY, IS REGISTERED WITH THE AIA
CONTINUING EDUCATION SYSTEM (AIA/CES) AND IS COMMITTED TO DEVELOPING QUALITY
LEARNING ACTIVITIES IN ACCORDANCE WITH THE AIA/CES CRITERIA.

KASSLER LECTURE

KOL/MAC STUDIO, "VERTICAL URBANISM: LO_RES / HI_RISE"
STUDIOWORKS, "DANGEROUS SUPPLEMENTS"
GRIFFIN ENRIGHT ARCHITECTS

PAID
PERMIT NO. 255
INGLEWOOD, CA

SCI·ARC FALL 2003

Southern California Institute of Architecture 960 East 3rd Street Los Angeles California 90013

9.11   STEVEN HOLL Architect, New York
9.17   AARON BETSKY Director, Netherlands Architecture Institute, Rotterdam
9.24   NATALIE JEREMIJENKO Artist, New Haven, Connecticut
9.29   STANLEY SAITOWITZ Architect, Stanley Saitowitz, San Francisco
10.01 ADA TOLLA & GIUSEPPE LIGNANO Architects, LOT-EK, New York
10.06 JEAN-LOUIS COHEN Prof., Inst. of Fine Arts, New York Univ., Ecole Francais d'Architecture, Paris
10.08 MACK SCOGIN & MERRILL ELAM Architects, Atlanta
10.15 AMMAR ELOUEINI Chair, Digital Media, School of Art, Univ. of Illinois, Chicago
10.27 GRAFT Architects, Berlin & Los Angeles
10.29 DOMINIQUE JAKOB & BRENDAN MACFARLANE Architects, Paris
11.03 SHEILA KENNEDY Architect, Kennedy & Violich Architecture, Boston
11.05 MICHAEL SKURA Vice-President, E-SDL, Los Angeles
11.19 CHARLES JENCKS Author-Historian-Designer, London
11.12 WILLIAM K. MASSIE Architect, New York
11.19 HENRY N. COBB Architect, Pei Cobb Freed & Partners, New York

One of the most renowned American architects practicing today, Mr. Holl is a graduate of the University of Washington and of London's Architectural Association. In 1976, he founded Steven Holl Architects in New York City, and he has taught at Columbia University since 1981. Together with William Stout, he founded the journal Pamphlet Architecture. He has written several seminal issues in the series, and his books: Anchoring, Intertwining, and Parallax, can each be found on most designers' bookshelves. His firm's work has been published in several monographs. El Croquis and A+U. Projects have been exhibited at the Museum of Modern Art, the Architectural League of New York and the Smithsonian's Cooper Hewitt Museum.

STEVEN HOLL ARCHITECTS NYC

STEVEN HOLL

Steven Holl has received a variety of honors including the Alvar Aalto Medal, the Chrysler Award for Innovation in Design and the Grand Medal d'Or of l'Academie d'Architecture. An honorary Fellow of the Royal Institute of British Architects, his work has received multiple Progressive Architecture and AIA awards. In July 2001, Time Magazine named Steven Holl as America's "Best Architect," for 'buildings that satisfy the spirit as well as the eye.' Holl's practice rose to international prominence with the design of the small but seminal Chapel of St. Ignatius at Seattle University. In the last five years, he has completed a prominent art museum in Helsinki and an acclaimed Visitor's Center in Langenlois, Austria, and is currently commencing projects in Beijing and Beirut. Recent American works include new undergraduate housing at MIT; an addition to the School of Architecture at the University of Minnesota in Minneapolis; the expansion of the Nelson-Atkins Museum of Art in Kansas City; and the Department of Art and Art History at the University of Iowa in Iowa City.

architecture.
washington university in st. louis

today. In recent buildings, the Museum of Contemporary Art in Helsinki, St. Ignatius Chapel at the University of Washington, the Museum of Art in Bellevue, Washington, and in his projects, he has set out an original program for architecture. Strongly influenced by

Steven HOLL
MOCKBA 12.03.04

ЗДАС "МОСКВА"
www.edas.kiprobew.net
http://shegallweat.ru

/ Postgraduate Prog

DEPARTMENT OF ARCHITECTURE
CURT F. DALE MEMORIAL LECTURE